Strategy OS

Implement an Advanced Business Operating System in Six Simple Steps

Steve Preda

ALSO BY STEVE PREDA

Insights of a Maverick Investment Banker

Insights of a Maverick Exit Advisor

Buyable: Your Guide to Building a Self-Managing, Fast-Growing and High-Profit Business

Pinnacle: Five Principles that Take Your Business to the Top of the Mountain (with Gregory Cleary)

ISBN: 979-8-9860636-5-2 (hardcover)
ISBN: 979-8-9860636-6-9 (paperback)
ISBN: 979-8-9860636-7-6 (e-book)
ISBN: 979-8-9860636-8-3 (audio book)

Amershire Publishing, Glen Allen, Virginia

Printed in the United States of America

Cover Design: Jason Anscomb

Text Design and Illustrations: Andy Meaden, Will Sargent, and Zoltan Ember

Editing: Christina Palaia

Indexing: Toni Culley

DEDICATION

To the memories of my late grandparents: Grandmas Ica and Nusi, and Grandpas Sanyi and Gyuszi. Thank you for teaching me love, courage, imagination, and the joy of life.

Contents

Preface

Seven years ago, when I embarked on teaching small business entrepreneurs the Entrepreneurial Operating System (EOS)—a set of tools and concepts that owners can implement to take their business to the next level—I had a vision. I loved EOS but was convinced that the framework had to be scalable. In my mind, business owners had to be able to continue implementing simplified tools in their businesses to thrive.

My plan was to master EOS as well as the best tools of other systems, such as Scaling Up and the Great Game of Business, and then create a complete next-level operating system for businesses. Companies that had mastered EOS and other entry-level systems would want to keep growing using a comprehensive business framework, right?

Then, just as I was getting into a routine of implementing EOS, on the first step toward my vision, something unexpected happened. EOS Worldwide, the owner of the EOS framework, decided to transition its business model from licensing EOS tools to business coaches like me, to becoming a franchise organization. EOS franchisees were asked to stick to teaching EOS tools exclusively and to give up their individual coaching brands as EOS implementers.

It was a scary moment. I loved the EOS concepts and tools and was not looking forward to upending my coaching practice just yet—I was rather hoping to build my own concepts on top of EOS's tools and keep guiding my clients higher up their business mountains.

But unless I gave up my vision, I'd be barred from teaching the EOS concepts as the foundation of a more extensive business-building framework.

After some soul searching, I decided to join a group called Pinnacle Business Guides (PBG), a coaching community founded by Gregory Cleary, a former top-ranked EOS implementer.

Pinnacle

PBG attracted me because of it's entrepreneurial ethos and philosophy. The idea behind PBG was for business owners to choose a *guide* rather than a *system* and then to let their chosen sherpa curate the tools they needed to grow their business. Pinnacle Business Guides gathered together a loose structure of state-of-the-art business tools that could be customized to the needs of each client.

I saw in PBG the potential for a scalable business system. Each guide was responsible for continuing to grow with his or her clients, helping them expand their businesses indefinitely.

My challenge was figuring out how to explain the Pinnacle system to my clients and prospects. I needed complete clarity on what a distinct Pinnacle business operating system would look like, and how it was different from EOS and other systems.

Further, I wanted to explain Pinnacle by drawing its tools on a whiteboard. This would only be possible if I understood all the details and was sure they all made sense and were internally consistent. Greg had come up with the Five Pinnacle Principles of: People, Purpose, Playbooks, Performance, and Profit, which were brilliant.

I wanted to figure out the three most important concepts that formed each of these Principles, draw them, and explain them. I called these the 15 Pinnacle Practices, and soon the drawings morphed into the draft of a book. Then I called Greg and asked him to join me in this project to produce a definitive guide to the Pinnacle business operating system.

Greg and I spent several days discussing the designs, adding stories, and tweaking concepts and illustrations to make sure they were in line with his ideas and teachings about Pinnacle. The result was our coauthored book published in 2022: *Pinnacle: Five Principles that Take Your Business to the Top of the Mountain.*

But What About Strategy?

Pinnacle: Five Principles broached a couple of the strategy concepts I am including in this book, but only at a surface level. After all, strategy was just one of the 15 Practices in the *Pinnacle* book, and we could not devote more than fifteen to twenty pages to it without upsetting the simplicity of the book.

In particular, we talked about positioning and differentiating a business and outlined the concept of the Strategy Stack, but we did not explain how to create one beyond a couple of examples.

After the publication of *Pinnacle*, I felt this was sorely missing. If I could crack the nut of building a Strategy Stack, that is, an interlocking system of Unique Activities, it would help business owners create sustainable differentiation. It would allow them to dig a moat around their business, like IKEA had done thirty years ago.

I spent the following six months devouring all the important strategy books that I had not yet read, including the works of Michael Porter, Richard Rumelt, Jim Collins, Joan Magretta, Henry Mintzberg, and Bruce Henderson and his colleagues at the Boston Consulting Group; Marvin Bower's books about McKinsey & Company; the strategy articles published by the *Harvard Business Review*; and others.

Although several of these authors argued that strategy was more an art than a science, I could not accept this as an explanation. I was convinced that there had to be more science behind strategy, and I wanted to organize and refine its most important concepts into a sequential toolkit—a "Strategy Operating System" that would allow any business owner to build a winning strategy by following a step-by-step blueprint.

Strategy OS

The result is a six-step system that leads you to build up and reinforce a successful growth strategy for your business. In the first four steps, I show you how to position your business well and use your constraints to differentiate and eventually corner a niche market with a unique Strategy Stack.

Step 1 is about positioning. I show you how to define your Core Business and how to view your business through the lens of Michael Porter's five competitive forces, plus the force of government regulations. Then, we position your business by choosing one of the quadrants of Economy, Variety, Focus, or Luxury on the Positioning Matrix.

Step 2 helps you zoom out and find the biggest blocker of your progress: your Crux Challenge. We'll ask, which one piece of one of your most critical challenges could be resolved so that the dam of your company's growth can be reopened? How can you respond and what are the coherent actions that will help you solve that Crux Challenge?

Step 3 discusses identifying your Business Constraints because these carry your business's seeds of greatness. Great strategy is about turning lemons into lemonade. What brand promises can emerge from your challenges and what are the Unique Activities that will manifest them?

In Step 4, I show how you can author further Unique Activities by determining your Core Market and ideating an Advanced Profit per X metric and your Strategic Flywheel. I analyzed dozens of companies I've advised to understand the most potent forces that drove their respective flywheels. These same factors will enable you too to create further Unique Activities for your business.

Step 5 is about ensuring that your Unique Activities fit your business and then forging them into a sustainable Strategy Stack. This chapter explores how you can grow your niche leader business by expanding into adjacent geographies, channels, markets, products, and industries. We discuss network effects and how you could tap into them for faster growth.

Finally, in Step 6 we explore ways you can eventually build a perpetual growth machine by creating a culture of innovation and selective acquisitions and disposals.

In the final chapter, we examine the nuclear option: reinventing your business when disruption, commoditization, or other competitive threats force you to make a dramatic shift.

So, there you have it—a complete Strategy Operating System for your business. Is it perfect? Absolutely not, but it will give you 80 percent of the results you want from your strategy with only 20 percent of the effort.

Have fun applying these simple strategy steps and building the business you have hitherto not even dared to dream about.

Steve Preda

Glen Allen, Virginia, February 2023

Introduction

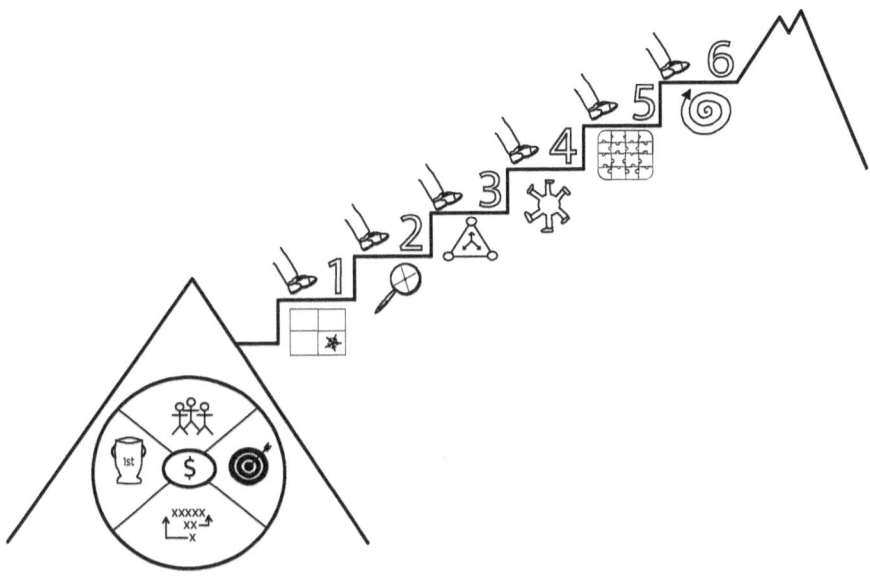

Tactics without strategy is the noise before defeat.

—Sun Tzu

You are an ambitious entrepreneur or CEO who wants to build a successful company—and not just a small lifestyle business for you and your family to live comfortably.

You want to create something that will be bigger than anything on your city's Fast Fifty list. You're aiming for the *Inc.* 5000 and possibly even the *Fortune* 500.

In some respects, you are already on your way. You discovered and implemented a robust business operating system, such as the Entrepreneurial Operating System® (EOS), Scaling Up, OKRs, or Pinnacle.

You already have most of the right people in the right seats and they are setting and establishing annual and quarterly objectives. Your business has a vision, and a mission, and you are making progress toward them.

However, you have hit a ceiling. And your basic business operating system is no longer enough to help you push through. Although you have mastered the tools of these systems, your quarterly meetings are becoming repetitive and boring. You have fallen into a rut.

But, wait! There are higher-level strategy concepts that the iconic companies of our age—Apple, Amazon, Adobe—use. Couldn't you study these masters and apply what they have done in your own business?

Yes, there is a plethora of strategy books out there. However, you'll find many of them arcane, academic, and even confusing. Most were written a long time ago and use out-of-date examples from well before the tech age. Many are no longer relevant.

Worse, a lot of the concepts are incoherent and you'd be hard pressed to find any reasonable sequence of implementation.

Further, several authors argue that strategy is an art, not a science, and that it is not even possible to build a coherent system for strategy creation...

Now, what if I told you that these authors are wrong and that strategy is more of a science than an art?

What if these concepts actually *could be* "toolified" and sequenced, like what EOS did with the methods of small business execution?

For the past five years, I've been obsessed by the idea of creating a Strategy Operating System, and I've spent the past twelve months figuring out how to design one.

During that time, I read and reread the most important strategy books of the past half century, including those from Michael Porter, Bruce Henderson, Richard Rumelt, Henry Mintzberg, Jim Collins, and others, and the top strategy articles in the *Harvard Business Review*.

My goal was to extract and simplify their essential ideas. I then figured out the right sequence for these concepts and illustrated them with simple drawings and fresh examples. I want you, the ambitious entrepreneur, to understand these steps so clearly that you could explain them to your people and implement these concepts in your business.

I have clustered and organized these ideas into six consecutive steps that will enable you, the smart business owner or CEO, to gradually build up a coherent strategy from scratch. Strategy OS can be implemented on top of your existing business operating system, and you can manage it using a digital platform such as Ninety.io.

But I have to warn you: This system can lead you to the peaks of the highest business mountains in the world, but it will be no light trekking. Implementing the Strategy Operating System requires commitment, disciplined thinking, teamwork, and consistent execution.

I also highly recommend that you hire a Steve Preda Business Growth Guide™, someone who has mastered the Strategy Operating System, to help you navigate the journey and hold you and your team accountable for your self-promises.

As incentive, I can promise you that we will get you a couple of early wins on this journey. Within the first couple of days, we will find the right Strategic Position for your business and devise a road map for navigating the Six Competitive Forces so you can carve out a more profitable position in the force field of your business sector.

Next, we can help you intuit your business's Crux Challenge—the biggest impediment of your further growth—and orchestrate a set of coherent actions with which to overcome it.

From there, the hard work really begins...

We have to dig deep into the constraints of your business to discover the unique brand promises your company was created to deliver on, for your Core Market customers. Then, we must discover and spawn a combination of Unique Activities to dig a moat around your business.

Next, we will build an unassailable Strategy Stack for your organization using the Unique Activity Generator. To scale your business, we'll leverage the Six Dimensions of Expansion, network effects, and other state-of-the-art approaches.

In the final step of implementing the Strategy OS, you will learn how to foster an Innovation Culture in your organization and how to augment it with Smart M&A so that your maturing business continues to grow at a healthy pace.

In the last chapter, we explore eleven ways businesses have reinvented themselves and how you can do the same should you face disruption or opportunity.

Are you ready for the business adventure of your lifetime?

Welcome to the Strategy OS!

Ralph Waldo Emerson said, "The mind, once stretched by a new idea, never returns to its original dimensions."

A word of warning! After you've read this book, the genie is out of the bottle and you will no longer be able to return to your old lifestyle business.

I wish you much luck and wide-open blue skies for your exhilarating journey!

PICK A POSITION

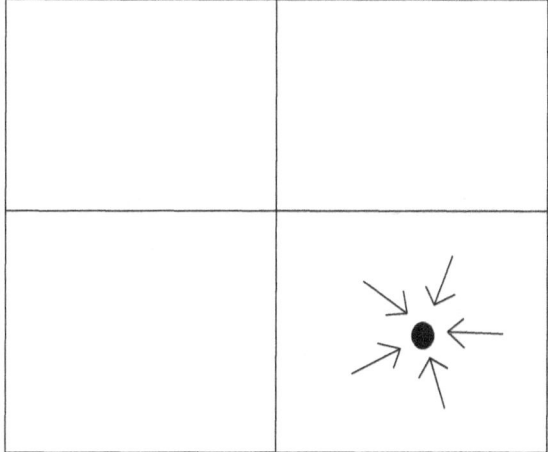

The essence of positioning is sacrifice. You must be willing to give up something to establish that unique position.

—Al Ries

In 1959, in its toad-looking PV544, Volvo introduced the three-point seat belt that mechanical engineer Nils Bohlin had designed. Soon thereafter, the company decided to waive its patent on the invention, and car seat belts proliferated and went on to save over a million lives in the coming six decades.[1]

Volvo followed up on the success of the seat belt by designing the rearward-facing child seat (in 1972), the booster seat (in 1976), side-impact airbags (in 1994),[2] and the City Safety system (in 2008) that autonomously brakes the car to prevent collisions. Volvo improves the safety of its cars in a state-of-the-art crash-testing facility. The company employs accident researchers who visit the scenes of all Volvo accidents in Sweden in order to gather data to perfect future models. Volvo's stated objective is that no one should be killed or seriously injured in a Volvo.

Volvo's reputation for safety has become legendary, and risk-averse drivers often choose the brand over trendier, faster, more luxurious and affordable models. Volvo is the car of choice if you are looking for peace of mind about protecting yourself and your loved ones.

Volvo is not competing to produce the *best* car. It is known for producing the *safest* car.

Competing to Be the Best

Michael Porter, in his seminal book *On Competition*, explains how "competing to be the best" is a trap that prevents you from being successful.[3] Being the best, producing better quality products with more features, is expensive and copyable, which leads to price competition and erodes profit margins over time.

Think of the Japanese consumer electronics companies of the 1980s and 1990s, like Sony, Sanyo, Panasonic, and Pioneer, that kept adding features and making their products smaller, more feature-rich, and more ergonomic—but none of this increased industry profitability.

The products of these companies were great and constantly improving, but prices kept dropping because these brands were hardly distinguishable from one another in the eyes of customers. Sony stayed slightly ahead of the pack by out-advertising its rivals, the cost of which only canceled out much of the profit margin advantage it might have had over them.

No company can win in the marketplace without making money. Without healthy profits, you cannot afford the best employees or to innovate the next generation of products and services.

To produce superior profits, your products must be seen to be serving your target customers *uniquely*, such that they cannot substitute your competitors' offerings for your products without sacrifice. Positioning is your first step to creating such uniqueness in the eyes of your Core Market.

Positioning your products and services (hereinafter, I use "products" as a synonym for both) is a three-step process.

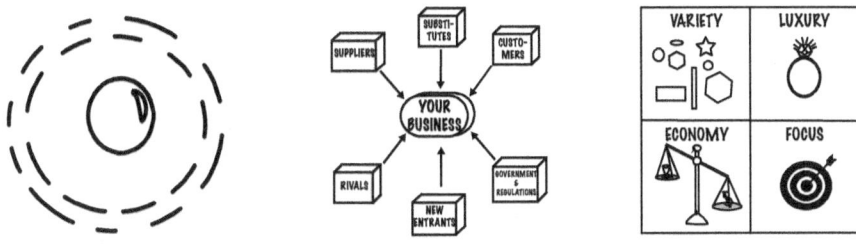

- In Chapter 1, we identify your Core Business to understand where to leverage your inherent advantages and make the most impact.

- In Chapter 2, we evaluate your products through the lens of the Six Competitive Forces to understand the profitability force field that your business is operating in.

- In Chapter 3, we position your product in one of four categories on the basis of the mix of features and performance you deliver to customers.

Let's begin your strategy quest by identifying your Core Business.

CHAPTER ONE

Identify Your Core Business

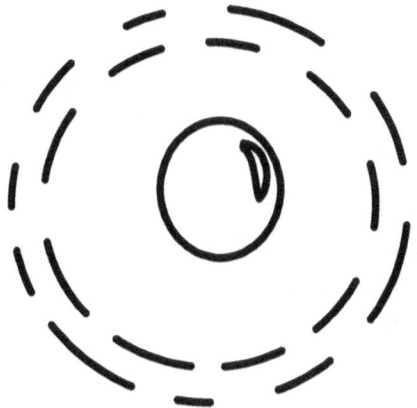

Control your cash. Stick to your core business.
Know your numbers.

—Marcus Lemonis

A company's *Core Business* is the main source of that company's profit and success. It is often, but not always, the activity that the company was originally set up to carry out.[1] More broadly, your Core Business describes a set of functions, processes, and capabilities that produce most of the value in your business.

Apple's Core Business is high-tech consumer electronics and digital services. Tesla's Core Business is electric cars. Amazon's Core Business is online retail. Coca-Cola's is nonalcoholic beverages.

Companies are often unclear about their Core Business or lose focus of it over time as they try to increase revenues and serve their clients more comprehensively.

If you deliver a quality product or service, your customers will want to rely on you more, and they will likely ask you to help them with a broadening array of their needs. You will be tempted to respond. In the short term, it is easier to serve existing clients by being flexible than it is to find new clients that need your Core Business offerings.

The danger of this kind of "flexibility" is that your experience will broaden rather than deepen. You risk becoming all things to all people rather than the best there is in a narrow segment you have mastered and where you can make a real difference. You might become a commodity.

Further, by focusing on more broadly serving existing clients, you risk growing dependent on a handful of customers for your revenues and profit. This is a slippery slope because saying no to certain clients who generate more and more of your income becomes increasingly hard.

The Pressure to Grow Distracts from the Core

One of my former clients, DataCo, a venture-funded data security Software-as-a-Service (SaaS) company, fell into this trap. DataCo identified a niche where there was a high demand for its services by fast-growing cloud businesses. DataCo approached investors and proposed to build a scalable SaaS product to serve this market, which would eventually allow the business to be sold in an initial public offering (IPO).

DataCo stormed out of the gate by landing a handful of prominent customers. It needed to hire developers and upgrade its management team to keep up with its initial growth. This hiring spree burned cash and necessitated further rounds of capital raises.

The company's impressive client list and its plan to develop a scalable product kept investors interested. However, high growth expectations forced

DataCo to accommodate its marquee customers and customize its offering instead of developing its Core Business, a self-service, scalable SaaS product, that the company's investors wanted.

Notwithstanding its growth, the profit margin of customized professional services was insufficient to generate the returns required by DataCo's venture capital investors. Consequently, further financing rounds became increasingly expensive and dilutive to the company's founders.

Focusing on your Core Business allows you to stick to where you create the most value. You will be tempted to diverge for the sake of expediency or short-term revenues, but that will harm your long-term growth prospects.

Core Business Mistakes

In DataCo's case, the company allowed pressures to distract it from its core SaaS mandate. In another example, a business starting out as a consulting practice had to discover its core after it hit a growth ceiling.

This is what happened to a managed service provider (MSP) I'll call RightSyst. Two software engineers started the business when they felt constrained by the culture of their employer, a large IT consulting firm. The two founders assumed that their strength lay in system integration: putting together IT systems for midsize corporate clients, including developing websites and custom apps.

However, during a Core Business discovery exercise, these business owners realized that the company's forte was client service rather than software development. In servicing clients they really shone and were creating the most value. Software projects were hard to price, stressful to execute, and required skills that were difficult to scale.

Moreover, in many cases software development clients would not turn into the recurring-revenue customers that the RightSyst founders wanted. Redefining the company's Core Business as "supporting growth through technology" allowed RightSyst to dial back development and instead focus on managing clients' technology infrastructure.

In a third type of scenario, the original Core Business does not gain enough traction and the company must pivot and follow market needs.

For example, I launched my own consulting business twenty years ago to give advice on management buyouts. However, my team soon discovered that most buyout firms did not use advisors, and buy-in managers had little money to pay for our services. Therefore, we pivoted to capital raising and later to advising business owners on how to prepare and sell their businesses to corporate and private equity buyers.

In our example, our original Core Business turned out not to create enough value, and we had to develop a new, adjacent core.

Seven Questions to Figure Out Your Core Business

Whether your company has been around for a while or it's relatively young, it is worth reexamining your Core Business. You can ask yourself some of the following questions. (See Figure 1.1.)

Question 1: What are you best at? What is your core competency that allows you to create unique value?

The Core Business of Adriana Accounting, a SaaS company, is to modernize financial and accounting processes. This company has developed a software interface that allows accountants to align company accounts with the company's banking transactions. While creating its core software product, Adriana has developed a deep understanding of the challenges and time sinks accountants face.

This allows the team to innovate their existing software and develop other solutions that eliminate friction and errors in bookkeeping and that leverage data for the automation of accounting and reporting transactions.

Bramante Homes, a custom home builder, identifies "Providing Well-Guided Custom Home Experiences" as its Core Business. Building a custom home is a complex process that requires prospective homeowners to make hundreds of decisions and trade-offs.

Figure 1.1 Core Business Lens

Bramante's strength is helping customers translate their vision into reality by presenting tangible design choices and articulating the pros and cons of each. The company has developed a unique process to help homeowners make the right choices along the way and enjoy an inspiring— rather than a frustrating—homebuilding experience.

Question 2: What is the root cause of your competitive advantage? Is this advantage still relevant for the marketplace? Is your market still using your core assets?

For example, after losing the PC wars to Intel- and Microsoft-powered clones, IBM decided that its hardware business was no longer as relevant as its relationships and goodwill with *Fortune*-ranked clients. Serving blue-chip clients and securing their trust were, in fact, IBM's core, not its computer equipment. Big Blue soon repositioned itself as a consulting business and regained much of its lost footing.

Question 3: Is what your business focuses on a strength of the current business or that of the original founders, who may no longer be around?

An imaging software company, Media Cybernetics, when still owned by a global conglomerate, used to define its Core Business as follows:

> *"Developing image analysis software used in scientific industries and applications"*

Since then, an entrepreneurial ownership bought out the business. The new team dug deep to explore where the company's power lay and then redefined its Core Business as

> *"Developing microscope-agnostic image analysis solutions to targeted verticals"*

The new definition is much more granular and niched, making it easier for everyone in the company to understand what to focus on, in which direction to develop the company's product, and how to position its business to customers.

The Core Business of Media Cybernetics is not developing software but providing imaging solutions, including services, to advance innovation in partnership with the scientific community.

Question 4: Which of your products or services are the most distinctive?

When Steve Jobs took over Apple again, he ditched most of the company's tired product portfolio and launched the colorful computer-in-monitor iMac desktop. Jobs's goal was to return to the creative and innovative Core Business that had made Apple famous. Next came the iPod, iTunes, and the iPhone, and Apple was on its way to topping *Fortune's* rankings.

Questions 5: Which of your products or services are the most profitable?

The Pareto principle comes in handy here for triaging your portfolio. Focus on the 20 percent of your products that deliver 80 percent of your profits. These are most likely to represent your Core Business.

One of my former clients, a regional managed services provider (let's call it Regional MSP), initially thought that its Core Business was

"Solving tech problems that impact business"

However, as we dug into understanding what the company was really good at and where it created the most value, the picture changed. This service company was at its best when it was

"Serving the complex technology needs of professional service firms"

Regional MSP's forte was serving law firms whose attorneys wanted to spend their time doing billable work efficiently from anywhere without having to worry about being hacked or getting stuck. These customers were ready to pay premium prices for a premium level of service. Regional MSP had the technology, the customer service skills, and the expert chief information officers on hand to provide a white glove client experience.

Question 6: Which of your customers are the most satisfied?

I have found that my best customers are service-driven and technology-enabled. These are the ones I most resonate with, understand the best, and love helping. Regional MSP's most satisfied clients were large law firms that were in geographical proximity to their managed service providers.

Ask yourself what your ideal customers look like. How can *you* acquire and serve more clients like them?

Question 7: Which of your customers, channels, or purchase occasions are the most profitable?

My best customers have found me through my books. They already liked me and wanted what I have, and I enjoy helping their businesses grow. These are my kind of people.

On the other hand, I have had a patchy experience with requests for proposals (RFPs). RFPs are designed to commoditize suppliers so that a business can procure the lowest-cost service. RFP prospects often pay lip service to considering intangibles but, in my experience, are rarely interested in building a mutually rewarding business relationship.

Ask yourself who *your* best customers are, and *through which channels* did they find your business? Is there a pattern you can observe that will help you define your Core Business?

By asking these seven questions, your Core Business will become apparent. Your job, then, is to buckle down and make sure you are exploiting it to its maximum potential.

Steve Jobs, after his return to Apple, steered the company back to its Core Business of intuitive, well-designed consumer products that serve as the "bicycle to the mind" and amplify the power of the human brain.[2] By sticking to that idea, Apple followed up the iMac with the iPod, the iPhone, the iPad, the Apple Watch, and the HomePod.

What is *your* Core Business and how do *you* make sure you stay in it?

Key takeaways from Chapter 1

• Identify your Core Business and double down on it to maximize your growth and profit opportunity.

• Notice whether pressures to grow have distracted you from your core or your original attributes or key assets have lost their luster.

• Ask the seven clarifying questions to get to the bottom of your Core Business.

Having clarified your Core Business, it's time to assess the field for your products. It is not enough to have a robust Core Business if you are at the mercy of customers or suppliers who will not allow you to grow profitably. You need to know more than just your Core Business when the risk of substitution or new entrants threatens your business. Let's find out about these forces next.

CHAPTER TWO

Assess Your Six Competitive Forces

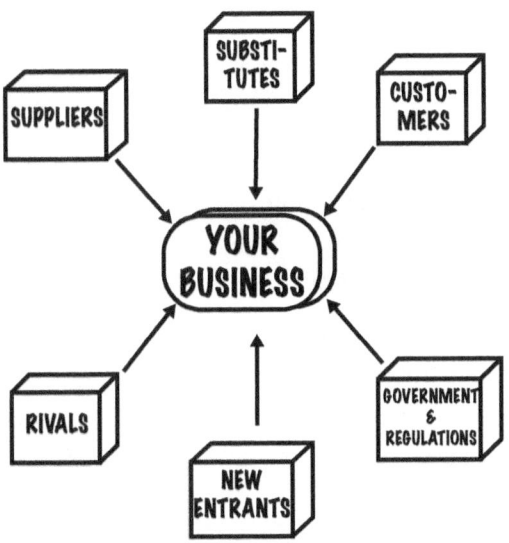

The strongest competitive force or forces determine the profitability of an industry and become the most important to strategy formulation. The most salient force, however, is not always obvious.

—**Michael Porter**

Perhaps the most-quoted authority on strategy, Michael Porter introduced the "five forces of competitive position analysis" at Harvard Business School in 1979. The Five Forces are competition in the industry, potential of new entrants into the industry, power of suppliers, power of customers, and threat of substitute products. This model became an instant favorite of business consultants and corporate strategists for evaluating the competitive force field that affects an industry.

In *On Competition*, Porter asserts that competition is not about beating rivals but about earning profits. Competing for profits *is* a more complex equation than dealing with head-on rivalries because it includes multiple players, not just direct competitors, who are responsible for the profitability of an industry.

These players might include powerful suppliers that force you to pay high for their inputs as well as mighty customers that can negotiate discounts and rebates on your products.

A former client of mine, a household paper product manufacturer I'll call PaperCo, was squeezed by a monopolistic paper mill on the supply side and a handful of superstore customers on the demand side.

His paper supplier enjoyed a regional monopoly on paper production that forced my client to pay high prices for raw materials. At the same time, PaperCo's main customers, large retail chains, chose to buy the white-label version of his paper tissues and rolls and market these products under their store brand.

PaperCo was stuck in the middle, with a single-digit net profit margin, until the company fought back by strengthening its brand. It took years, but eventually PaperCo's branded goods made it onto superstore shelves, improving the company's bottom line.

Sources of Disruption and Profit Pressures

Your product may also face competition from substitutes. Video rental giant Blockbuster got disrupted by Redbox DVD kiosks, which in turn fell victim to online streaming services such as Netflix.

Disruption is nothing new. In the second half of the twentieth century, railway services got disrupted by trucking and air freight. Skype disrupted long-distance phone services around the millennium.

New entrants may threaten your business when barriers to entry are low. Gillette thought it controlled the razor blade business with its giant advertising budget. Remember "The best a man can get"? However, Dollar Shave Club came along and disrupted it with the founder's David versus Goliath videos that went viral on the internet.

Powerful rivals, mighty customers, strong substitutes, and able new entrants put pressure on your prices, while rivals and powerful suppliers increase your costs. These pressures can accumulate and, if you are in a commodity business, potentially eliminate your profitability.

A sixth force that Porter does not talk about is the potential for direct government interference in your business through subsidies, regulations, and eminent domain exercised through changing taxes and tariffs and in other ways. For example, environmental regulations can benefit green energy businesses and harm fossil fuel producers. Tobacco companies suffered losses when tobacco advertising and the flavors of vaping products were restricted through legislation and regulation. During World War II, the U.S. government mandated that large companies such as General Motors reorient to war production at regulated prices.

Hereafter, I refer to the combination of this sixth force and Porter's Five Forces as the "Six Competitive Forces." See Figure 2.1.

Figure 2.1 The impact of the Six Competitive Forces on your profitability[1]

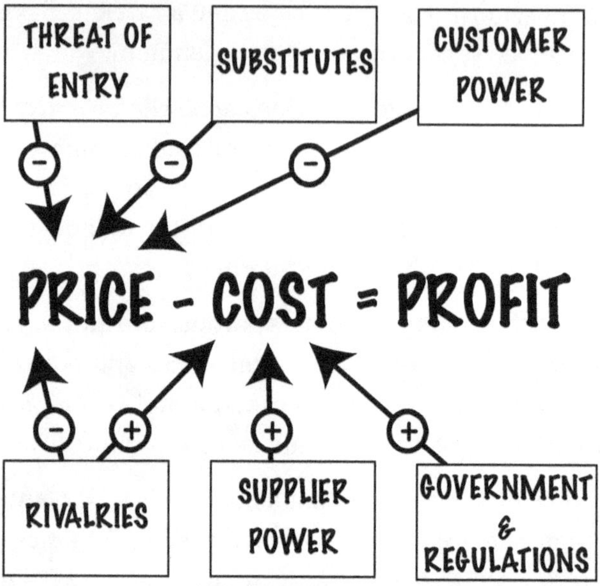

Inspired by Joan Magretta, *Understanding Michael Porter* (Boston: Harvard Business Review Press, 2012), 54.

Now let's see how you can use the Six Competitive Forces model to assess the power of your business.

Analyze Your Industry Scope

Start by delineating the market you are competing in. Is your industry scope limited by market segregation or geographic or cultural barriers?

Porter warns that his model must be used at an industry level rather than in the context of the environment of a middle-market company. I believe this is true when your Core Market is *Fortune*-ranked companies, as I suspect Porter's was. The largest players often control a significant market share and their context becomes the whole industry.

However, the Six Competitive Forces model works just as well in the context of smaller companies that operate in segmented markets, face geographic or cultural barriers, or operate in a niche. In such cases, you would do well to consider only the businesses that potentially play a material role in your geography or niche, and there is no need to look at the whole industry.

Let's look at some examples.

Market Segmentation

Your industry may not be defined by your product. Porter brings up the motor oil market, which is segmented into products offered for cars and offerings tailored to trucks and stationary engines. The engine oils for these two distinct audiences are marketed and distributed in separate channels and at different prices, and they don't compete with each other. (Car owners pay more for their oil than truckers do.)

The same is happening in broadband internet. Retail customers enjoy lower prices for higher bandwidths than business customers do. Corporate users are prepared to pay for a more stable connection and a fixed IP address, options that are not offered to retail customers in order to keep the two markets segmented.

Even in professional services, markets can be segmented out of convenience. *Fortune*-ranked companies tend to prefer working with global law firms and advertising agencies that have offices in all potential geographies. These global firms may not offer the best level of service and they are almost certainly more expensive than their local and regional competitors, but using them makes life easier for the time-starved executives of giant companies.

Geographic Barriers

Some products don't travel well and thereby avoid global or even regional competition. One example is prefabricated concrete, which is not economical to ship beyond two hundred miles.

I knew a prefabricated concrete manufacturer who enjoyed a competitive advantage by not having a sophisticated facility, as depreciation expense burdened him less than it did his competitors. As a result, he could afford to underprice his company's rivals and regularly won business while making a healthy profit.

The owner of the business hired my firm to sell his company, and we found multiple interested buyers. However, the sale did not close because the buyers felt that the company had inferior technology and would not sustain its competitive position. In fact, the company continued to prosper, even after the death of the owner and under new management.

Another example is a regional real estate brokerage and property management company that I'll call RealEstateCo, or REC. REC operates in the metro area of a medium-size midwestern U.S. city and only does business within a 150-mile radius of its headquarters. REC uses the Six Competitive Forces framework by considering only those customers and rivals that are active in its geographic area.

RealEstateCo's suppliers are local employees, contractors, and software vendors. REC has no reason to consider industry-wide employment and contractor conditions because they may be less relevant than what the company experiences locally. However, its software suppliers and software-based substitutes competing for profits in REC's brokerage business can and should be considered at the industry level.

Now let's look at a different example, one in which the industry-level perspective is more relevant. An e-commerce agency based in Maryland that I'll call eCommerceCorp (ECC) serves consumer brands, retailers, and business-to-business (B2B) manufacturers nationwide. ECC can serve clients in any U.S. time zone and competes with other digital e-commerce firms nationwide.

eCommerceCorp's competitive context with respect to customers is the whole of North America. However, ECC's suppliers may include other remote and cost-competitive geographies, as well, such as Brazil, India, and the Philippines.

This brings up another type of industry barrier, so let's look at that next.

Cultural Barriers

ECC is unlikely to have to compete with companies that have no major presence in North America because there are cultural barriers to winning business here. Without a strong workforce on the ground, European companies, let alone Indian or Philippine ones, face an uphill challenge in relating to and communicating with American executives and creating the confidence needed to win substantive contracts.

Traditional consumer food products such as coffee and candy also don't face fierce global competition. In parts of the world, such as in Central Europe and Latin America, consumers prefer the brands that they grew up with and will insist on drinking locally percolated coffees and buying their kids the candy brands of their own childhood. These products enjoy a level of insulation from rivals and substitutes.

Now that we have got the industry scope exceptions of the Six Competitive Forces framework out of the way, let's look at each force and consider how it might impact the business of our example company, eCommerceCorp (ECC).

Evaluate the Players and Their Powers for Each Force

ECC builds websites and provides search engine optimization (SEO), pay-per-click (PPC) advertising, and social media management (SMM) services. eCommerceCorp's **RIVALS** may be national advertising firms, local and regional boutique agencies, and solopreneurs who market themselves through networking and freelance websites, and they may be offshore.

ECC targets midsize companies that can spend at least $50,000 a year on a full-service agency that will focus on engineering ways to grow their business. Smaller rivals will not be able to match ECC's offerings, whereas large national firms will lack the nimbleness and brainpower ECC can dedicate to these midsize firms. Therefore, rivals represent a **MEDIUM**-strength force.

eCommerceCorp's target **CUSTOMERS** are consumer brands and online retailers that can afford professional help and that have internal marketing staff but don't yet have the scale to run an e-commerce operation in-house. These customers probably have annual revenues of $10 million to $200 million.

ECC's customers are not yet big enough to use procurement techniques to commoditize and drive down ECC's fees. This is not their focus yet. These customers want to select an agency with a solid reputation for thought leadership, one with which they can build a collaborative relationship.

Figure 2.2 eCommerceCo's Six Competitive Forces Map

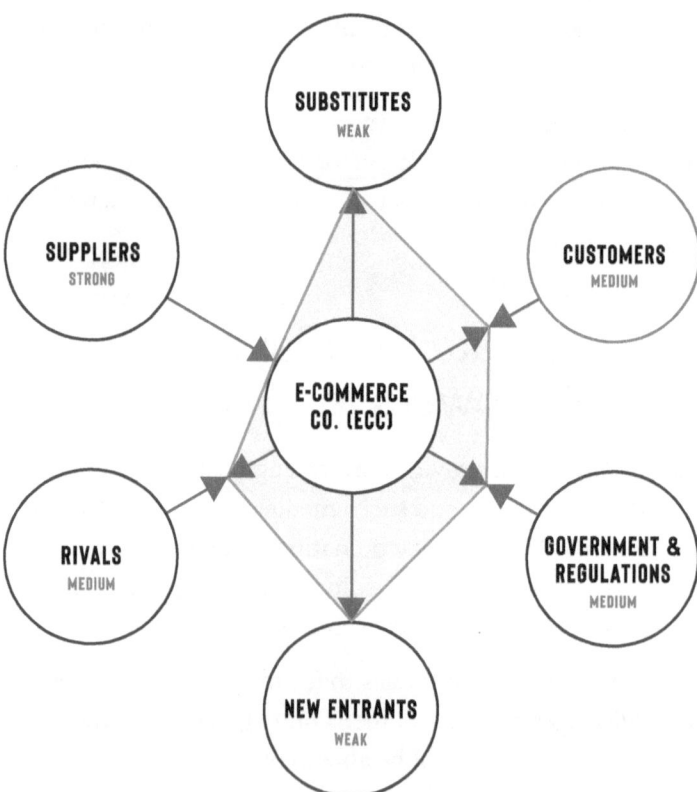

Some customers referred by software providers, such as BigCommerce, Magento, and Shopify, may shop around for an agency. However, they will likely not dictate payment and contractual terms and instead will follow ECC's lead in shaping the collaboration. Customers therefore can be considered to be **MEDIUM**-strength.

What about **SUPPLIERS**? ECC does not have to rely on local talent. It can tap the whole U.S. labor market through remote employment, whereas integrating low-cost offshore contractors from India and the Philippines, for example, would be more difficult because of the communication barriers arising from divergent cultures and time zones. Also, overcoming cultural barriers that can prevent team members socialized in remote cultures from taking on client-facing roles requires hands-on instruction.

ECC's other suppliers are the major e-commerce platforms mentioned above, which require ECC employees to carry licenses and certifications. These suppliers expect ECC to deliver a minimum number of engagements per year, even at cost or at a loss if necessary. Such platforms often control the supply of projects and eat up a substantial chunk of the end customer's wallet, putting pressure on the fees ECC can earn. Customers can also more easily shop around for platform projects. Therefore, power of suppliers is relatively **STRONG**.

So, what **SUBSTITUTES** exist for ECC's services? Targeted projects are complex and cannot be easily outsourced to technologies, such as self-service SaaS solutions. Customers might try to market their services themselves through third-party platforms, such as Amazon, but that is difficult to do without SEO and PPC support.

Most e-commerce roles have become specialized, and midmarket customers can't afford to employ or leverage full-time experts. Therefore, building internal e-commerce capacities is not a viable option for customers and substitutes represent a **WEAK** force for eCommerceCorp.

What about **NEW ENTRANTS**? Could companies set up shop overnight and intensify competition for ECC? E-commerce consulting is a people business with relatively low capital barriers to entry. However, ECC's

Core Market companies are unlikely to commit to working with small or new teams at the risk of disruption if team members depart with no backup. Attaining partnership levels with the major e-commerce platforms is also a challenge. Therefore, substitutes is a **WEAK** competitive force.

GOVERNMENT actions and regulations represent the sixth competitive force. Is it difficult to comply with Electronic Communications Privacy Act (ECPA) and General Data Protection Regulation (GDPR) rules and regulations? What about Google's changing algorithms and Apple's shifting privacy settings? Is there a risk of further governmental or platform restrictions that might limit the effectiveness and marketability of e-commerce consulting work?

Though the regulatory landscape is constantly changing, it is unlikely to substantially limit the functioning e-commerce consulting sector. This power is **MEDIUM** strong.

Assess Overall Industry Structure

Let's now assess the power dynamic in your industry by asking the following questions about *your* business:

Which forces control your industry's profitability?

- *Are there technology companies that control the software and platforms you use?*

- *Is your business dependent on the specialized skills of your employees, giving employees the power?*

- *Do your customers hold all the cards? This could be the case if, for example, there is only a small number of customers to pitch your services to.*

- *Do you have established rivals that dominate your industry, such as the Big Four accounting firms dominate the audit and assurance business?*

- *Are there barriers that prevent new entrants from getting a foothold in the market, such as high up-front capital investment, brand power, or proprietary patents or technologies?*

Are you more or less profitable than your industry average? Can you sustain or improve your position?

- *Can you increase your prices or improve the packaging of your services?*

- *Can you develop a method or a digital product or API that will give you the edge and allow you to price better?*

- *Can you develop your thought leadership by writing books or hosting industry conferences?*

Are the more profitable players better positioned in regard to the Six Competitive Forces? Why?

- *Do competitors have access to intellectual property (IP) that insulates them from competition?*

- *Are they more prominent and plugged-in with industry associations?*

- *Do they have better strategic partnerships with critical distribution channels?*

What are recent and likely future changes for each of the Six Competitive Forces?

- *Which power is on the ascendant? Are software platforms consolidating power or being disrupted?*

- *Are your customers consolidating, shrinking the industry pie, or is your market expanding, with new clients entering the fray?*

- *Are substitutes being developed? Are their start-ups peddling an automated version of your services?*

- *Are there regulatory changes on the horizon? Are privacy regulations getting more stringent or being liberalized?*

How can you best position your business?

- *Can you find a position where forces are weakest? Can you develop a niche offering that has no direct competition?*

- *Can you exploit industry change? Do you have or can you develop skills that will give your business a competitive advantage using emergent technologies?*

- *Can you reshape industry structure in your favor? Is there a software application or proprietary process that you can develop to disrupt competitors or to offer a unique advantage to your customers?*

- *Can you bypass or replace your suppliers by building your own platform? Can you raise venture capital money to do that?*

Ask yourself these and your own questions and you will soon have a vivid picture of where you stand against your competitors. You can start by listing the strengths and weaknesses of each force and then evaluate whether it has a WEAK, MEDIUM, or STRONG power over your business.

Brainstorm what moves you could make to position yourself to take advantage of your strengths and avoid exposure of your weaknesses.

Key takeaways from Chapter 2

- Analyze your industry scope for market segmentation, geographic barriers, and cultural barriers.

- Evaluate each of the Six Competitive Forces of Rivals, Customers, Suppliers, Substitutes, New Entrants, and the Government, for the power they wield in your market and over your business.

- Assess the power dynamic in your industry and determine how you can best position your business to maximize profitability.

Now that you know your Core Business and have analyzed the Six Competitive Forces and your industry structure, it is time to choose your Strategic Position. This is what we will do in the next chapter.

CHAPTER THREE

Choose a Strategic Position

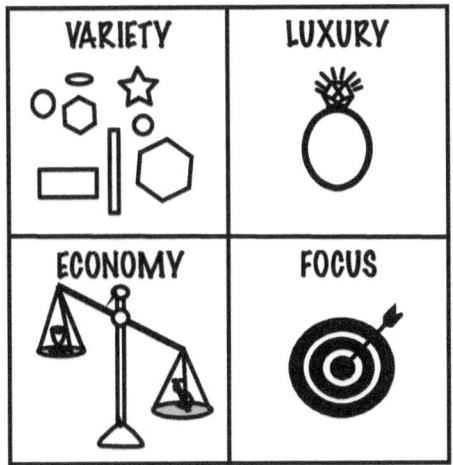

A great product isn't just a collection of features.
It's how it all works together.

—Tim Cook

You can improve your power against the Six Competitive Forces that vie for profit dollars in your industry by finding a new position in the market. Is there a position that can woo customers from established positions or attract new customers into the market?

Over recent years, big-box stores, such as Best Buy, Dick's Sporting Goods, and Home Goods, have taken market share from broad-line retailers like Walmart and Sears. Uber and CarMax recognized poorly served customer groups and started catering to them.

New positions can open because of changes in customer groups, purchase occasions, societal needs, and emerging technologies, among other changes.

There are different ways to think about the broad positioning categories available for your business. Michael Porter talks about "variety-based," "needs-based," and "access-based" positions. (See Figure 3.1.)

Figure 3.1 Porter's Positioning Triangle

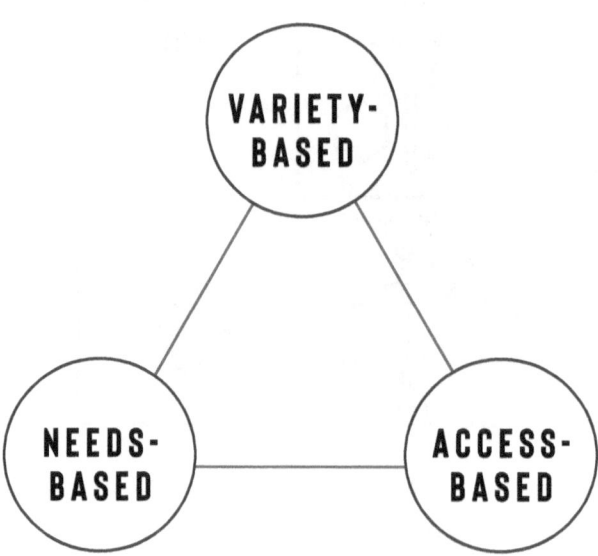

- **Variety-based positioning:** Limited product line offers superior value. Jiffy Lube focuses on simple car maintenance such as oil changes, filter replacements, and tire repairs. However, it targets a broad market of motorists, including ones whose warranties have expired and owners of new vehicles who have no time to schedule an appointment with their dealership.

- **Needs-based positioning:** A broad range of products is tailored to a distinct demographic. IKEA targets young middle-class families and offers them all types of home furnishings, household goods, and interior decoration products.

- **Access-based positioning:** Customers in poorly served geographies or with low incomes are targeted with barebones offerings. Checkers fast-food chain and Dollar Tree use this positioning stance.

The Positioning Matrix

I find Porter's presentation somewhat confusing. In my mind, needs and access don't drive positioning so much as the business's decision to offer a narrow set or a wide range of *features,* while delivering a low- or high-*performance* product.

Naturally, low-income people cannot afford high-performance products, and offering them variety often is not economically feasible. On the other hand, luxury markets will pay for both variety and performance.

Therefore, a positioning grid describing four major positions may be more meaningful and helpful. The Positioning Matrix in Figure 3.2 allows you to clearly visualize your options and evaluate what makes the most sense for *your* business.

Figure 3.2 The Positioning Matrix

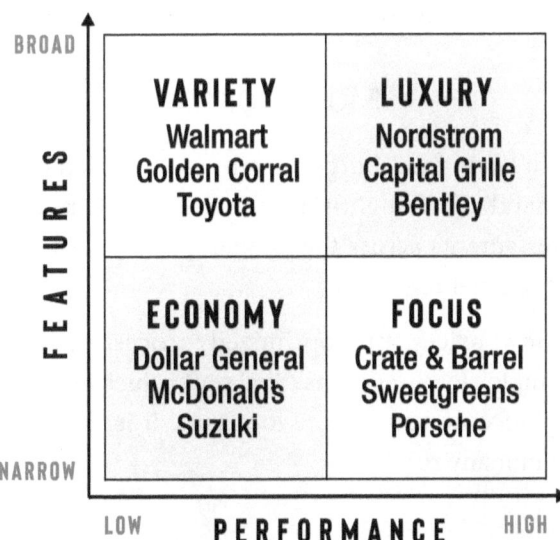

The Economy Quadrant

The bottom left quadrant, called Economy, is the positioning to attract low-income consumers who represent limited purchasing power. If you serve this consumer group, you will have to offer low prices and only a limited selection of the essential products and services that are regularly consumed by this group. This is similar to Porter's "access-based" positioning.

Dollar General

Companies that operate in the Economy positioning include Dollar General, a general chain store that serves remote and low-income locations where people often don't own cars and where supermarkets and grocery stores can't operate profitably.

Many times, Dollar General, which runs over 18,000 locations in the United States, is the only accessible retailer for the local populace, selling food, snacks, health and beauty aids, cleaning supplies, basic apparel, housewares, seasonal items, and paper products.[1]

By being the only retailer in most of its locations, Dollar General can set its prices higher than supermarkets and variety stores, which face more competition in the metropolitan areas where they operate.

McDonald's

The McDonald's fast-food burger chain serves a demographic similar to Dollar General's, but slightly more upscale. There are over 13,000 McDonald's restaurants across the United States offering $1, $2, and $3 items on a limited menu.

With its low prices and optimized processes, McDonald's can productively employ low-wage, unskilled staff, which allows it to profitably operate in low-income and remote locations. It is the only food service establishment in many rural areas.

Suzuki

Among automakers, Suzuki has been the most successful at serving low-income consumers around the world with barebones, rugged vehicles. Suzuki focuses on middle-income markets such as India and Eastern Europe where it uses local manufacturing bases. It often enjoys government tax breaks, which allows the company to offer highly affordable, value-for-money vehicles.

In the United States, the most affordable car is the Chevrolet Spark,[2] which retailed for $13,600 in 2022. It is a small passenger vehicle offering fuel efficiency, but it has a small fuel tank and lacks standard safety features, such as forward-collision warning, automated emergency braking, and cruise control. However, it is a rugged and reliable vehicle with low cost of maintenance.

Diego

The strategy in the Economy positioning is finding a formula for becoming the low-cost provider. Many years ago, I advised Diego, a flooring and interior decoration company serving DIY customers and contractors. Diego devised an operating model that allowed it to sell franchise units to entrepreneurs serving small towns and villages in Hungary, Slovakia, and Romania that catered to low-income populations.

Diego's lean business model, savvy local marketing, and charismatic founder allowed it to sell low-cost franchises and mobilize the entrepreneurial energy and networks of its franchisee partners to operate profitably in marginal markets, with minimal, if any competition.

The Variety Quadrant

The Variety positioning is about offering a wide selection of products and features at an affordable price. This quadrant often targets lower-middle-class consumers who aspire to a middle-class lifestyle but can only afford it on a budget.

Walmart

Perhaps the most iconic company serving this sector is Walmart, a retailer of groceries, entertainment, and sport and craft goods across the United States. Walmart's marketing motto is "Save Money, Live Better," which celebrates the "smart" consumer. The corporation's stated goal is to "deliver unbeatable prices on the brands you trust, in an easy, fast, one-stop shopping experience."[3]

Walmart has staked out a position where it offers the widest selection of grocery and home and office consumer goods at low prices, targeting middle-income consumers. Walmart covers all U.S. cities with a population of 10,000 or more and operates 4,700 stores, of which 3,500 are superstores (a big-box store that combines a grocery and a department store).

Golden Corral

The Golden Corral franchise restaurant chain offers low-cost buffet dining with a wide selection of dishes, including steak, fish, seafood, mashed potatoes, self-built burgers, salads, and desserts—its "famous carrot cake" among them. Golden Corral focuses on offering a broad variety of options to a loyal crowd of middle-class, often millennial, consumers.

Golden Corral operates 400 restaurants across the United States, offering an array of all-you-can-eat food for as little as $10.50 per dining experience.

Toyota

The most prominent carmaker in the Variety segment is Toyota, which offers feature-rich, dependable cars and trucks for middle-class customers in the thirty-year to fifty-year age group. Toyota's largest market is the United States, where it sold 2.3 million cars in 2021. Toyota is positioned broadly to reach a wide market, including affluent buyers with its premium Lexus brand.[4]

Toyotas are reliable and quality vehicles, and the company offers all mainstream technology options and multiple trim levels. However, even its premium Lexus models don't offer high-end speed, comfort, or technical performance characteristics.

The Focus Quadrant

The Focus positioning may be the most interesting one of the four. This is the home of those companies that want to appeal to one or more narrow markets with products tailored to the segment's specific needs. Focus quadrant products tend to limit features and accept trade-offs as the price of success. The companies here believe that "less is more" and that "one-size-fits-all fits no one."

Crate and Barrel

A successful retailer with the Focus positioning is Crate and Barrel, which sells contemporary and modern furniture, housewares, and decor through a chain of over a hundred U.S. stores. The company is known for traditional, rustic, and modern farmhouse furniture, and it targets middle-class homeowners. Crate and Barrel's selection is limited, but its products are high quality, with trendy designs. The company's motto is "Let life in."

Importantly, Crate and Barrel offers only a limited selection of items, exclusively for living spaces, baths, and kitchens for a stylish middle-class audience.

Sweetgreen

The Sweetgreen fast-food chain is a successful salad bar that is "connecting people to real food." This means that it operates a transparent supply network of local producers and prepares dishes from scratch, on the spot. Sweetgreen offers a limited menu of salads and bowls plus self-combined dishes. The drinks menu includes healthy kombuchas and other nonalcoholic beverages. The Core Market is young, health-oriented, mostly female consumers.

Notably, Sweetgreen is a food service chain that sells no comfort foods, such as burgers, fries, sugary or caffeinated beverages, or alcohol.

Porsche

One of the car brands in the Focus segment is Porsche, the sports car brand of the Volkswagen group. Porsche's vehicles are positioned as high-priced, high-quality, exclusive sports cars that offer high performance and German engineering. Porsche caters to "privileged and upscale" consumers. The brand's Core Market is college graduates with a household income of more than $100,000 a year, 85 percent of whom are male.[5]

Equally importantly, Porsche is *not* a safety-focused family car, *nor* is it inexpensive to maintain or fuel-efficient, and it offers a comparatively cramped cabin and limited space for luggage.

The Luxury Quadrant

The Luxury quadrant is the opposite of the Economy quadrant—consumers are looking for both maximum features *and* maximum performance. They might not need it all, but why compromise if you don't have to? This quadrant is about service, status, and a VIP experience. Price is secondary for the customers here.

Nordstrom

One well-known department store in this quadrant is Nordstrom, which operates a hundred stores across the United States. Nordstrom's customer service is legendary, including lifetime refund guarantees and sales assistants who are encouraged to nurture their own client list in any way they deem appropriate. According to company lore, one customer even received a refund for faulty tires he had purchased from a different company that had earlier leased Nordstrom's building.

Shortly after moving to America, I bought a suit and a sports jacket at our local Nordstrom from a young gentleman named Mitchell, who subsequently kept in touch with me and called whenever an item of clothing that he felt I might like was on sale. Years later when I walked into the store, Mitchell remembered my name and inquired about a jacket I had bought from him. When he heard that I'd stopped wearing it, he immediately offered a refund, which I could not even accept in good conscience.

Nordstrom's got it all. Variety, high performance, and raving patrons who are happy to pay premium prices for the privilege of enjoying Nordi membership and late-night VIP shopping trips.

Capital Grille

If you are looking for a chain restaurant with a premium food selection and dining experience, try Providence, Rhode Island–based Capital Grille. Founder Ned Grace envisioned an eatery that would be popular with the local business and political elite. Founded in 1990, his steakhouse chain has expanded to twenty-five states, Washington, DC, and Mexico City.

Capital Grille offers a wide selection of premium-priced meals, from soups and salads to steaks, sushi, fish, seafood, and a variety of gourmet desserts. The restaurant chain's tagline is "Wine, Dine and Dazzle," and it offers a variety of gourmet dishes and a memorable culinary experience to patrons, who are happy to open their checkbooks.

Bentley Motors

A well-known car company in the Luxury position is Bentley Motors Limited, a British designer, manufacturer, and marketer of luxury cars and SUVs, now owned by the German Volkswagen Group. The Bentley brand was formerly owned by Rolls-Royce, possibly the most iconic luxury car brand of the last hundred years.

Bentleys are equipped with all the latest technologies, and their interior is high-end. Models are equipped with 12.3-inch high-resolution touchscreens, traffic sign recognition, leather upholstery, suede-like Dinamica accents, and optional embroidery, piping, and specialty stitchings.

Bentley cars are powerful, too. Customers can choose a 6.0-liter W12 engine that offers zero to sixty miles per hour in just 3.8 seconds, with 542 horsepower and a top speed of 190 mph, or a 2.9-liter V6 hybrid engine. All vehicles come with Bentley's Active All-Wheel Drive system and four different driving modes.

Bentley pulls out all the stops on both the variety of the best equipment and materials and the driving power and performance, for a starting price of $227,000.[6]

How to Choose Your Strategic Position

If you are looking to scale a midmarket business, you may find that the Focus (low variety, high performance) position is where it's safest and easiest to begin. By picking a niche to serve, you give yourself the best chance of understanding a well-defined Core Market and can focus your energies to address it exceptionally well.

On the other hand, niche markets offer marginal payoffs for large companies that need to make big moves to make a difference for their shareholders. But with a midmarket business, you will likely find the Six Competitive Forces relatively weak, allowing you to potentially stake out a powerful position and generate profits for growth.

In 1959, Swedish carmaker Volvo staked out a unique position that has allowed it to maintain a distinctive brand in a highly competitive market without having to compete on price, performance, or quality with its Asian, European, or American rivals. It chose the Focus position, concentrating on enhancing the *safety* of its vehicles. Over the years, Volvo developed innovations that have since become standards in the auto industry.

Your job is to choose one of the positions of Economy, Variety, Focus, or Luxury where you can be most successful. Emerging companies often do best by choosing the Focus positioning in a niche where they have the potential to grow to dominance over time.

Key takeaways from Chapter 3

- Study the Positioning Matrix and your options to choose Economy, Variety, Focus, or Luxury as your position.

- Try to identify a niche where you can execute a Focus strategy of low variety and high performance—this is the easiest position in which to build a profitable business.

- You can broaden your appeal later, when your niche has been exhausted. We cover strategies to do so later in Steps 5 and 6 of the Strategy OS.

Now that you have identified your Strategic Position, let's find the critical obstacle preventing the growth of your business: your Crux Challenge.

CRACK THE CRUX

The Crux is… that the vast majority of the mass of the universe seems to be missing.

—William J. Broad

Richard Rumelt, author of *Good Strategy/Bad Strategy* and *The Crux*,[1] uses a rock-climbing analogy to describe the critical challenge of a business, "the crux," the solving of which opens the floodgates to growth.

In the movie *Free Solo*, rock climber extraordinaire Alex Honnold climbs the three-Eiffel-Towers-high (7,573 feet) El Capitan granite wall in the Yosemite Valley without a rope. In a YouTube video, Honnold demonstrates how he conquers the Crux Challenge of the El Capitan climb, what he calls the "boulder problem."[2] In an incredible scene, he switches hands while holding himself with a single thumb pressed into a minuscule crevice. From this position he executes a "karate kick" to reach a wall six feet away.

What is the Crux Challenge in *your* business? What is the problem that, if resolved, would boost your forward momentum?

The Crux Challenge of El Capitan is the boulder problem. That is the stickiest part of the climb that trumps all other challenges in complexity. If a climber can make it through the boulder problem, they will likely reach the pinnacle.

The Crux Challenge of World War II (WWII) was arguably the Battle of Britain, the fight for air supremacy in the skies over the British Isles between July and September 1940.

Britain was still the leading naval power in the world and could repel an invasion over the English Channel, provided it could deliver air cover to its fleet. However, Germany's Luftwaffe had more planes than Britain's Royal Air Force (RAF), and its pilots had gained superior experience during the Spanish Civil War.

The German air assault gradually intensified, and during two weeks in late August and early September in 1940, the RAF suffered significant losses in planes and pilots that it could not replace. Three more weeks of such losses would have depleted Britain's air defenses. However, Germany was unaware of the RAF's predicament and failed to capitalize on its momentum.

Sticking out the Battle of Britain turned out to be the pivotal event for UK prime minister Winston Churchill because it gained him time to persuade Franklin Roosevelt to rearm Britain and allowed FDR to shift public opinion in favor of U.S. engagement in the war.

This success was due to Churchill correctly identifying *aircraft production* as the crux of his strategic challenge to keep Britain in the game. After becoming prime minister in May 1940, one of the "Old Man's" first appointments was Lord Beaverbrook as Minister of Aircraft Production.

Beaverbrook was a shrewd media magnate and forceful leader who cut through government bureaucracy and forced a 50 percent increase in the available fighter aircraft in the next three months following his appointment.[3]

In this Step 2 of the Strategy OS, I show you how to (1) intuit the Crux Challenge of your business; (2) stimulate potential responses to it; and (3) take coherent actions to resolve your Crux Challenge.

- In Chapter 4, we prioritize your obstacles and intuit your Crux Challenge.

- Chapter 5 discusses ways to stimulate possible responses to solve the Crux Challenge we have identified.

- In Chapter 6, we design a set of coherent actions to move your business through the Crux Challenge and beyond.

Now let's start by exploring how to identify your Crux Challenge.

CHAPTER FOUR

Prioritize Challenges

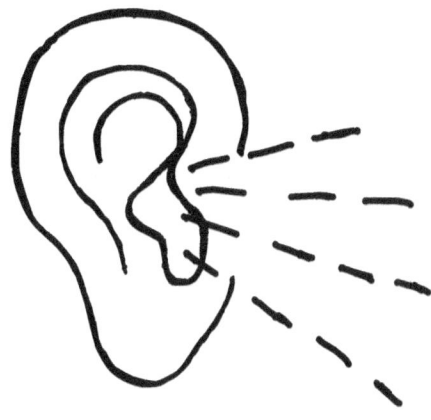

If it's a priority, you'll find a way. If it isn't, you'll find an excuse.

—Jim Rohn

In 1984, Andy Grove, Intel's legendary CEO, faced an existential decision.

Intel's Core Business, the production of dynamic random-access memory (DRAM) semiconductors, at one point accounted for 90 percent of the company's revenue and made Intel a dominating leader with over 80 percent market share. However, by the early 1980s, Japanese competitors had copied multiple generations of the product.

By continuously improving their manufacturing processes, Intel's leading competitors accumulated a significant cost advantage that eroded the American memory chipmaker's market share to less than 2 percent.

In 1984, Intel faced the decision of whether or not to invest another $100 million into DRAM production to try to regain technology leadership. Incidentally, around the same time, Busicom, a calculator manufacturer, hired Intel to design a computer chipset for its new product. An Intel employee convinced Intel's management to buy the rights to use the design in other non-calculator applications, and this created a new opening for the embattled chipmaker.[1]

But giving up on the memory business would go against the company's deeply ingrained beliefs. Memory production provided the technology skills that allowed Intel to develop other follow-on products. Furthermore, Grove and Intel's chairman, Gordon Moore, worried that without keeping memories in the product line, Intel could not offer a one-stop-shop experience, possibly losing key customers.

Andy Grove's biographer, Richard Tedlow, chronicles what happened next:[2]

> *At one point in mid-1985, after a year of "aimless wandering," Grove said to Moore, "If we get kicked out and the board brings in a new CEO, what do you think he would do?" Moore immediately replied, "He would get us out of memories." "I stared at him, numb, then said, 'Why shouldn't you and I walk out the door, come back, and do it ourselves?'"*

This was Intel's Crux Challenge. The company said no to memories and refocused on the microchip business. Within a few years, Intel has grown into a dominant force in microprocessors, just as it had been in memories a decade earlier. "Intel Inside" became an essential core of all IBM PCs and clones (disrupting Big Blue in the process).

The Three Steps to Intuiting Your Crux Challenge

Now that you have identified your Core Business, let's get you a quick win in your strategy quest.

Every business faces challenges, but not all challenges are created equal. If we can isolate your most critical challenges and find one that is solvable, we can generate an initial momentum toward creating a winning strategy for your business.

So, what exactly is a *critical* challenge?

A challenge is critical if it represents a major impact on your business, or if solving it would provide a major opportunity. To define an impact or opportunity as *major*, let's rely on the Pareto principle, or the rule of the precious few: 20 percent of your actions will create 80 percent of the impact on your business.

Accordingly, intuiting the Crux Challenge is a three-step process:

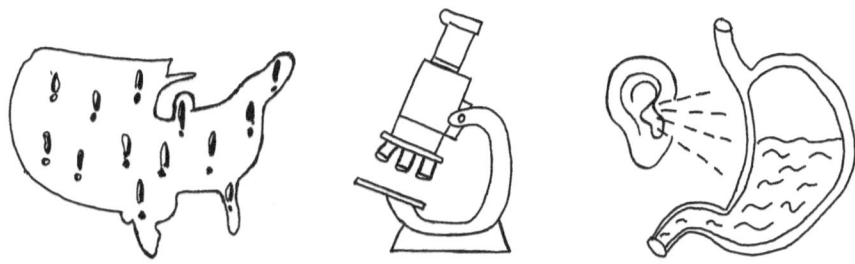

1. Identify your most important challenges.

2. Analyze these challenges.

3. Listen to your gut or intuition to determine the Crux Challenge.

   Now let's start with number one.

1. Identify Your Most Important Challenges

Canvassing your challenges requires curiosity, honesty, and willingness to face the brutal facts of your business. In order for these values to be observed, you need a culture of psychological safety in your business. After all, if you have a tendency to shoot the messenger, people won't tell you the truth.

The challenge facing charismatic leaders is to avoid drowning out the voices of caution around them. Intel's Andy Grove was famous for creating a culture of "constructive confrontation," which empowered employees to address difficult issues without regard to seniority.

Intelers believed that the company would benefit from embracing fierce discussions of conflicting views by intelligent, well-meaning individuals.

The challenge with constructive confrontation is that it can potentially provide jerks cover to bully subordinates and peers. However, a lack of open communication creates similar results, where, without being challenged, leaders become entitled to their opinions by virtue of their seniority. These "put up or shut up" cultures prevent leaders from spotting and addressing problems in real time.

Force People to Bring Issues

Alfred Sloan, the legendary CEO who built carmaker General Motors into a dominant force, demanded that his executive team act as the devil's advocate. He reportedly canceled discussions of new initiatives whenever his team had not researched valid counterarguments against a project. He considered consensus a sign of weakness rather than strength.

Similarly, venture capitalists routinely pass over opportunities when capital seekers fail to present credible research of existing or potential competitors. Every company and each product have alternatives and face risks that need to be carefully vetted and considered before a sound decision can be made.

Ask for Challenges and Opportunities in Multiple Ways

Every person's brain operates in a different way, and it is worth asking the same question multiple times to get answers. Questions are powerful because listeners cannot help but respond. But will they share their answers with you? Police officers and prosecutors use this psychology by cross-examining suspects and witnesses. This approach is so effective that suspects need to be legally reminded that they might inadvertently incriminate themselves by sharing information.

Below are questions you can ask to dig for challenges:

- *What could be working better?*

- *What is not perfect yet?*

- *What can be improved?*

- *What is the one thing that, if we could resolve it, it would make a big difference?*

- *What is the elephant in the room?*

- *What are three things that we could be doing better?*

- *What would you do if you were a competitor and wanted to put us out of business?*

- *What would be an audacious action to try if we knew we could not fail?*

- *What are the biggest gaps you see in the company?*

- *What are the two biggest issues we need to address in our upcoming session?*

- *What are the highest-impact moves we could make if we had the guts, the time, and the money to do it?*

- *What have you wanted to solve for a very long time?*

- *What issue would you bring up if you knew for sure no one could get hurt?*

Use a Facilitator to Elicit Your Challenges

Richard Rumelt in *The Crux* describes his approach to discovering hidden challenges in client organizations. As a consultant, he requests access to leaders and other key individuals and interviews them in confidence, both in person and through written follow-up questions, about the issues and opportunities facing the business. He grants anonymity to his internal sources in return for the permission to raise their issues during executive strategy sessions he facilitates.

It is natural for leaders and difference-makers to want to share sensitive information with a trusted party. These are successful individuals who want their companies to thrive and desire thorny business problems to be resolved.

I have encountered many high-powered CEOs who had the self-awareness to recognize that they were intimidating people around them. However, they just could not hold back from overselling their vision.

In many cases, smart leaders fall under the spell of the infallible CEO and unconsciously suspend their judgment, self-censor, or second-guess themselves. The late Steve Jobs was famous for projecting a "reality distortion field" around him that would sway the minds of his subordinates against their premeditated, debate-tested, and logically sound convictions.

Bringing in an outside facilitator can level the playing field on the executive team and allow less-dominant voices to be heard. This will help the CEO cover their blind spots and empower the group to harvest all good ideas.

Now that you have discovered all the potential challenges facing your business, let's dig deeper to get closer to your Crux Challenge.

2. Analyze Your Challenges

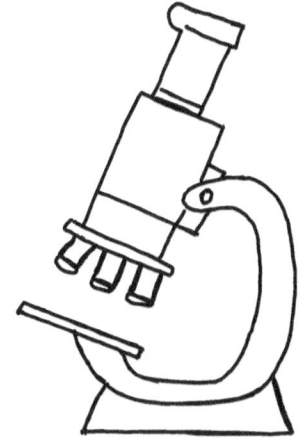

How do you analyze your challenges? Remember, we want to find the most critical ones that can be solved. In *The Crux*, Richard Rumelt gives us some suggestions on how to parse the list.

Break Them Apart

Some challenges are tricky and look unsolvable. Try to break them apart to see whether there is an element of the challenge that could be solved to create a shift. Isolate this solvable part of the challenge and add it to your list. Write each challenge on a separate sticky note or index card.

Cluster Them into Related Groups

Can you sort the challenges into clusters of items that belong together? After each possible challenge is written on a separate sticky note, I like to ask my leadership teams to sort them on a whiteboard into four to six clusters. I give no instructions on what these groups might be—they have to figure it out themselves. Smart executives often enjoy unstructured puzzles, and the CEO gets a chance to observe the team problem-solve.

Isolate Immediate Challenges

Which urgent issues must be tackled immediately? These are the ones you need to consider more deeply. The less urgent ones may wither away over time or be resolved while you traverse the Crux Challenge.

Rate Your Short List of Challenges by Importance and Solvability

Force-rank the remaining challenges. Which is the most critical one to solve? Can it be overcome? If not, can it be dissected further? Compile a list of addressable challenges and subproblems.

When you are down to your short list of standalone challenges, it's time to use your intuition.

3. Listen to Your Gut

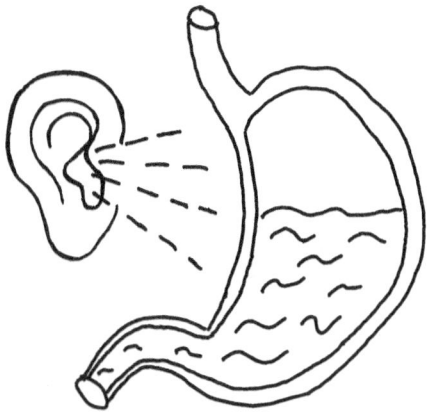

Look at your final short list of solvable challenges. Which one, if solved, would make the biggest difference for your business?

Meditate on the problem. Try to feel your way to a solution. Your subconscious is a fine-tuned instrument that allows you to synthesize information. Learn to detect and articulate your gut feelings. Tune in to hear your intuition. Don't be afraid to give yourself time. Sleep on it.

In early 2005, Apple designer Bas Ording received a call from Steve Jobs, who asked him to come up with a scrolling design for a buttonless phone. Ording started playing around with an iGesture Pad, a gesture-sensitive touchpad developed by FingerWorks, a consumer tech company Apple had acquired earlier.

As Ording was finger-scrolling a contact list, he noticed that the screen abruptly stopped at the top of the list, as if the phone was frozen. Then, while trying to make the scroll stop look natural and unfrozen, Ording intuitively stumbled upon what later became known as Apple's famous "rubber band effect."[3] He likely could never have invented such an ingenious design by following a step-by-step logical process. Intuition played a part.

Let's look at another, unrelated example of intuition at work. As a Roger Federer fan, I will never forget how he lost the 2019 Wimbledon final against archrival Novak Djokovic after having held two championship points.

Actually, Federer did nothing wrong in those points. It was Djokovic who tuned in to his intuition and played two brilliant, aggressive returns, landing winners for both. It was a manifestation of self-belief and self-trust—perhaps something helped by the intense spirituality he exhibits after wins.

Here is how another athlete, Dan Brodsky-Chenfeld, skydiving champion, articulated how instinct or intuition works.

> *Trusting our instincts is not limited to sports. In every walk of life, regardless of how well trained our instincts are, we will usually do our best by trusting them. Recent brain-scanning technology has shown that the brain unconsciously makes rational decisions, quickly analyzing the data it gets, and reaches a decision sometimes seconds before our conscious minds "think up" that same decision. Actions that feel like random choices or instinctive responses are often logical thought processes using available information carried out in the unconscious mind. Many successful business people say their best decisions are the ones they make using "gut feelings" or instinct.*

So, after brainstorming your long list of challenges and analyzing it to find a short list of solvable problems, use your intuition to home in on your Crux Challenge.

Key takeaways from Chapter 4

- Start by inventorying your most important challenges. Try to use trick questions, if you must, and perhaps a facilitator to help extract them from your team.

- Analyze these challenges by clustering them, breaking them apart, and picking and prioritizing the solvable ones.

- Use your intuition to feel your way to the most critical, solvable problem facing your business, the Crux Challenge.

- Now that you have discovered your Crux Challenge, let's generate potential solutions to overcome it.

CHAPTER FIVE

Stimulate Responses

What's in a question, you ask? Everything. It is evoking, stimulating response or stultifying inquiry. It is, in essence, the very core of teaching.

—John Dewey

On May 10, 1940, Winston Churchill was appointed prime minister of Britain in the wake of Hitler's invasion of Belgium, Luxembourg, and the Netherlands. Within weeks, the war outlook darkened considerably after France capitulated and the British Expeditionary Force had to be rescued from Dunkirk. It seemed just a matter of days before Britain would be forced to surrender and make peace with Germany, an idea that much of Churchill's cabinet, led by Foreign Secretary Lord Halifax, favored.

Churchill was generally unpopular and considered a "warmonger" in Parliament, and he only got the job because there was no one in the cabinet who showed the level of leadership required in "Britain's finest hour." The British Empire faced impossible odds against the German war machine that already occupied half of Europe and that could draw on the economic resources and people of much of the Continent for support in its war effort.

Churchill's vision was to somehow keep Britain in the game until America and its vast economy could be mobilized as an ally. This was no trifling task because U.S. public opinion overwhelmingly favored neutrality at that time.

Churchill believed in taking action and that Britain's best chance was to go on the offensive and take the war to the Axis powers. In the weeks and months following his appointment as prime minister, he initiated some of the following actions: [1,2]

- He flew to France behind enemy lines to try to convince the French government to fight on.

- He evacuated over 450,000 British and French troops as German forces were closing in on Dunkirk.

- He promoted colonel Charles de Gaulle by allowing him to broadcast his call for a French resistance through the BBC.

- He ordered the destruction of the French fleet, which was about to fall into German hands.

- He mobilized public support with speeches projecting a vision of heroic resistance and eventual victory over Hitler.

- He won over his national-unity cabinet to support fighting Germany against the odds.

- He started persuading Franklin D. Roosevelt to support Britain with weapons and munitions, which eventually led to the Lend-Lease program.

- He boosted aircraft production and upleveled the Royal Air Force to protect the skies.

- He won the Battle of Britain, when the RAF repelled the Luftwaffe over England.

- He kept morale up and national unity alive during the bombing of London, which he called the Blitz.

- He distracted Hitler by opening a new front in North Africa.

- He reinforced the Mediterranean war theater to protect the Middle East and Greece.

- He retaliated for the Blitz by bombing Berlin, Dresden, and other German cities.

- He built a network of spies to infiltrate and sabotage the Axis alliance.

- He built a relationship with Stalin to weaken Germany in Russia.

After Germany lost the Battle of Britain and its offensive stalled near Moscow, on December 7, 1941, Japan bombed Pearl Harbor, and four days later the United States entered the war against Germany.

Churchill's resistance strategy succeeded. He generated diverse responses and succeeded in creating public support and strengthening his executive power in the cabinet. Then, by orchestrating a multipronged and aggressive response, he slowed Hitler's momentum and distracted him. These actions won him time to persuade Roosevelt to help, and to ripen American opinion to supporting the war.

Roger Federer and the Tennis GOAT Race

A more recent and less violent example describes the three-man race to win the most Grand Slam tournaments in tennis history involving Roger Federer, Rafael Nadal, and Novak Djokovic.

After Federer won seventeen Grand Slam titles between 2003 and 2012, Nadal and Djokovic started to catch up with him and they prevented Federer from winning another major title for the next five years. In early 2016, Federer injured his knee in a bathroom accident and later strained his back. Consequently, after the Wimbledon Championships in early July, he decided to retire for the rest of the season.

However, after this forced break, he returned in 2017 and won three more Grand Slam titles in the next eighteen months. Federer's renaissance increased his lead in the Greatest of All Time (GOAT) race for the first time since 2009. How did he do it?

Clearly, by 2017 Roger Federer was years past his prime and faced stiff competition from younger opponents: Djokovic, Nadal, Andy Murray, and Stan Wawrinka. He had to come up with new responses to have a chance to conquer his Crux Challenge, which was suffering aging-related injuries. His efforts were focused around an eight-week unbroken practice period on the tennis courts of Dubai and Switzerland after finishing rehab for his knee injury.

Roger Federer came up with the following responses to reignite his tennis career at age thirty-five:

- He improved his backhand shots so that he could play more aggressively and defeat Nadal three times in a row, after years of unfavorable head-to-head results.

- He took physical and mental breaks, which rejuvenated him and allowed him to play more relaxed, with more joy. He even took a playful approach in his pre-serve rituals.

- He developed a shot called SABR (Sneak Attack By Roger), where he would move forward to the edge of the service box while his opponent tossed the ball, to surprise him with an aggressive half volley.

- He devised a subtle block return with a slight topspin to start return points more effectively, gaining an advantage against all but the best servers.

- He mastered a new racket with a bigger head and sweet spot allowing for more stable play, a stronger spin, and more successful reaction shots.

- He hired Ivan Ljubicic, a former world number three, who had played against him and who understood his weaknesses as well as those of his rivals. As a bonus Ljubicic lived next door to Djokovic in Monte Carlo and could potentially spy on his practices.[3]

- Finally, in the first Grand Slam tournament final, at the Australian Open, Federer decided to take the ball early and not let Nadal get into his usual topspin groove he had been using to fire opponents off the court.

The cumulative impact of all the above changes allowed the veteran Swiss tennis master to win another three Grand Slam tournaments and enjoy a rebirth on the courts.

How to Stimulate Responses to Solve *Your* Crux Challenge

Now that you have identified your highest-impact *solvable* challenge, it is time to generate potential responses. This requires creating and testing hypotheses. Let's look at various ways to generate such ideas.

Brainstorming Principles

Brainstorming is a group creativity technique where people generate ideas and solutions around a specific topic.[4] The technique was first introduced by advertising executive Alex Osborn when his employees were unable to generate good enough ideas for ad campaigns.

Osborn first named the process "organized ideation," but the term *brainstorming*, meaning "the brain to storm a problem," stuck.

Osborn believed that brainstorming is only effective for clearly stated problems because, otherwise, the structure of complex problems can derail the ideation process. He also stated four rules for effective brainstorming:

1. **Go for quantity** because the more ideas that are generated, the higher the chance that radical and effective solutions will be found.

2. **Withhold criticism** as suspending judgment allows participants to come up with unusual ideas.

3. **Welcome wild ideas** by avoiding assumptions and looking at problems from different perspectives.

4. **Combine and improve ideas** with a process of association.

Types of Brainstorming

There are several variations on brainstorming and these are worth mixing up so that people stay engaged with the technique. The facilitator should project energy and prime the group for the exercises beforehand, to induce all participants to embrace the process.

Let's look at the most popular brainstorming approaches:

- The **nominal group technique** is where participants write down their ideas autonomously and then share them with the group. The team votes on the ideas and the top-ranked ones are sent back to the team or to break-out groups for further brainstorming.

- In the **group passing technique**, each participant in a circular group writes down one idea and then passes the paper to the next person, who then builds upon it with another idea. The process is complete when the paper returns to the first contributor.

- A variation of this method is called **idea book**, when a person lists their ideas in a notebook and then passes the book to the next person on a circulation list. Each person adds their original and derived ideas, and the list eventually is discussed and prioritized in a group meeting.

- The **team idea-mapping method** is when participants brainstorm individually and contribute their ideas to a whiteboard or a mind map, an amoeba-shaped drawing of linked ideas drawn by a facilitator. In the ensuing discussion, new ideas emerge and are added to the board or the mind map, and eventually the group prioritizes the list and agrees on an action plan.

- In a **directed brainstorming**, the facilitator establishes a set of criteria that will be used to evaluate ideas. These established constraints serve as a forcing function to trigger creative ideas. Participants "brain dump" their ideas on a piece of paper and then randomly swap papers with others so that other participants can improve the ideas or use them to trigger ideas of their own. This process is repeated three or four times.

- **Guided brainstorming** is a process where participants brainstorm individually or in a group from a predetermined perspective for a set time period and all ideas are displayed on a mind map. In subsequent rounds, group members are asked to use different inventive principles to examine the problem. According to the Theory of Inventive Problem Solving, there are forty inventive principles that can be applied to solve virtually any problem.[5]

- Finally, **question brainstorming**, or **quest-storming**, is a technique to start a brainstorm by brainstorming the questions to ask to begin with. In this method, the pressure to find solutions is removed, which frees up the creativity of the group. Then questions are prioritized and the group brainstorms answers to the most important ones.

Other Brainstorming Techniques

Visualization techniques help people imagine a future state of things, which then can be verbalized.

A variation of this method is the Dan Sullivan Question, coined by the legendary business coach, which asks the respondent to transport themselves mentally to a future date and look back over the period between now and then to survey what has been accomplished.

This technique allows people to reverse-engineer the stepping-stones to the future they want.

Another technique is asking **"what if" hypothetical questions** to break down mental resistance in evaluating "unthinkable" scenarios. For example, you could ask: "What audacious plan would you attempt to accomplish if I could guarantee that you would not fail?" or "What would your ideal solution look like if money was no object?"

Richard Rumelt suggests **using past or imaginary mentors** who inspired you, or others. Ask yourself what Steve Jobs, Albert Einstein, or Abraham Lincoln would do or ask in this situation.

Edison was known to practice **hypnagogia** in generating ideas for the incandescent light bulb. He would take a nap holding a small hand weight, which would fall out of his relaxing hand and wake him at the moment he was falling asleep. He's said to have had great ideas come to him in that half-awake mental state.

Another masterly technique is to **draw on analogies** to a given situation to explore possible implications. Analogies help you recognize, simplify, and share your understanding of complex problems. I recall how the chairman of the Hungarian National Bank explained why the national currency had to be devalued by using the analogy of an overstretched family budget.

When exploring responses, **make assumptions and question why** you made them. This technique can help you spot unconscious constraints in your thinking. What biases underlie your assumptions? What if they are not valid?

Try applying the scientific approach by **establishing a testable hypothesis** to see whether it stands up to scrutiny. Do not rest if your early ideas appear good. Keep going and generate more ideas. Breakthroughs often emerge only after all conventional ideas have been exhausted.

Finally, ask yourself, **"what makes that challenge so hard to solve?"** to shed light on the nature of the difficulty. Perhaps answering this question will reveal a way to break up the problem or develop a unique insight that gets you closer to a solution.

There are almost infinite ways to brainstorm solutions. Use this handy list to apply different techniques to keep your team engaged with the process.

Key takeaways from Chapter 5

- Stimulate responses to your Crux Challenge by using brainstorming techniques. Consider using a trained facilitator, such as a Steve Preda Business Growth (SPBG) Guide. SPBG Guides are trained experts in helping you find your Crux Challenge.

- The four principles of brainstorming are to (1) generate a high quantity of ideas; (2) suspend judgment of the quality of the ideas during brainstorming; (3) invite wild and out-of-the-box thoughts; and (4) combine ideas and improve them.

- Try different brainstorming methods to maximize the number and quality of ideas that you can harvest from the group and to keep people highly engaged in the process.

- Brainstorming techniques include visualization, asking hypothetical questions, interviewing imaginary mentors, drawing on analogies, and building and challenging hypotheses.

Having generated responses that most likely would work, it is time to take coherent action to address your Crux Challenge. We will review how to formulate an action plan in Chapter 6.

CHAPTER SIX

Design Coherent Action

The path to success is to take massive, determined action.

—Tony Robbins

In 1997, Gil Amelio, the CEO of Apple, was stuck. His company was rapidly losing market share, but Amelio hoped that acquiring a new operating system might revive its fortunes.

He turned out to be right, but not in the way he intended to be.

There were two obvious options available for Apple. One was to acquire BeOS, an operating system developed by Be Inc., a fledgling competitor to Microsoft Windows founded by a former Apple executive. The other was to buy or license NeXTSTEP, a UNIX-based operating system developed by a company called NeXT Software. NeXT Software was run by Apple cofounder Steve Jobs.

Amelio chose NeXT Software. However, the *real* operating system that came with the acquisition was not NeXTSTEP but Steve Jobs himself. Jobs signed up as an advisor to Apple, but took Amelio's job within months.

Jobs's second coming to Apple was a great example of having a strategy and taking coherent action.

Steve Jobs had a clear vision and strategy since the early eighties, as the founding CEO of Apple. However, he did not yet have enough management experience at that time to execute it. He was volatile and abrasive, and he eventually got pushed out of his own company.

The Apple cofounder then launched NeXT Computing, later renamed NeXT Software, which created innovative, well-reviewed products. The company developed a following, but never became commercially successful.

Steve Jobs's Vision

Jobs's vision for Apple was for it to be a consumer product company with integrated hardware and software offerings to create intuitive and trouble-free user experiences. He positioned Apple products to appeal to creative people, changemakers, and free thinkers who ignored the status quo.

Upon his return to Apple, Jobs saw why the company was drifting. It had stopped focusing on its Core Business. Instead of creating intuitive computers, it had expanded its product line, bundled Hewlett-Packard printers and other peripherals, and licensed its operating system to competitors, which then became Mac clones that cannibalized Apple's high-margin computer sales.

In other words, Apple tried to stand for everything and it stood for nothing.

So, upon taking the reins, as an "advisor" and later as CEO, Jobs righted the ship to get back on course to his original strategy. His first priority, or Crux Challenge, was to stem Apple's losses and bring it back from the brink of bankruptcy.

Apple 2.0's Coherent Actions

Specifically, Steve Jobs took thirteen coherent actions within months of returning to Apple.[1] These tactics reversed the company's fortunes. Within a calendar quarter, Apple shifted from an organization hemorrhaging cash and people to a company that was reenergized and profitable. Apple's stock price quickly doubled.

Jobs took these specific actions to turn the tide:

1. He arranged for NeXT engineers to replace Apple executives in key technical functions.

2. He stopped the company losing employees by reducing the exercise price of employee stock options to the prevailing market price. (This was a legal but unorthodox step that was frowned upon by public markets.)

3. He asked 90 percent of his board to resign and replaced them with directors who backed the new strategy.

4. He killed the Newton stylus-powered handheld device developed by Jobs's "assassin" John Scully for $100 million.[2] Axing the gadget freed up engineers for other products and future mobile devices.

5. He cut Apple's product line by 70 percent to four principal products: one laptop and one desktop model each for the consumer and the professional Core Markets.

6. He got the company out of printers and servers to redirect engineering and marketing to focus on core products.

7. He spearheaded the development of the iMac, a new line of affordable home desktops.

8. He made peace with Bill Gates by dropping patent infringement litigation. In return, Microsoft committed to long-term software licensing and invested $150 million in nonvoting Apple stock.

9. He got involved in all aspects of the business, including product design, where to cut expenses, supplier negotiations and ad agency selection.

10. He repositioned Apple as a lifestyle consumer brand by devising and launching the "Think Different" campaign.

11. He involved his ad agency with new products to transmit his passion into each Apple ad.

12. He installed the G3 PowerPC microprocessor in all computer models, which ran faster than Intel's Pentiums.

13. He terminated the licensing of the MacOS to protect Apple's premium positioning from clone manufacturers.

Jobs also took the painful step of laying off three hundred employees, which helped erase over $1 billion in quarterly losses and produced a modest profit in his first full calendar quarter as CEO.

In the following fourteen years, until Steve Jobs's death, Apple created $500 billion in shareholder value. Jobs left a legacy of an enduring innovative business, which became the world's most valuable company under his handpicked successor, Tim Cook.

When Jobs had taken over, Apple was "90 days from bankruptcy."[3] Jobs addressed this Crux Challenge by taking coherent actions to revive the company's focus, inspire its staff, rebuild its strategic relationships, reenergize execution, and revive its brand.

So, let's take a closer look at what makes actions coherent.

What Are Coherent Actions?

According to the *Oxford Dictionary*, *coherent* means "logical, consistent and forming a whole." Coherent actions are those with these three characteristics that address the Crux Challenge of your strategy. Let's look at each characteristic in turn.

Logical Actions

According to *Merriam-Webster's* thesaurus, *logical* means capable of reasoning or using reason in an orderly, cogent fashion. You must clearly explain your actions to resolve your Crux Challenge to your team. Your people must understand why you are taking these actions and how they will address the principal challenge your organization is facing.

When Steve Jobs announced the narrowing of Apple's product portfolio, he drew a four-quadrant matrix and labeled the top row "Desktop," the bottom row "Portable," the left column "Consumer," and the right column "Pro." (See Figure 6.1.) It became immediately obvious to his audience that these four options were sufficient to serve Apple's Core Markets. Offering a wider product portfolio would only confuse consumers and lengthen development cycles.

Figure 6.1 Apple's product matrix in 1997

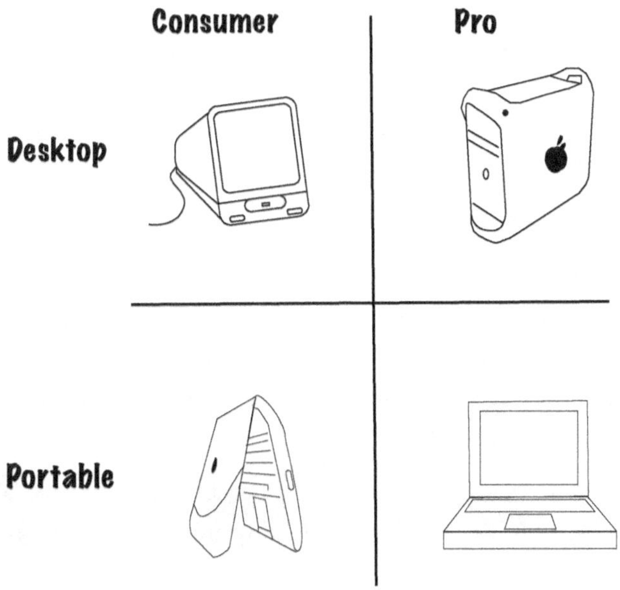

Consumer | **Pro**

Desktop

Portable

Consistent Actions

Consistent means "acting or done in the same way over time, especially so as to be fair or accurate." Jobs's Crux Challenge was to save Apple, and the actions he took over time were consistent with this purpose and with each other.

For example, narrowing the product portfolio and redeploying staff to accelerate the release cycle were both actions consistent with improving product quality and profitability. The same applied to canceling licensing agreements to strengthen the Mac's brand by enhancing pricing and quality consistency.

Replacing the board was also consistent with Apple's new direction and leadership style. Jobs ousted the consensus culture and invited in strong, visionary leadership. He needed a board to replace the Amelio and Scully loyalists who might have wanted to second-guess his decisions.

Burying the hatchet with Gates was also consistent with saving the business. It's no use holding out for a settlement windfall if you don't survive to see it. The company also needed Microsoft's popular Office products to run on Macs.

The only inconsistency in Jobs's actions may have been the axing of the Newton handheld device, which with Jobs's support might have become what the PalmPilot personal digital assistant (PDA) ended up being.

Actions Forming a Whole

Coherent actions should all link together and further the solution to the Crux Challenge. In the case of Apple, all thirteen actions evidently contributed to the shift in Apple's fortunes. Some of the moves have had longer-term impact, too, such as the board changes, the processor upgrade, and the Microsoft peace treaty.

However, all moves were coherent and consistent with Jobs's longer-term vision in which Apple regained its leadership in the premium consumer tech segment.

Bringing Big Blue into the Twenty-First Century

IBM was the dominant computer company in the world up until the late 1980s. It was the go-to supplier to *Fortune*-ranked companies, where "no one got fired for choosing IBM."

However, Big Blue was slow to acknowledge the advent of the personal computer era. When it finally did, it became dominant in this segment for a while but soon stumbled and handed industry leadership to Microsoft and Intel.

To escape its own slow bureaucracy, IBM allowed Bill Gates to keep the rights to the DOS operating system, which it could then license to IBM-clone manufacturers. By the time Big Blue developed its own system, called OS/2, Microsoft Windows already owned the market for PC operating systems.

IBM lost control of the microchip for a similar reason. It wanted a powerful machine quickly, so it opted for an off-the-shelf chip from Intel. Using aggressive litigation and the "Intel Inside" branding tactic, Intel suppressed IBM's second sourcing partner, AMD, in the IBM-clone market and became the dominant chipmaker for PCs.

As the computer market continued to shift away from mainframes toward PCs, IBM was slow to neutralize clone manufacturers, fearing government antitrust action. Thus, IBM's market share in PCs plummeted from over 80 percent to below 20 percent by the mid-1990s. Big Blue was losing ground fast.[4]

Lou Gerstner to the Rescue

From the late 1980s, IBM saw the writing on the wall. CEO John Akers launched a sweeping restructuring to reinvigorate the company after years of drifting. This included decentralizing innovation, design, and manufacturing into autonomous organizations called "Baby Blues" to be led by a younger generation of IBM executives.

To cut costs, Akers reduced IBM's 400,000-strong workforce by 10 percent and pushed to split the company into autonomous business units that could compete with their more focused and agile competitors.[5]

However, the company kept making losses, and the board decided to replace Akers with the former CEO of RJR Nabisco, Lou Gerstner. Gerstner was chosen after none of the IBM competitor CEOs approached was interested in taking the job.

Gerstner identified slow execution as the Crux Challenge. He wanted to break the gridlock by further simplifying the organization and accelerating decision-making. However, as he studied Akers's decentralization plans, he saw a bigger opportunity: IBM was uniquely positioned to integrate the separate computing technologies that were emerging.

IBM's brand and client relationships were its biggest asset, and the company could provide complete IT solutions to customers who had already bought IBM computers. For others, the barely profitable IBM hardware could open the door to more profitable consulting deals.

IBM 2.0 Coherent Actions

As Gerstner explained in his book *Who Says Elephants Can't Dance?*, he carried out the following coherent actions to activate IBM's system integration strategy:[6]

1. Tied employee compensation to company rather than division performance. This forced people to cooperate and venture outside of their fiefdoms.

2. Consolidated advertising agencies down to one to create a single, common brand message for all IBM products and services around the world.

3. Began rewarding teamwork and put an end to consensus building to break the bureaucratic gridlock in decision-making.

4. Created a new way to measure results. Employees needed to know who their competitors were outside of IBM, not across the corridor.

5. Launched a crusade against perfectionism and analysis paralysis. In the new IBM, people would be rewarded for getting things done fast.

6. Required every employee to make three personal commitments to fulfill broader IBM goals. Salary was tied to performance against these commitments.

7. Pulled the plug on the OS/2 operating system, which lost to Windows despite its technical superiority.

8. Canceled the development of big corporate software applications that IBM spent mightily to develop but made no money on.

Lou Gerstner was an outsider without any emotional bonds to IBM's past. This allowed him to see a new direction unthinkable to the Big Blue faithful.

He saw that IBM's decades-old hardware business and short-lived dominance in PCs had been disrupted. However, the power of the brand—its customer relationships and the quality of its engineers—pointed to a potentially bright future in services.

Thanks to Lou Gerstner's coherent actions, IBM's market capitalization grew from $12 billion to $100 billion between 1993 and 2002, surpassing its previous peaks. However, Big Blue was eventually left behind by the giants of the Internet Age.

Key takeaways from Chapter 6

- Coherent action means consistent, multipronged, aligned steps taken by the whole company to overwhelm its Crux Challenge.

- Explain why you are taking these actions and how they will address the principal challenge your organization is facing.

- Be consistent—act in the same way over time—so that your tactics have time to yield results and be embraced by the company.

- Make your actions all link together and further the solution to the Crux Challenge you identified.

Having found the right Strategic Position for your business and solved the Crux Challenge that has held you back, it is time to discover the constraints your business faces and the brand promises that these predispose you to offer.

We will do this next in Step 3.

CAPITALIZE ON
CONSTRAINTS

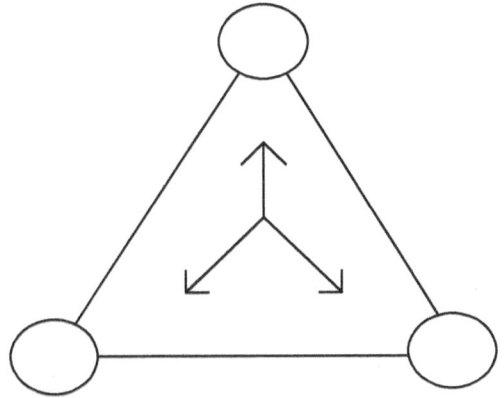

Design is the beauty of turning constraints into advantages.

—Aza Raskin

In 1943, a Swedish teenager named **Ingvar Kamprad**, from Elmtaryd Farm in **Agunnaryd** Parish, started a business called **IKEA**. He first sold matches, self-caught fish, and Christmas cards.

Then, at high school he heard a lecture on Frederick Taylor, the father of scientific management. The efficiency that systemized production created excited the boy and he wondered why such methods were ignored by distributors. He decided that he would try to fix that.

Kamprad envisioned revolutionizing distribution. His business evolved into an import–export venture, where he purchased pens, watches, and nylon stockings from Switzerland and sold them using sales letters and small brochures via mail order. His customers were country folk like himself whose life and thinking he understood and whom he could convince to buy his products.

At the end of the 1940s, IKEA's main rival started selling furniture. Kamprad liked the idea of selling local goods by mail and jumped into that business.

From Mail Order to Trade Fairs

In the early 1950s, IKEA's sales letters and brochures evolved into the IKEA Catalog, which decades later became the most printed publication in the world.

Local demand for mail-order furniture was brisk, and in 1950, Kamprad decided to step out of his region and exhibit at a Stockholm trade fair. His innovation was to display retail prices that were much lower than his competition's. IKEA could sell low because the company had no showroom, salesforce, or factory and had very low overhead.[1]

However, IKEA's discounting strategy created a backlash, and the Swedish furniture industry boycotted the company—IKEA was banned from trade fairs and Swedish suppliers were warned not to trade with the company. IKEA fought back by exhibiting under different names and via joint venture partners. Kamprad also created a separate company for procurement to get around the boycott.

Eventually, the exhibition ban forced the company to open its own stores in Sweden, Norway, and Denmark. It was at that time that Kamprad witnessed a store manager struggling to load a table into his car, and the man broke the legs off the table in frustration.[2] This triggered Kamprad's idea of modular furniture that could be shipped home and assembled by the customer.

The Supply Chain Emerges

The supplier boycotts also helped IKEA evolve. Kamprad ventured across the Baltic Sea to outsource production to state-owned factories in Poland, Romania, and East Germany. These Eastern Bloc governments needed hard currency revenues and produced cheaply, strengthening IKEA's price competitiveness. This cost advantage helped IKEA expand rapidly in Western Europe, Japan, and the United States.

The fall of the Berlin Wall disrupted IKEA's supply chain, so the company shifted to building its own factories in Eastern Europe and later in Asia.

In the ensuing decades, IKEA expanded to over 400 stores in fifty countries and developed a slew of Unique Activities, including using Swedish-sounding names for its products to save customers from having to remember product codes.[3] Typical showrooms were giant buildings with easy parking near major motorways. Stores included childcare and dining facilities and sold cheap toys to keep kids entertained while their parents shopped.

Unique Activities are singular approaches to overcoming the constraints facing your business. The more constraints you overcome the more different your business can become from competitors, accumulating an unassailable advantage over time.

Business Constraints Catalyze Differentiations

IKEA's story is instructive because the constraints it faced forced it to innovate. These innovations led to unique capabilities and enabled the company to make differentiated brand promises.

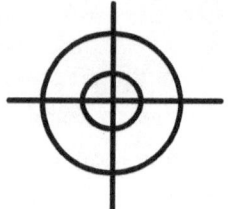  

In Step 3, I show you how to use your constraints to develop Unique Activities for your business.

- In Chapter 7, we examine how identifying your business's constraints allows you to be different and offer unique value and thus brand promises to your customers. Your Business Constraints show you who you are *not* and what you should *not* try to do.

- Once you know your Business Constraints, find something else your business can do that others can't or that others have not yet discovered. This could be your unique way, your Unique Activities, that allow you to swim out into a blue ocean of low-competition growth. We cover these in Chapter 8.

- In Chapter 9, we talk about how your brand promises will manifest in Unique Activities, which are your way of getting around your weaknesses and building on your strengths.

You probably already have a few of the Unique Activities figured out. We will map them and discover others along the way in Steps 4 and 5 of the Strategy OS. We will ultimately forge these into a unique Strategy Stack that will make your business sustainably different, like IKEA is.

CHAPTER SEVEN

Find Your Business Constraints

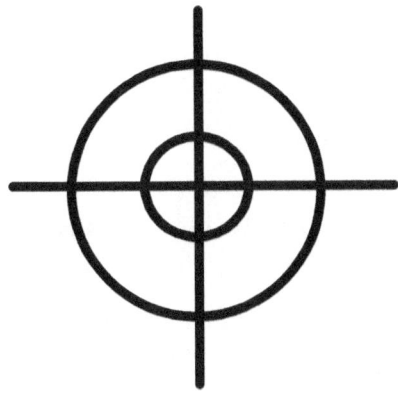

Innovation is born from the interaction between constraint and vision.

—Marissa Mayer

The constraints in your business are the most important compass to your strategy. They demarcate the line which you can push against to differentiate your business.

IKEA

Let's look at our immediate example, IKEA. Which constraints helped it evolve to a hyper-dominant furniture retailer in the past forty years?

The first constraint the company's founder, Ingvar Kamprad, came up against was that his business was based in Älmhult, Sweden, a small town of only 18,000 inhabitants in 2021. Back when IKEA was founded, there were few if any businesses around, no infrastructure to help him expand.

Kamprad responded by developing his writing skills. He convinced pen and watch companies in Switzerland to treat him as a distributor and he learned how to compose effective sales letters to peddle his imported gadgets to local customers.

When Kamprad saturated his small local market, he was forced to look at other products to sell. This led him to entering the furniture business, in which a Swedish company could actually have an edge.

Then IKEA hit another constraint. Mail-order sales were insufficient to feed growth in larger cities, where people had access to stores. Kamprad turned this apparent handicap into another weapon. He disrupted established competitors by exhibiting at trade fairs and offering transparent and low prices, which was unheard of at the time in Sweden.

The old boys then fought him by banning IKEA from exhibiting at these trade fairs, which forced Kamprad to open his own stores, which drove sales further. Everyone loves an underdog, and Kamprad capitalized on the "Robin Hood positioning" gifted him by the "Swedish furniture guild."

When manufacturers boycotted IKEA, the company was forced to look outside Sweden for suppliers, and it found a much cheaper source in Eastern Europe that none of its competitors had discovered. Another unique opportunity that improved margins and fueled growth for the business.

When one of Kamprad's managers broke a table in frustration while trying to load it into a customer's car, it led to another breakthrough: modular furniture.

The disruption of East European suppliers gave IKEA a further push. The company was forced to develop its own manufacturing operation from that point, which opened the opportunity for IKEA to expand the modularity concept and find still lower-cost suppliers farther east.

Turn by turn, every constraint created a unique opportunity to improve the business and leave competitors in the dust. IKEA could have caved and given up, but it didn't. What doesn't kill you makes you stronger. Every crisis the business survived made it more competitive.

Germany's Postwar Productivity Secret

I have witnessed a phenomenon time and again in business, as well as in politics. Beginning in the 1960s, West Germany's economy became a powerhouse in Europe. Western Europe, America, and later Eastern Europe and Asia continued to buy German cars and machinery. A few countries in Northern Europe kept pace, but the rest of Europe, especially Italy, Spain, Greece, and the UK, regularly devalued their currencies against the strengthening deutsche mark to restore their nations' export competitiveness.

As an example of the gradual strengthening of the deutsche mark, the value of DM100 grew from $24 in 1960 to $61 at the end of 1999, a 2.5× revaluation.[1]

Every time its export partners devalued their currencies against the deutsche mark, suddenly German cars and machines became more expensive in those countries. German companies had to cut prices to remain competitive in these foreign markets, which reduced their profitability.

However, these exporters reacted by rapidly improving productivity and restoring their pre-devaluation profit margins. In the meantime, the mighty deutsche mark allowed German tourists to travel like royalty.

Germany's export constraint, the regular devaluations, allowed it to register the fastest productivity growth in the postwar Western world.

In 1999, after adopting the euro as a common European currency, Germany no longer faced revaluations against the currencies of its traditional European trading partners. This productivity pressure lifted from German industry and apparent productivity improvements slowed. To the casual observer, Germany no longer feels that much more prosperous than its southern neighbors. The gap stopped widening and has possibly narrowed in the past two decades.

Business Constraints and Their Strategic Implications

The Business Constraints facing your business force you to decide to *not do* things. It is helpful to articulate these Strategic Implications because they will help you discover your potential brand promises. (More on that in Chapter 8.) Figure 7.1 shows the Business Constraints and their Strategic Implications that IKEA was facing.

Figure 7.1 Constraint–implication examples: IKEA

CONSTRAINTS	IMPLICATIONS
Few local customers	Operating retail stores is uneconomic
Can't afford salespeople to sell products	Must use self-service sales model
No local manufacturers to procure from	Can't offer locally produced goods
Furniture hard to transport	Assembled furniture cannot be retailed for instant use
East European supplies get disrupted	Must set up own manufacturing operations in Eastern Europe. Spurs modularity and design innovation and streamlines logistics and warehousing

Ryanair

Ryanair is an ultra-low-cost carrier that was founded near Dublin, Ireland, in 1984. It grew from a small airline that flew the short journey from Waterford, Dublin, to London Gatwick, into Europe's largest carrier.

Initially, Ryanair faced serious Business Constraints in a highly regulated European airline industry. The market for decades was dominated by state-subsidized flagship carriers, many of which were government owned and unprofitable.

How could Ryanair compete?

The company's first coup was to exploit a legal loophole and enter the profitable Dublin–Luton route, which to that point had been a duopoly of the British and Irish national carriers. Ryanair followed this up with an acquisition of London European Airways, which allowed the company to start connecting flights from Luton to Amsterdam and Brussels.

However, by the end of the 1980s, Ryanair was unprofitable, and CFO Michael O'Leary suggested closing it down. CEO Tony Ryan proposed instead that they visit Herb Kelleher, the CEO of low-cost regional airline Southwest, and study how he was managing to run a profitable business.

O'Leary and Ryan were astounded to see that Southwest turned planes around in twenty-five minutes, while European airlines needed at least seventy-five minutes to do so. Fast turnaround meant that Southwest's planes could fly more trips each day than its competitors could, so that the company was making a good return on its expensive Boeing fleet, by far the biggest cost in the business.

The two Ryanair executives returned from their U.S. trip inspired. All they needed to do was to slim down to a single fleet, reduce turnaround time to twenty-five minutes, and pick secondary airports where fees and traffic were substantially lower.[2]

Ryanair transitioned to using Boeing 737s only, which allowed it to reduce its maintenance, repair, and overhaul costs; reduce staff training; and increase its flexibility in staff allocation.

Ryanair was further helped by the deregulation of the airline industry in Europe in 1992, which gave carriers from one EU country the right to operate scheduled services between other EU states. By the late 2010s, Ryanair became Europe's largest airline, employing 19,000 people.[3]

While Southwest in the United States positioned itself as the "fun carrier," Ryanair embraced being the bad guys that cut costs to the bone in their quest to democratize air travel.

The company charged passengers for checking in at the airport, printing boarding passes, paying with a credit card, and carrying hand luggage beyond a laptop case or small backpack that fit under the seat. Passengers were only allowed to bring on food and drink that fit in their handbag, and on-flight services were offered for a king's ransom.[4]

To further reduce costs, the airline installed nonreclining seats with no back pockets and stored life jackets overhead to create more room for more seats and faster cleaning of aircraft.

Instead of worrying about the negative publicity that these changes created, O'Leary—who took over as CEO in 1994—embraced it as free PR. He courted controversy by suggesting that Ryanair might redesign its aircraft to allow standing passengers traveling in "vertical seats," charge passengers for using the toilet, charge extra to overweight passengers, and ask travelers to carry their checked-in luggage to the aircraft.

Now let's look at Ryanair's Business Constraints and their Strategic Implications in Figure 7.2.

Figure 7.2 Constraint–implication examples: Ryanair

CONSTRAINTS	IMPLICATIONS
Full-service airlines are often unprofitable	The flying experience must be stripped down to make money
High airport fees at major cities	Must use cheaper, out-of-city airports
Late start and low brand awareness compared to flag carriers	Build a brand embracing the outsider bad boy status
Small, remote destinations are unprofitable	Reduce price point to generate demand to scale flights and make them profitable

MB Partners

The story of the investment banking firm that my wife and I founded in 2002 in Budapest, Hungary, also demonstrates how constraints shape a business and create opportunities.

Around the time we started the company, I was obsessed with management and leveraged buyouts (LBOs). I read *Barbarians at the Gate*, the story of RJR Nabisco's LBO by Kohlberg Kravis Roberts & Co, and books about Michael Milken, the junk bond king, and many others. I believed that twelve years after the fall of the Berlin Wall and a decade following the privatization of state-owned companies, a buyout wave could happen in Hungary too.

I thought that enterprising managers in their thirties and forties were ready to become owners. These managers, who, like me, would have studied in Western Europe and learned finance and marketing from Western corporations, would want to control their destinies by becoming owner-managers.

Interest rates were coming down and banks were more open to financing management buyouts. I worked at one of these banks myself, arranging such loans. I felt qualified in the field and believed that I could play a leading role creating the buyout market.

As it turned out, I grossly overestimated the market opportunity. In our first year in business, we worked on only two such engagements, and only one of them turned into a deal. Few middle-aged managers appeared willing to risk their jobs to strike out on their own. Even fewer had savings or collateral to put skin in the game. Without these, banks wouldn't finance deals.

The First Pivot

Since it was too late to turn back and take a job, we pivoted the business to help midcap companies access an equity line from the Hungarian Development Bank (HDB). This was a new program, and we were the first boutique firm to recognize and "mass-promote" the opportunity and our consulting services to midcap businesses. After twelve months of cooperation, HDB decided that it had more opportunities than it could handle and would cut out the middlemen. Us.

The Second Pivot

After HDB pulled the plug, we were in trouble. The buyout business never got off the ground and we were now kicked out of HDB's equity program. I was paying three full-time employees at this point and started to panic.

The flicker of hope was a fledgling market for representing small business owners and helping them sell their business to international strategic buyers.

During the privatization wave of the 1990s, a handful of Austrian and Dutch investment banks controlled the mergers and acquisitions (M&A) advisory space, with Big Four accounting firms performing transaction support services. However, a growing number of middle-aged owners who had started their businesses under the thawing of the communist regime were getting ready to retire. Therefore, a new market would emerge to help these business owners exit.

But MB Partners had no international M&A network. Without connections to international buyers, we had no credibility with business owners to act as their sell-side advisors. There was little local demand for acquisitions at the time.

I reached out to several international M&A networks that aggregated independent M&A firms, but none of them wanted to partner with a small firm like us. But this gave me an idea: What if *I* formed such a network with like-minded small boutique firms across Central Europe?

Within three months, M&A Central Eastern Europe (MACEE) was formed at the Absint Restaurant in downtown Budapest with eight founding members, and I became its first president.

Our small group was extremely entrepreneurial and collaborative, and we all started signing up sell-side M&A clients virtually overnight.

Project Acceleration

Eighteen months later, we were hired by a stationery product distributor. It had a loyal roster of corporate customers to whom it was selling all kinds of consumable office products, from paper cups to rolling chairs. The business was owned by three partners who claimed that they had gotten burned out running their fast-growing, but low-margin business. They wanted out.

We quickly lined up a Romanian buyer, a swashbuckling entrepreneur, through our MACEE colleagues. The buyer liked the selling memorandum and business plan we'd prepared, and they hired KPMG to start a due diligence review of the company.

However, the morning of the kickoff, the CEO called us in for an urgent meeting where he confessed that the company's warehouse data had been falsified to keep bankers at bay. The company had a multi-million-dollar hole in its balance sheet, and consequently its book value was negative. The company was worthless.

This dramatic development happened at the worst possible moment for MB Partners. We were just coming out of a long "dry spell," when we had closed no transactions, and had hired a group of young talent in the hope of growing the firm. MB Partners was quickly running out of cash.

The problem was not sales but execution. Each of our engagements required the research and production of a compelling selling memorandum describing the business and a financial model projecting a multiyear business plan for our client's business.

We charged monthly retainers during a three-month go-to-market process of producing these documents. Learning from our mistake with the stationery company, our process now included a light due diligence of the business as well. I realized that we could only stay solvent if we accelerated our retainer billings *and* processed deals *much* faster.

Earlier in the year, we had merged MACEE with one of the leading international M&A networks called IMAP. After the merger, I visited the most successful partner firms and interviewed partners about their best practices, from producing sales memoranda and financial models to running auction processes.

I spent the following two weekends in my office completely redesigning and documenting our memorandum and modeling processes. I figured out that by modularizing these documents, we could farm out the research and number-crunching to junior members of our team and accelerate our production process dramatically.

Better still, we could collect the three months' retainer up front and produce documents in three weeks instead of three months. This would make our clients happy, because they could go to market faster, while our services would become more competitive. The move would also dramatically improve our cash flow and allow us to do more deals with the same staff. Win win win.

Now let's look at the Business Constraints MB Partners faced and their respective Strategic Implications in Figure 7.3.

Figure 7.3 Constraint–implication examples: MB Partners

CONSTRAINTS	IMPLICATIONS
Buyout and government-funded equity markets dry up	Have to compete with other sell-side M&A firms for traditional engagements
International networks are not available	Must form own network to have affiliations
Can't afford to finance drawn-out delivery cycle	Must bill up front and increase velocity of production

Key takeaways from Chapter 7

- Devise how you can turn lemons into lemonade. Business Constraints catalyze creativity and allow you to find a differentiated growth opportunity. The Strategic Implications of your constraints may suggest points of leverage that your competitors won't have.

- Consider the constraints IKEA, Ryanair, and MB Partners faced and their respective implications.

In the following chapter, we will explore how such Business Constraints and their Strategic Implications can be used as leverage to articulate brand promises. When one door closes, another opens. Your goal is to find the opportunity your Business Constraints offer. Pushing against constraints is a powerful source of creativity and business model innovation.

CHAPTER EIGHT

Articulate Brand Promises

A brand is a promise. A good brand is a promise kept.

—Muhtar Kent

What are brand promises and why should you make them?

Your brand promises communicate the compelling benefits that you consistently deliver to your customers. The more unique and useful your brand promises are to your Core Market (more on that later in Chapter 10), the more consistently powerful your brand will become.

A brand promise is only as impactful as the sacrifices you've made to be able to offer it. If you have not made trade-offs, then you are still offering a generic product. If your Porsche is safe, family-friendly, and gives a smooth ride, then it's not a sports car.

Some of these trade-offs arise naturally, that is, they derive from the Business Constraints facing your business and the Strategic Implications you must confront as a result. Let's look at the brand promises of the companies that we examined in the previous chapter.

IKEA's Brand Promises over the Years

Convenient Mail-Order Purchases

Ingvar Kamprad started IKEA in a small Swedish municipality with few customers. The low foot-traffic made opening a store uneconomic. Further, Kamprad did not have the capital to fund such a venture.

However, he understood local customers intimately, being one of them. This allowed him to appeal to their wants and desires through sales letters and small brochures and to offer products that were not otherwise available. He sourced these from imports through correspondence with overseas manufacturers and sold them by mail order for home delivery. IKEA's brand promises evolved over the years (see Figure 8.1).

Figure 8.1 The evolution of IKEA's brand promises

CONSTRAINTS	IMPLICATIONS	BRAND PROMISES
Few local customers	Operating retail stores is uneconomic	**Convenient mail-order purchase**
Can't afford salespeople to sell products	Must use self-service sales model	**Furniture at transparent, discounted prices** (at trade fairs)
Swedish furniture manufacturers' boycott	Can't offer locally produced furniture	**Quality, inexpensive furniture** (sourced from Eastern Europe)
Furniture hard to transport	Assembled furniture cannot be retailed for instant use. Spurs modularity and design innovation	**Flat-pack, "drive-it-home" furniture with easy self-assembly**
East European supplies get disrupted	Must set up own manufacturing operations in Eastern Europe. Allows the company to improve logistics and develop its own unique designs	**Wide selection of "enjoy-from-day-of-purchase" products, in attractive designs**

Furniture at Transparent, Discounted Prices

As IKEA grew and exhausted its local market and as its imports became more widely available to customers, Kamprad had to find other products to sell. His biggest competitor started selling furniture, so he decided to follow suit.

Quality, Inexpensive Furniture

IKEA's next constraint was that it lacked stores and warehouses. Therefore, the company needed an alternative venue to display its products: trade fairs. Kamprad had no need to spend on showrooms and warehousing and could offer discounted prices as a result. Because he had no salesforce, these prices were openly displayed, a stark departure from the industry practice of negotiated prices.

This angered his established competitors, who lobbied the industry association to have manufacturers boycott IKEA. This created another constraint: the company could no longer procure furniture in Sweden, with the implication that it now had to import its products.

These circumstances forced another innovation: sourcing quality inexpensive furniture from Poland and other East European countries. IKEA could now offer lower prices and, running a fast-growing, profitable business, could soon afford to open its own stores in Sweden, and gradually, all over Europe.

Flat-Pack, "Drive-It-Home" Furniture with Easy Self-Assembly

When Kamprad witnessed his customers' frustration with transporting assembled furniture, he stumbled upon the idea of self-assembly. The constraint of furniture retail was the warehousing and transporting of assembled furniture. Traditionally, cupboards, beds, and sofas were sold to order in showrooms, and customers had to wait for the product to be manufactured and delivered. This could take weeks or even months, denying shoppers the satisfaction of impulse buying and limiting the general demand for furniture.

The implication was that if customers were empowered to assemble the products themselves, it would revolutionize furniture retail. Goods could be packaged in flat, no-air boxes and then shipped to and warehoused in stores. Customers could take furniture home in their cars or by public transport and assemble it themselves in their homes. This would allow tremendous cost savings to IKEA and immediate gratification to its customers.

Wide Selection of "Enjoy-from-Day-of-Purchase" Products, in Attractive Designs

Following the fall of communism, IKEA's supply chain was disrupted. This forced the company to set up its own manufacturing facilities in nearby low-cost countries. Developing its own manufacturing allowed IKEA to design and engineer a wide selection of furniture ideal for flat packaging and same-day self-assembly.

Further, the furniture retailer could consolidate the design and use fewer parts, thereby reducing the complexity of manufacturing and streamlining logistics and warehousing. Self-assembly with fewer modules became simpler, flattening customers' learning curves.

Ryanair's Brand Promises

As you can see in the IKEA example above, the company's brand promises were all the result of constraints-triggered experimentation. Let's look at our second case study, Irish low-cost airline Ryanair, for further examples of how overcoming constraints creates unique offerings. (See Figure 8.2.)

Figure 8.2 The evolution of Ryanair's brand promises

CONSTRAINTS	IMPLICATIONS	BRAND PROMISES
Full-service airlines are often unprofitable	The flying experience must be stripped down to make money	**Lowest airfares**
High airport fees at major cities	Must use cheaper, out-of-city airports	**No flight delays and less airport congestion**
Late start and low brand awareness compared to flag carriers	Build a brand embracing the outsider, bad boy status	**We embrace extreme cost-saving measures so that you can fly cheaper**
Small, remote destinations are unprofitable	Reduce price point to generate demand to scale flights and make them profitable	**Affordable, exotic vacations for low-income passengers**

Lowest Air Fares

After a profitable start, when Ryanair entered the duopolistic Dublin–London route, the company realized the challenges of running a full-service airline. Ryanair was close to folding when its executives learned about Southwest Airlines' low-cost model. Adopting that approach required simplifying the airline's fleet, focusing on point-to-point destinations, reducing turnaround times, and implementing other cost-saving measures.

After transitioning to a Boeing-only fleet, cramming more seats into planes, and launching new routes as Europe deregulated in the early nineties, Ryanair was able to offer some of the cheapest flights in Europe. At the same time, the company became profitable.

No Flight Delays and Less Airport Congestion

Airports charge high landing fees. For example, the landing fee at London Heathrow was $36 per passenger in 2022. By using less-frequented airports, such as Luton near London, Ryanair was able to cut costs while promising on-time departures and low congestion.

We Embrace Extreme Cost-Saving Measures So That You Can Fly Cheaper

Ryanair's aggressive drive to cut costs went well beyond the Southwest model and earned the scorn of British tabloids. Passengers had to pay for checking in at airports and eventually were denied this privilege altogether. Seats became nonreclining and no luggage was allowed on board without extra fees.

Instead of becoming defensive about it, the company embraced the negative press as free publicity. The CEO, Michael O'Leary, felt that the criticism was helping the company by implying that Ryanair must be the lowest-cost airline and by implication was probably able to offer the lowest prices.

Affordable, Exotic Vacations for Low-Income Passengers

The drive to cut costs aggressively allowed low-income passengers—for the first time—to reach remote European holiday destinations in Greece, Croatia, and Eastern Europe from Liverpool, Manchester, and other cities. Ryanair could fill Boeing-737s with families and retirees who could not have afforded visiting these places without cheap airfares. Many had never flown before and did not know the difference to complain about inconvenient conditions.

This example demonstrates that Ryanair managed to turn its low level of service into an asset by using it to imply that it must be the cheapest airline. Further, its low prices allowed access to flights to low-income consumers who had no fixed expectations about flying other than reaching remote destinations.

Now let's look at our third example for constraints-induced brand promises.

MB Partners' Brand Promises

The brand promises our former investment banking business offered evolved over time as the constraints we were facing morphed and shifted. (See Figure 8.3.)

Figure 8.3 The evolution of MB Partners' brand promises

CONSTRAINTS	IMPLICATIONS	BRAND PROMISES
Buyout and government-funded equity markets dry up	Have to compete with other sell-side M&A firms for traditional engagements	**Reach traditional buyers plus buy-in managers and financiers**
International networks are not available	Must form own network to have affiliations	**Best international reach in CEE region through unique alliance**
Can't afford to finance drawn-out delivery cycle	Must bill up front and increase velocity of production	**Fastest to market**

Reach Traditional Buyers Plus Buy-In Managers and Financiers

MB Partner's original positioning did not work out, but the experience we gained allowed us to offer access to a wider pool of potential investors than any of our competitors. Most M&A advisors were stumped if no strategic or private equity buyer showed interest. We weren't, because MB Partners had the buyout card up our sleeves, and we could "manufacture" investors when needed.

For example, when the owner-managers of an HVAC company wanted to retire without succession, we attracted an oil industry executive to buy out the HVAC company that was unattractive to mainstream buyers.

At another time, we found a former automotive CEO, who was ready to come out of retirement, to lead a buy-in for a car parts manufacturing business. He had little cash to invest, but we found an adult entertainment company that wanted to diversify into promotable activities, to put up most of the equity for the acquisition.

Best International Reach in Central Eastern Europe through Unique Alliance

The biggest obstacle MB Partners faced in entering the M&A advisor market was lack of access to international advisory partners. Necessity is the mother of invention, so we went out and launched our own network with other Central Eastern European (CEE) partners. This gave us a unique angle because the most likely international investors for Hungarian companies were already in CEE and we now had a direct line to reach them.

Fastest to Market

Just when MB Partners finally managed to attract a talented junior team and had a good flow of quality client candidates, we no longer had the cash reserves to support our own delivery cycle. This forced us to completely rethink and redesign our transaction playbook.

The result was a consistent process, with an effective division of labor, fully leveraging our less-experienced team members. Switching from monthly to up-front retainers accelerated our cash flow, and our new process allowed us to compress our work from three months down to three weeks.

Best of all, we could go to market in less than a month, running circles around our competitors. It also made MB Partners the preferred advisor for clients who wanted to time the market and sell out quickly just as their business was peaking.

Embrace Your Business Constraints

You should welcome—not curse—the constraints facing your business. You can leverage these obstacles by turning them into brand promises. These challenges carry the seeds of competitive advantage and differentiation. Business Constraints can force your dormant creativity to come alive, mobilize your untapped resources, and turn them into enduring competitive advantages.

I've observed over the years that the most successful entrepreneurs are the ones who are willing to face down their company's greatest constraints and put themselves under pressure to overcome them.

This is the equivalent to the Roman armies burning bridges behind them. By cutting off the escape route for his soldiers, the general irrevocably commits himself and his troops to fighting till the last.

Elon Musk was willing to sacrifice his health and relationships when in the summer of 2018 he locked himself in at Tesla and slept under his desk for days at a time. He personally supervised ramping up the production of the Model 3 to 5,000 a week in order to prevent Tesla's banks from pulling their credit lines and pushing the company into insolvency. [1]

Key takeaways from Chapter 8

- Your brand promises communicate the compelling benefits that you consistently deliver to your customers.

- The more unique and useful your brand promises are, the more powerful your brand will become.

- A brand promise is only as impactful as the sacrifice you made to provide it. If you have not made trade-offs for your brand promises, then you are still offering a generic product.

- Use your way of overcoming the constraints in your business to create unique brand promises. The constraints that your competitors never faced could not force them to innovate your unique ways of doing business. What doesn't kill you makes you stronger.

Now that you have extracted your brand promises from your Business Constraints and leverage points, it's time to develop tactics to manifest them for your customers in the form of Unique Activities.

CHAPTER NINE

Turn Promises into Activities

A brand is the promise of an experience.

—Alexander Isley

In his book *On Competition*, Michael Porter talks about how strategic differentiation manifests in your business through performing a set of differentiating activities, what I call Unique Activities. Your strategy is really only different from that of other companies to the extent that you carry out different activities than your competitors.

For example, fast-food restaurant chain Chick-fil-A performs the following differentiated activities:[1]

- It is closed on Sundays to ensure that employees can share a day of rest with their families.

- Employees are trained to make eye contact with patrons, smile, and say "my pleasure."

- Servers take customer orders in the parking lot when the restaurant is busy.

- Drinks and refills are served at your table for your convenience and so that servers can respond by saying "my pleasure" when you thank them.

- The fast-food brand uses proprietary recipes such as the Chick-fil-A Pickle Brine.

- The chain deploys quirky cow billboards where cows direct you in broken English to eat chicken.

- A low-investment franchise model where each operator may only manage a single restaurant ensures consistently high standards of customer service.

- Meticulously cleaned and maintained bathrooms make young mothers feel comfortable changing nappies.

Your Unique Activities are your way of delivering on your brand promises. Recognizing, documenting, and consistently executing your Unique Activities is how you will create a sustainably different and profitable firm. I call the complete web of Unique Activities your Strategy Stack, which we will discuss in more detail in Step 6: Strategize a Stack.

Designing your Unique Activities is a multistep process. The first step involves identifying the activities that you are already executing while delivering on your brand promises. Let's review the Unique Activities our example companies have employed to deliver on their constraint-triggered brand promises.

Recognizing Unique Activities

Let's first look at how IKEA's Business Constraint and the resulting brand promises led to the initial Unique Activities of the company from the 1940s to the 1980s and beyond. Figure 9.1 shows some of IKEA's Unique Activities.

Figure 9.1 IKEA's Unique Activities

CONSTRAINTS	IMPLICATIONS	BRAND PROMISES	UNIQUE ACTIVITIES
Few local customers	Operating retail stores is uneconomic	Convenient mail-order purchase	**Sales letters and brochures tailored to local tastes.** **The IKEA Catalog.**
Can't afford salespeople to sell products	Must use self-service sales model	Furniture at transparent, discounted prices	**Listed prices at trade fairs.** **Transparent price displays in stores.**
Swedish furniture manufacturers' boycott	Can't offer locally produced furniture	Quality, inexpensive furniture	**Strategic partnerships to circumvent bans and boycott.** **Source furniture from Polish state-owned companies.**
Furniture hard to transport	Assembled furniture cannot be retailed for instant use	Flat-pack, "drive-it-home" furniture with easy self-assembly	**Modular furniture designs.** **Step-by-step assembly instructions.** **No-air packaging process.**
East European supplies get disrupted	Must set up own manufacturing operations in Eastern Europe. Spurs modularity and design innovation and streamlines logistics and warehousing	Wide selection of "enjoy-from-day-of-purchase" furniture, in attractive designs	**Optimized packaging.** **Special naming system for easy product identification.** **Winding-path showroom with pick-yourself warehouse near counters.**

Unique Activities for the 1940s Brand Promise: "Convenient mail-order purchase"

- **Sales letters and brochures tailored to local tastes:** IKEA's founder, Ingvar Kamprad, wasn't a top student, but he understood the people who lived in his tiny municipality of Älmhult, Sweden, and the surrounding towns. He taught himself to write simple sales letters and brochures offering his imported wares, such as pens and stockings.

- **The IKEA Catalog:** As IKEA's business evolved to selling furniture, the sales brochure was replaced by a growing product catalog, first published in 1951 in southern Sweden, at sixty-eight pages. At its peak, the IKEA Catalog was published in 300 million copies, and was translated into thirty languages. In 2021, after seventy years, the IKEA Catalog was discontinued and merged into the company's website.[2,3]

Unique Activities for the 1950s Brand Promise: "Furniture at transparent, discounted prices"

- **Exhibits at trade fairs with prices displayed:** After exhausting the mail-order market, IKEA started exhibiting its furniture at trade fairs. This Unique Activity was short-lived because established competitors revolted against IKEA's approach of price transparency and discounting tactics, which they considered to be "destroying the market."

Unique Activities for the 1960s–1980s Brand Promise: "Quality, inexpensive furniture"

- **Strategic partnerships to circumvent bans and boycotts:** IKEA partnered with other companies to have them front IKEA at trade fairs to which the furniture retailer was not invited.

- **Source furniture from Polish state-owned companies:** After IKEA was boycotted by Swedish manufacturers, it started outsourcing its manufacturing to state-owned companies in Poland and Romania.

Unique Activities for the 1980s-and-beyond Brand Promise: "Flat-pack, 'drive-it-home' furniture with easy self-assembly"

- **Modular furniture designs and step-by-step assembly instructions:** IKEA developed modular, easy-to-assemble furniture to cut production and logistical costs and to allow customers to drive their purchases home for self-assembly. Customers receive a dummy-proof instruction guide with each piece of furniture.

- **Design and manufacture own furniture:** After the Berlin Wall crumbled, IKEA set up its own manufacturing plants, and today it has design studios in Sweden, India, and China. In 2022, the IKEA Group had fifty manufacturing sites in ten countries employing 16,000 people.[4]

- **Step-by-step assembly instructions:** IKEA's cartoon characters, including the now retired Allen Wrench and the Blue Shark, instruct shoppers on how to assemble their furniture.

- **No-air packaging process:** Furniture elements are designed to fit in closely assembled flat boxes, using the mantra "we hate air." These packages usually fit into passenger vehicles and are easy to maneuver into small apartments and rooms.

Unique Activities for the Brand Promise: "Wide selection of 'enjoy-from-day-of-purchase' furniture, in attractive designs"

- **Optimizing packaging:** IKEA is obsessed with eliminating waste in its packaging to save materials, storage and handling, fuel consumption and emissions and to eliminate the number of damaged and returned goods and other types of waste.[5]

- **Special naming system for easy product identification:** IKEA uses a naming system invented by Ingvar Kamprad, who was dyslexic and had trouble remembering item codes. Kamprad named each product after towns in Denmark or Sweden or used a Swedish word based on the product. For example, bed and bath accessories are named after flowers and plants.[6]

- **Winding-path showroom with pick-yourself warehouse near counters:** This Unique Activity was designed to lead customers through the different living spaces that can be furnished with IKEA products. Customers can collect smaller items in their shopping cart, make notes about the larger products selected, and pick and load these items onto large shopping trolleys in the warehouse, en route to checkout counters.

These are the most well-recognized IKEA Unique Activities, but there are many others, including offering Swedish meatballs and in-shop playgrounds.

Ryanair's Unique Activities

Now let's look at Ryanair's brand promise–driven Unique Activities, as presented in Figure 9.2.

Figure 9.2 Ryanair's Unique Activities

CONSTRAINTS	IMPLICATIONS	BRAND PROMISES	UNIQUE ACTIVITIES
Full-service airlines are often unprofitable	The flying experience must be stripped down to make money	Lowest air fares	**Hyper-low basic airfares with lots of optional "extras".** **No unpaid luggage on board and life vests are overhead.** **Food service is optional and very expensive.**
High airport fees at major cities	Must use cheaper, out-of-city airports	Less airport congestion and no flight delays	**Use obscure airports, often 50+ miles from target destination.** **25-minute aircraft turns.** **No assigned seating with family exceptions.**
Late start and low brand awareness compared to flag carriers	Build a brand embracing the outsider bad boy status	We save money so that you can fly cheaper	**No-recline, no-back-pocket seats.** **Boeing-737s only.**
Small, remote destinations are unprofitable	Reduce price point to generate high demand that makes low-cost flights profitable	Affordable, exotic vacations for low-income passengers	**Direct connections from secondary UK cities to smaller tourist destinations.**

Unique Activities for the Brand Promise: "Lowest airfares"

- **Hyper-low basic airfares with lots of optional "extras":** Dublin to London round-trip fares were as low as $23 on Trip.com at the end of 2022. However, Ryanair charges extra for airport check-in, misspelled boarding cards, and priority boarding.

- **No unpaid luggage on board and life vests are overhead:** Taking your hand luggage on board could cost $30 or more.[7]

- **Food service is optional and very expensive:** Pack your own food, but make sure it fits into the small lap bag you are allowed to carry on board.

Unique Activities for the Brand Promise: "Less airport congestion and no flight delays"

- **Use obscure airports, often 50+ miles from the target destination:** Paris-Beauvais Airport, 53 miles from Paris; Stockholm Skavsta Airport, 52 miles from Stockholm; and Reus Airport, 55 miles from Barcelona.[8]

- **25-minute aircraft turns:** Ryanair achieves this by having passengers disembark by stairs both at the front and at the rear of aircrafts. With no seat-back pockets, passengers take their trash with them, eliminating cleaning time. The airline often starts boarding before all passengers have left the airplane, a practice referred to as "boarding not boarding." Only priority boarding passengers can take luggage on board, and seats are allocated on a first come, first served basis.[9]

- **No assigned seating with family exceptions:** Ryanair allows children ages twelve or younger to sit next to their parent without a surcharge, as required by law.

Unique Activities for the Brand Promise: "We save money so that you can fly cheaper"

- **No-recline, no-back-pocket seats:** These practices allow Ryanair to squeeze more seats into planes and ensure faster turnarounds by eliminating the need for trash removal.

- **Boeing-737s only:** Having a uniform fleet allows Ryanair to save money on the training of staff and pilots and allows maintenance and scheduling flexibility, because any staff member can be deployed on any route.

Unique Activities for the Brand Promise: "Affordable, exotic vacations for low-income passengers"

- **Direct connections from secondary UK cities to smaller tourist destinations:** Ryanair flies from fifteen different cities in the UK and has hubs in Ireland, the UK, Belgium, Germany, Italy, and Spain that serve over a hundred destinations each.[10]

Now let's look at the Unique Activities MB Partners developed to deliver its brand promises.

MB Partner's Unique Activities

MB Partners' Unique Activities evolved from our brand promises as follows. See them laid out in Figure 9.3. Let's review the first three of these activities based on the company's earliest brand promise.

Figure 9.3 MB Partners' Unique Activities

CONSTRAINTS	IMPLICATIONS	BRAND PROMISES	UNIQUE ACTIVITIES
Buyout and government-funded equity markets dry up	Have to compete with other sell-side M&A firms for traditional engagements	Reach traditional buyers plus buy-in managers and financiers	**Proprietary buyer research methodology using own and paid databases, international network, and brainstorming system.** **Customized information memoranda to debt financiers.** **Proprietary relationships with buyout lenders.**
International networks are not available	Must form own network to have affiliations	Best international reach in CEE region through unique alliance	**Regular, structured deal exchange meetings between M&A network members.** **Access to all CFA charterholders in Europe through AIMR Global Council.**
Can't afford to finance drawn-out delivery cycle	Must bill up front and increase velocity of production	Fastest to market	**Go to market in three weeks.** **Modular information memoranda and business plans with multilevel quality control.**

Unique Activities for the Brand Promise: "Reach traditional buyers plus buy-in managers and financiers"

- **Proprietary buyer research methodology using own and paid databases, international network, and brainstorming system:** MB Partners developed a complete playbook on how to systematically research all possible buyer prospects. These included access to paid databases, such as Amadeus, Dun & Bradstreet, and others; canvassing buyers from our international-affiliated M&A network partners; and drawing from our own database of local financial and private individuals looking for deals. We also used a systematic brainstorming process to explore out-of-the-box ideas for generating unintuitive cross-industry acquirer ideas.

- **Customized information memoranda for debt financiers:** The firm produced a special version of the selling memorandum targeted at banks. This was necessary because debt financiers focused on the target company's ability to cover debt payments and offer collateral to buyout loans rather than the ability of the business to create equity value in the long term.

- **Proprietary relationships with buyout lenders:** MB Partners had a history of doing transactions with local banks and project managers in those banks, who often moved jobs. Deals depended on the quality of the bank executive championing our projects, their experience and drive in pushing for internal approvals, and the momentary willingness of the bank's leadership to offer cash flow–based financing.

How to Find Your Unique Activities

Having considered in the examples of IKEA, Ryanair, and MB Partners how these companies created Unique Activities, it is time for you to identify the Unique Activities of *your* business. You can do this by answering the following questions.

- *What constraints has your business faced in the past and how did you overcome them?*

- *What brand promises did these "solutions" allow you to make to your customers? What were the resulting trade-offs that you had to make?*

- *What was the respective Unique Activity in each case that resulted in overcoming your constraints and that has helped you make good on your brand promises?*

- *Have you defined, ingrained, and optimized these Unique Activities as part of your proprietary business recipe? Which ones?*

- *Have you given each of these Unique Activities a name? If so, what do you call them?*

- *What Unique Activities did you come up with to overcome Business Constraints, which you have since abandoned? Was this abandonment strategic or accidental?*

- *Which of these abandoned Unique Activities would be worth reviving, refining, and habitualizing for your business?*

Key takeaways from Chapter 9

- Find those Unique Activities that allow you to express your brand promises in a powerful way and make them part of your business's playbooks.

- In our examples, IKEA, Ryanair, and MB Partners have met with various Business Constraints and then responded to these constraints by turning them into valuable brand promises. They then manifested these brand promises through Unique Activities that gave each company a competitive edge in the marketplace.

- What were the brand promises your constraints have catalyzed and which Unique Activities are you practicing? Do you have any abandoned Unique Activities that would be worth reviving and re-adopting?

Now that you have figured out your Strategic Position, resolved the Crux Challenge that blocked your growth, and derived brand promises and Unique Activities from how you are overcoming your Business Constraints, it is time to build your business's perpetual motion device, your flywheel.

STEP

AUTHOR ACTIVITIES

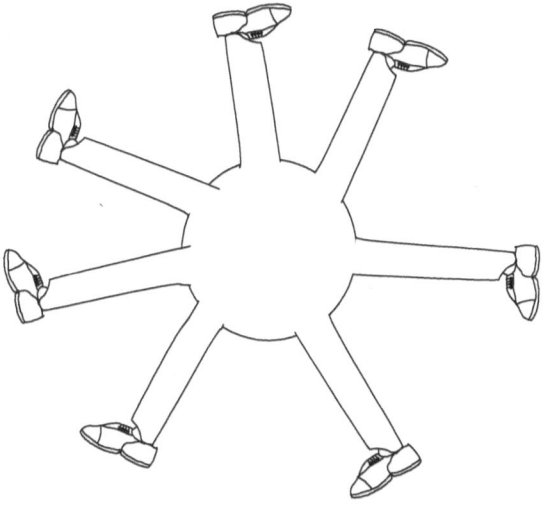

Everybody is a genius. But if you judge a fish by its ability to climb a ladder, it will live its whole life believing it is stupid.

—Albert Einstein

In April 2007 Justin Kan and Kyle Vogt launched a new reality TV–like website broadcasting Kan's life 24/7. Kan was wearing a webcam around the clock except while sleeping or in the bathroom, all the while chatting with viewers. The site was picked up by media outlets and the show became an immediate sensation.

People signed up to witness the life of a young man in real time. By the summer, Justin.tv (Justin TV) became a platform with scores of channels broadcasting a plethora of lives simultaneously from all over the world, catering to tens of thousands of viewers.

By 2008, Justin TV added selectable categories, such as People & Lifecasting, Sports, Music & Radio, Gaming, News & Tech, Animals, Entertainment, and Divas & Dudes. At that time, something curious happened. One of these categories took off like a rocket and trumped all others: Gaming.

It turned out that people loved watching others play and anchor video games. The screen would show the game screen with the player in the corner of the screen handling a console. Sometimes two or more gamers trash-talked while playing together, and a growing audience interacted with each other via a chat stream.[1]

In 2011, Justin TV's founders decided to go all in on Gaming and rebranded the channel Twitch, with reference to twitch gaming, a type of video game requiring fast player reactions. Twitch exploded and attracted tens of millions of users. Three years later Google and Amazon waged a bidding war to acquire Twitch. Jeff Bezos's company took the prize, paying $970 million for the streaming site.[2]

Soon Twitch turned into a cultural phenomenon and catalyzed the rise of a new form of entertainment: eSports.[3] In the coming years, the service started offering other "in real life" (IRL) streaming services, such as broadcasting music festivals, Bob Ross's painting marathon, and other reality programming, eventually fulfilling the original mission of Twitch's predecessor, Justin TV.

Step 4 of the Strategy OS is to develop a successful growth strategy by implementing three sequential activities that emulate some of the strategies Twitch employed.

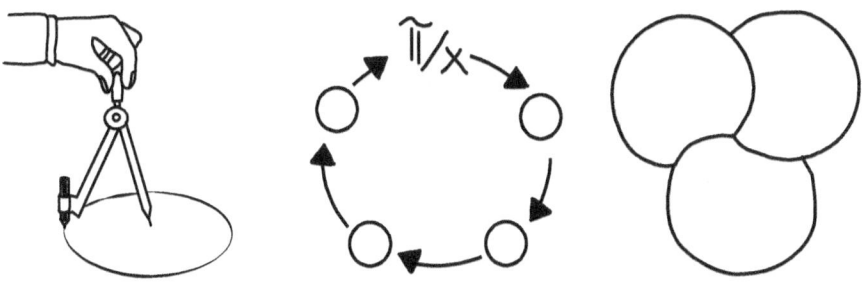

- In Chapter 10, I show you how to narrow your focus to a limited Core Market that resonates with your offering.

- In Chapter 11, we dissect how you can mold the key components of your business into a unique flywheel that, by serving your Core Market, fuels your business's growth momentum.

- Finally, in Chapter 12, we use that flywheel to ideate further Unique Activities to accelerate the individual cogs in your flywheel.

Let's start by zooming in on the Core Market that will best respond to your offering.

CHAPTER TEN

Delineate Your Core Market

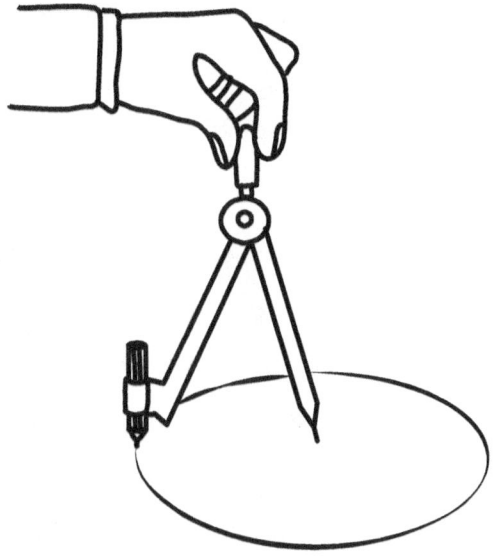

There is only one winning strategy. It is to carefully define the target market and direct a superior offering to that target market.

—Philip Kotler

In the previous three chapters, we identified the constraints facing your business and the resulting brand promises these Business Constraints allow you to make to your customers.

Further, we used these brand promises to identify the first set of Unique Activities that your business can perform to stand out in the marketplace.

These steps are critical in creating differentiation for your business. However, we still need to go further. Unless your business is massive and already on the *Fortune* list, you likely don't yet have the resources to serve everyone, everywhere. We need to find those select customers who will be the most responsive to your business's offerings. We also need to focus on the geographies that represent the low-hanging fruit for your business. (See Figure 10.1.)

Figure 10.1 The people and places you need to target

DEMOGRAPHICS   GEOGRAPHIES

Twitch (formerly called Justin TV) targeted all audiences with its "in real life" (IRL) content. Initially, the reality broadcasting of Justin Kan's life was a unique concept and voyeuristic audiences flocked to watch it.

However, as Twitch expanded to multiple genres, its growth slowed. The company could not serve a variety of audiences profitably, and its resources started dwindling.

Growth did not pick up until Twitch decided to focus all its resources on gamers, its most responsive Core Market, which represented the 20 percent of Twitch's market that generated over 80 percent of results.

Still, committing to gamers meant neglecting all other Core Markets for the time being. The cost of limiting the business was to become a niche player and to give up the dream, at least for now, of becoming "the leading company in IRL." It seemed like a desperate move to save the company.

And it was.

But Twitch offered a perfect product for gamers who wanted to learn from pros and to socialize with each other. These people were willing to pay for the privilege and generated enough revenue for the company to become profitable and eventually dedicate resources to other verticals.

Business-to-Business Core Markets

So, what are the steps to defining your target customers? Your approach will depend on whether you market to businesses or to consumers.

If you offer a business-to-business (B2B) service or product, then find your Core Market by answering the following questions. (Hereafter, I use the term *products* for both products and services.)

1. *Which industries and sectors can benefit the most from the use of your products?*

2. *Organizations of what type and size benefit most from using your products?*

3. *People in which functions within your target customers' organizations use your products?*

4. *People in which organizational positions will drive or influence purchase decisions for your products?*

1. Which industries can benefit the most from the use of your products?

Your product may be most useful for a specific type of business. A company mentioned earlier, Regional MSP, found that its service offering was most beneficial to law firms.

Legal advisory companies are obsessed with IT security. Their communications must be encrypted end to end, and all of their equipment must be regularly updated and patched in the office and at remote locations.

Law firms are also compliance-oriented and must ensure that they handle all client and third-party information securely, observing national and international laws and regulations. Firms don't just want to comply but also want to be seen to be compliant and to be able to prove it at any time.

Lawyers' time is expensive, and they need a concierge service where their MSP takes care of any internal IT staffing and training needs. Any potential disruptions must be minimized and crises should be handled according to proven protocols, without the loss of data, and with minimal stress.

Accordingly, law firms are often willing to pay a premium price for a premium level of service.

However, it is not easy to serve law firms. It requires a fully staffed team of specialist engineers who are available 24/7, easy access to tier-2 and tier-3 phone support, and a virtual chief information officer (VCIO) on call to provide expert advice and to solve intractable problems. This caliber of staff is hard to attract and takes a long time to train, requiring the MSP to be of a certain size and to have a strong work culture that keeps talent glued to the company.

But it is not just law firms that require premium services. There are highly-niched MSPs specialized in serving healthcare providers, private equity funds, educational organizations, and online retailers. These all require specialist skills and deep understanding of their target customers' domain.

In a different industry, GERSTEL, Inc. sells and supports specialized instruments for chemical analysis with emphasis on automation. Its products are used to prepare and introduce samples for analysis by gas chromatography – mass spectrometry (GC-MS) and liquid chromatography-mass spectrometry (LC-MS), to test the purity of a substance or to separate, identify, and quantify each component in a mixture.

GERSTEL's products are targeted at multiple industries that require the analysis and handling of chemical compounds, including food, flavor, fragrance, and beverage industries; consumer products; material emissions; environmental companies; polymers & chemicals; and forensics. Typical users are manufacturers, government institutions, colleges, and testing labs.

Adriana Accounting is Software-as-a-Service (SaaS) company that provides bank communication software that augments bookkeeping applications, similar to QuickBooks. Adriana's primary target industry is accounting firms that manage bookkeeping for multiple clients and need a potent solution for importing and processing large volumes of banking transactions. It also serves holding companies that perform accounting services for multiple businesses, and it offers a self-service solution for smaller businesses as well.

2. Organizations of what type and size benefit most from using your products?

What sales revenues or headcount do your sweet-spot customers have? How established does a prospect need to be to fully leverage your services and be able to afford them?

In the case of Regional MSP, the sweet-spot customer size for its services was law firms that employed 20–150 people. Smaller firms could not fully leverage MSP's services, and larger companies needed even more specialized services or they operated in multiple geographies that could be better served by a nationally present MSP.

GERSTEL's products are used by laboratories in government institutions, colleges, testing labs, and manufacturing organizations. Its Core Market includes small labs with a handful of employees as well as larger chemical manufacturing businesses. For an organization to include a chemical laboratory, it has to spend about $50,000 a year on equipment, comply with local zoning ordinances, and typically employ three or more people, which requires an annual budget of at least $300,000.[1]

3. People in which occupations within your target customers' organizations use your products?

Which people will benefit from the use of your product? In which functional areas do they work in your target customers' organizations? What influence do they have over decisions about which provider to choose?

Regional MSP's services are used by attorneys working in law firms. The influence of these individuals is only high when they express dissatisfaction with IT services at their organization. They have minimal direct influence on choosing a provider and thus are not worth targeting with marketing or sales messages.

The users of GERSTEL's instruments are chemists who perform research and development, quality control, or analytical services. These chemists tend to be vocal about the instruments they like and want to use and therefore are a worthy target for marketing messaging and thought leadership activities, such as workshops, video newsletters, and business reviews.

Adriana Accounting's software is used by accountants and bookkeepers who are potent opinion formers influencing purchasing decisions. They, too, should be targeted with education, testimonials, and free trials.

4. People in which organizational positions will drive or influence purchase decisions for your products?

Who are the decision makers that can initiate purchase decisions or that control the purse strings in your target organizations?

Large law firms employ full-time managers who decide on infrastructure spending such as MSP contracts. The managing partner may also be part of such decisions.

GERSTEL's institutional clients purchase their instruments through procurement processes or requests for proposals (RFPs). These are evaluated by purchasing staff and signed off on by CFOs or managing directors.

The purchase of Adriana Accounting's software is typically approved by the COO or managing director of client organizations or by the president of small to medium-sized business customers.

For B2B products, make sure you have a clear view of the industry and size of business that can use your product. You have to reach and educate both the influential users and the ultimate decision makers within those organizations.

Business-to-Consumer Core Markets

B2B marketing is all about targeting the right decision makers and influencers of the right organizations. It is aimed at selecting the target organizations first and then finding the right people inside them.

For business-to-consumer (B2C) markets, you will target individuals on the basis of their personal profile, interests, income level, and lifestyle.

Describe the avatars of the various ideal customer types who buy your product. What is their income level? What kind of lifestyle do they aspire to? What is their age and gender? Where do they live and what do they buy? What is their family situation? What are the problems they are trying to solve? How can your product help solve their problems?

Viking Capital syndicates investments in and manages its portfolio of multifamily real estate properties. The company's Core Market is high-income physicians who are looking for real estate investments as a way to diversify their income sources and build a residual income–earning asset.

Viking Capital's sweet-spot clients are "accredited power earners" who are midcareer, ages thirty-five to sixty-five. Many of them are doctors, which is the company founders' original profession, too, a space they are intimately familiar with.

The psychographic profile of Viking's customers includes that they seek financial freedom, they are willing to take measured risk, they are looking to maximize returns on a long-term horizon, they seek tax efficacy and the diversification of their income, and have disposable cash.

Your Target Geography

What is the ideal geography to target for your current business? The wider the net you cast, the more fragmented your message will be and the less its impact.

If you are operating a local dry-cleaner business, then your target geography is limited by the distance your customers are willing to drive to drop off or pick up their clothes. If you are an MSP that serves lawyers, your target geography may be your metropolitan area, or you may serve businesses remotely across your own and adjacent time zones.

Regional MSP targets customers in the DC Metro area. GERSTEL targets geographies in the United States and Canada. The company used to target Latin America, too, but later recognized that operating in these countries offered a marginal return on the complexity of the market and the extra time it took to succeed there.

Adriana Accounting's current target geography is Hungary, but it is getting ready to enter neighboring countries. Its challenge is to overcome regulatory and language barriers.

Viking Capital's Core Markets for real estate investment are the fast-growing Sunbelt states of the United States, the DC Metro area, and the Seattle area. These areas are where the company's principals have the strongest referral networks and they offer sufficient volume of potential investment opportunities for years to come.

Choosing a Broad or a Narrow Core Market

As a general rule, the narrower the Core Market, the more powerful your messaging and market awareness can be. If there is a sufficiently sized, addressable market in your current niche, your best opportunity will be to fully exploit it before moving to adjacent markets. (See Figure 10.2.)

Figure 10.2 Broad vs. narrow Core Market targeting

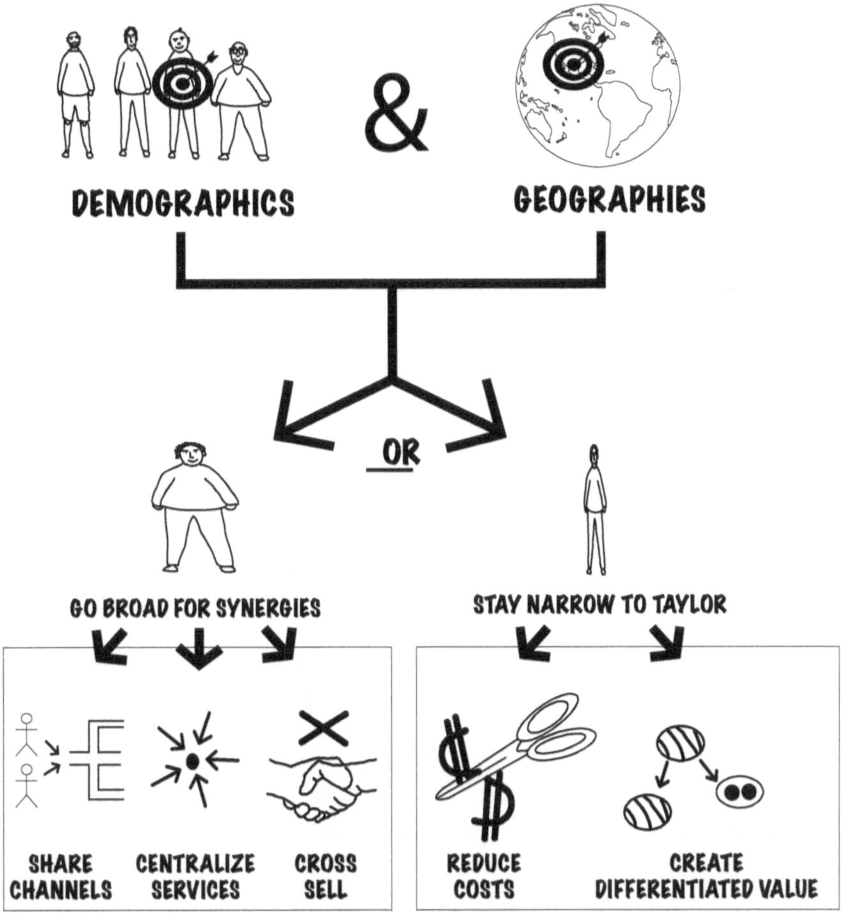

Broad Core Markets can be advantageous for large, established companies that have already exhausted the verticals where they enjoy the highest competitive advantages. These companies, such as Microsoft, can no longer grow in a niche. Instead, Microsoft's goal is to dominate a large segment of the market, which it defines as "people aged sixteen and above from both urban and rural places across the world."[2]

The advantages of broad Core Markets include the ability to share sales channels through different products, cross-sell services between your business lines, and outsource and improve the cost efficiency of your centralized services. However, the benefits of a narrow Core Market most often outweigh any potential loss of untapped opportunity. Studying a narrow group of clients or customers allows you to relate to their problems better and become an expert in servicing their needs.

Serving the same types of clients also helps increase processes and consistency of execution, which leads to cost savings. You will find it easier to create differentiated value by tailoring your products or services to the specific needs of your niche.

Key takeaways from Chapter 10

- Knowing and addressing your Core Market is a critical ingredient in an effective and economical marketing approach.

- Define your ideal type and size of customer and stay as narrow and "shallow" as possible to concentrate your limited resources on a single point where you can achieve a breakthrough.

- Develop B2B Core Markets by delineating your target organizations by industry, by size of customer, and the specific job functions to target for potential internal champions and decision makers.

- Your B2C Core Market depends on your customers' personal profiles, interests, income levels, and lifestyles.

- Choose a target geography. Casting a broad net feels easier, but you may find it difficult and suboptimal to seek and serve clients in other time zones and in countries that pose regulatory and language barriers.

Now that you have delineated your Core Market, in Chapter 11 we will look at how to construct a flywheel modeling the activities that will strengthen the growth momentum of your business.

CHAPTER ELEVEN

Construct Your Flywheel

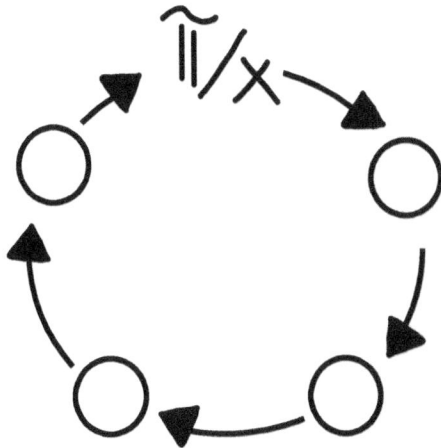

Habit is the enormous flywheel of society, its most precious conservative agent. There is no more miserable human being than one in whom nothing is habitual but indecision. Full half the time of such a man goes to the deciding, or regretting, of matters which ought to be so ingrained in him as practically not to exist for his consciousness at all.

—William James

Oft-quoted business strategist Jim Collins published a monograph about the concept of the business "flywheel."[1] Collins argues that the key to business success is to identify and innovate key elements in your business that can create a self-sustaining growth momentum. Then, you focus on improving these parts.

In his monograph, *Turning the Flywheel*, Collins describes how this idea crystallized in his mind during a consulting engagement he held with the top brass of Amazon.com in late 2001.

At the top of Amazon's flywheel is the cog of "low prices on more offerings" compared to its brick-and-mortar competitors, such as Walmart. (See Figure 11.1.) The wide selection of products generates a growing number of customer visits on Amazon.com, which in turn attracts third-party sellers to set up shop on the platform.

The revenue these sellers generate for Amazon then allows the company to expand its online store and widen its product range further, resulting in economies of scale: The company's fixed costs are spread over a larger revenue base, permitting Amazon to reduce its prices further.

The flywheel turns faster and faster, generating irresistible momentum.

Figure 11.1 The original flywheel of Amazon.com

Source: Jim Collins, *Turning the Flywheel*

The Amazon flywheel has obviously worked, propelling the online retailer to dominant status over the past two decades. According to Visualcapitalist.com, based on research published by Deloitte, as of mid-2019, Amazon was worth 30 percent more than the next nine publicly quoted U.S. retailers combined. See Figure 11.2.

Figure 11.2 The top ten U.S. publicly listed retailers compared by market size

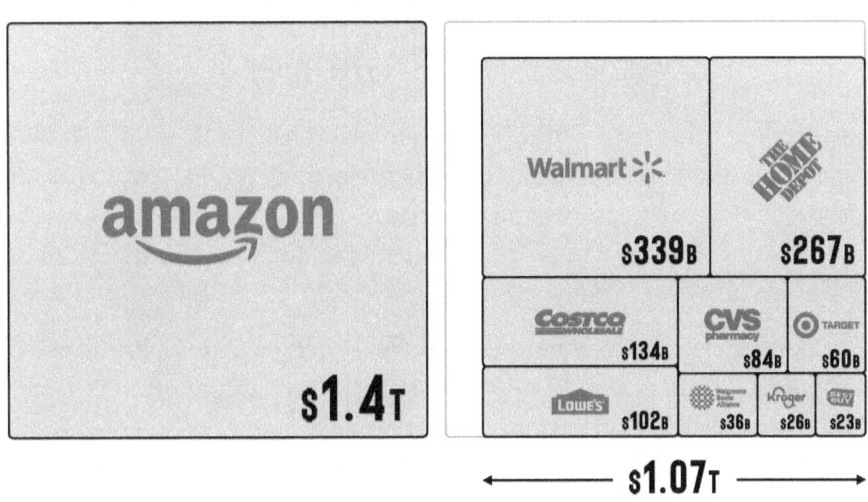

Source: Visualcapitalist.com

In our book *Pinnacle,* Greg Cleary and I discuss the flywheel concept and our experiences with several of our clients.

In this chapter, my goal is to dig deeper and identify the types of elements that propel the flywheels of my clients. I believe that I have cracked the code on the ideal flywheel to help you build the most effective "perpetual motion machine" for *your* business. Hereinafter, I will call it your Strategic Flywheel.

The stronger your Strategic Flywheel, the more useful it is for authoring Unique Activities that enable your organization to produce differentiated value for your customers.

So, what are the elements of a great Strategic Flywheel? During a conversation a couple of years ago with Verne Harnish, author of *Scaling Up*, he suggested starting each flywheel using Jim Collins's Profit per *X* formula at the top of the wheel.[2] This made perfect sense to me because every business must keep an eye on driving profitability, its oxygen for growth.

Advanced Profit per *X*

Jim Collins coined the Profit per *X* concept in his classic book: *Good to Great*.[3] On the basis of a study of high-performing public companies, he proposed that each company that managed to sustain outstanding results over multiple decades had an "economic engine" that could be described by a formula he called Profit per *X*.

Collins effectively argued that by developing a *unique* Profit per *X* formula, a business could find a "blue ocean" growth opportunity in the marketplace, with relatively low competition. He quoted Walgreens's Profit per Customer Visit formula that allowed the retailer to maximize profitable growth by clustering multiple stores in big cities to create local convenience and ubiquity.

Ever since I first read *Good to Great*, the Profit per *X* concept has intrigued me, and I have helped dozens of clients come up with their own unique formulas.

Over time, I have come to the realization that Collins's idea is all about constraints. More specifically, leveraging the most critical constraint in your business allows you to find a unique way to grow your company.

By understanding the deeper context of this exercise and considering the Profit per X formulas below, you can construct an Advanced Profit per X metric for your business. This will help crystallize your thinking on how to grow your business in a unique way, facing less direct competition than your industry peers.

Review the Constraints You Found

Recall that in Chapter 7 we discussed how overcoming the constraints of your business can help you articulate unique brand promises for your organization. We discussed IKEA, which used its Business Constraints to propel creative breakthroughs and turn by turn grow into a global furniture empire.

First, the lack of availability of local customers led to IKEA's founder discovering mail-order selling, which eventually catalyzed the IKEA Catalog. Later, the lack of funds to pay salespeople led to the self-service concept. The ensuing uproar in the Swedish furniture industry and the resulting boycott pushed IKEA to discover outsourced manufacturing and invent the IKEA supply chain, and so on.

Ryanair's Business Constraints also inspired creative responses, including stripping down the flying experience and using out-of-town airports to turn a profit. Instead of apologizing for poor service, the company leveraged its bad boy image into free publicity.

My business, MB Partners, evolved competitive advantages by facing down challenges when our market dried up for government-funded buyouts, with a lack of an international mergers network, and from cash flow issues.

So, what is the biggest constraint in *your* business? Let me give you some examples to help you answer this question.

Profit per *X* Formulas

Having analyzed a couple dozen companies, I have found that Profit per *X* formulas come in four main varieties. These are linked to customers, to scarce assets, to the center of activity of the business or the formula is based on units of time. Let's look at each one and review when using it is most appropriate.

Customer-Linked Profit per *X*

The Profit per *X* formula is linked to customers when the company's biggest constraint is getting customers, which is the case for about 30 percent of businesses. When gaining new customers is the biggest barrier, the easiest way to grow is to make the most of each customer you already have.

Ways of farming existing customers are to cross-sell or upsell them other products or services, to turn them into recurring-revenue customers, and to increase the frequency of transactions with them.

Examples:

- **Profit per Client:** For a professional services firm trying to expand the slate of services used by its clients (e.g., bookkeeping, accounting, tax preparation, consulting).

- **Profit per Customer:** For a bootstrapped IT product company that is financing its growth from the cash profits it generates.

- **MRR per Customer:** (MRR is monthly recurring revenue.) For a venture-backed SaaS company that is burning cash and is racing to dominate its market by leveraging investor funds.

- **Profit per Active Investor:** For a real estate syndication firm that is looking to grow its active investor base that is interested in investing in multiple opportunities.

Scarce Asset–Linked Profit per *X*

Linking Profit per *X* to scarce assets is useful when the business is constrained by an expensive, hard-to-acquire, or limited-availability asset. I have seen this type of formula applied in about 25 percent of companies.

Examples:

- **Profit per Service Truck:** For an energy-efficiency contracting company that delivers its installations using fully equipped and manned trucks costing over $100,000 each. Such trucks must be maximized before the company invests in equipping an expensive new vehicle.

- **Profit per Relationship:** This is the formula used by a real estate consulting business that generates business by cross-selling brokerage and property management services via word of mouth of happy customers and through referrals by real estate agents. This formula is well suited for commoditized service businesses that depend on personal relationships to create customers.

- **Profit per Trainer:** This is the growth formula used by a company providing premium personal fitness training services to busy professionals. Well-educated, trained, and socially skilled instructors are expensive to develop and retaining their services and keeping them productive are critical for attracting customers and creating raving fans that refer new patrons.

- **Profit per Associate:** This formula is used by a leading e-commerce agency that sells premium-priced website builds and expert marketing services to create recurring customers. Associates may be local or outsourced, but they need to have state-of-the-art marketing skills and be inculcated with the culture and the processes of the company.

Center of Activity–Based Profit per *X*

Formulas based on centers of activity are used in situations where a limited resource resides outside of the company's control. This formula applies to about 20 percent of companies.

Examples:

- **Profit per User:** This is the formula used by an MSP that serves different sized clients. Some employ only a handful of users; others, scores of them. The profitability of the business depends on maximizing the value provided to each user within client entities. This can be done by constantly seeking out and offering ways to enhance productivity, security, and mobility for each user.

- **Profit per Engagement:** I have seen this formula used by a company that is challenged to generate new client engagements because of a weak new business function. As soon as this company is hired, it has no problem upselling and cross-selling services and converting customers into a recurring source of new business.

- **Profit per Image Lab:** This ratio is used by an imaging software development company. This business has developed a niche product used by imaging laboratories all over the world. Because there exist only a few hundred image labs that can afford its product, this software company seeks to maximize its "wallet share" in each laboratory it has penetrated.

Unit of Time–Based Profit per *X*

This formula based on unit of time is useful for organizations that sell the expertise of individuals. These organizations can maximize production by making sure that their costly experts are as fully utilized as possible and that their work is organized effectively and efficiently. Any such expert time not sold or inefficiently used is lost forever. About 20 percent of companies use this type of formula.

Examples:

- **Profit per Customer Month:** A high-end custom homebuilder uses this formula because it has found that its most profitable projects are large-value homes that are built quickly. The formula keeps the spotlight on increasing the size of homes it sells and improving their delivery times by organizing the work well and by obtaining building permits promptly.

- **Profit per Associate Hour:** A consulting firm advising government contractors on a success basis uses this formula. Similar to the previous example, large projects, engineered to deliver success, and efficiently executed deliver maximum profitability for this business. The most profitable projects often require expensive contractors who know what they are doing and who can deliver timely and lucrative results.

- **Profit per Session Day:** This is the ratio I use for my coaching and consulting activities. My goal is to maximize earnings while working 100–125 days a year, which allows me to provide maximum value and impact to ambitious, coachable clients, while setting time aside for research, writing, speaking, and recreation.

Cogs in Your Stategic Flywheel

Having built scores of flywheels for clients, it was time to analyze the data and deconstruct what a Strategic Flywheel is made of. I have found that 99 percent of flywheel cogs represent one of the following nine themes, which are listed in order of frequency:

1. Improve Profitability

2. Create Customer Success

3. Strengthen Brand

4. Expand Production Capacity

5. Grow Volume of Business

6. Innovate Offerings

7. Deepen Customer Engagement

8. Upgrade Service Delivery

9. Increase Productivity

I found analyzing this list eye-opening. Over 25 percent of the companies reviewed forgot to include a cog in their flywheel for *business volume growth*, which exposed their obsession with customer service at the expense of creating new customers.

This, in the long term, can be deadly. No customer stays forever, and even if they did, you can't afford to completely rely on growing your existing clients. Clients that grow faster than your total revenue create dependence and diminish your ability to do the right thing in the relationship.

The results are scope creep, undue customization, eroding client profitability, and the atrophying of your new business muscles. Every company must maintain an inside sales engine vigorously used and in good repair.

Another 25 percent of the companies I examined had no flywheel cog responsible for strengthening their brand. Lacking brand focus can lead to commoditization and margin erosion, with predictable results.

Another quarter of the companies I analyzed failed to focus on expanding their capacity to produce. Again, without attracting and training people and constantly refining and optimizing delivery processes you will cap your capacity and hunger for new business, and growth will remain elusive.

Finally, 20 percent of the companies I scrutinized had no cog focused on improving profitability. Profit is oxygen for businesses, and it is necessary for innovating, taking advantage of opportunities, and looking after your people and shareholders.

Therefore, I believe that most companies must include cogs in their flywheel that cover profitability, customer success, growth, and productivity. You may skimp if you must on improving your brand, on innovation, and on improving service delivery or customer engagement—for a while.

Your challenge is to pick a profitability metric and an additional four to six of the nine essential flywheel cogs for *your* business. Trying to do more than five to seven in total will make your business too complex and will slow your growth.

The Nine Essential Themes for a Strategic Flywheel

Now it is time to populate your flywheel. A finished Strategic Flywheel looks like a clockface, as shown in Figure 11.3.[4] I invite you to ponder which flywheel cogs would be the most critical for *your* type of business and make sure to include them in your Strategic Flywheel. Here, we will discuss the nine Flywheel Themes, and in the next section we will review the two most common Strategic Flywheel structures that apply to the majority of businesses. You may choose to use one of those as your starting point or to create your own from scratch.

Figure 11.3 Examples of complete Strategic Flywheels

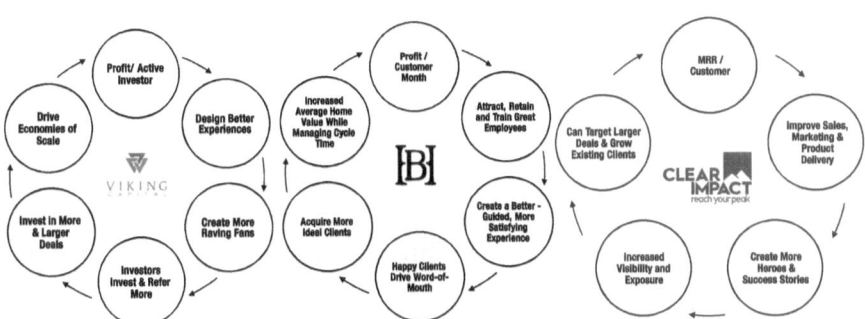

Theme 1: Improve Profitability

We already covered improving profitability in the Profit per *X* discussion above. I recommend that you start your Strategic Flywheel by figuring out your Advanced Profit per *X* metric and then use it as the cog that stands at the twelve o'clock position on your flywheel clockface. This is the "starting and finishing point" of your flywheel.

Theme 2: Make Customers Successful

Without happy clients, your business is unlikely to thrive—unless, perhaps, you are a government-regulated monopoly.

Strategic Flywheel cog examples:

- Custom homebuilder: "Provide better-guided, more satisfying experiences"

- Software developer: "Delight our customers"

- Fitness-training company: "Deliver remarkable workouts and customer service"

Theme 3: Strengthen Brand

Strengthening your brand is important for creating a differentiated client experience that allows your business to develop a following and improve profitability through premium pricing.

Strategic Flywheel cog examples:

- Results-based accountability software developer: "Drive increased visibility and exposure"

- Precision instrument distributor: "Clients call us first and refer us"

- Fitness-training company: "Retain premium-price clients and drive referrals without ad spend"

Theme 4: Expand Production Capacity

The cog of expanding production capacity helps build your foundation for continued growth.

Strategic Flywheel cog examples:

- Software developer: "Refine the client success process"

- MSP: "Hire new employees"

- Fitness-training company: "Provide exercise science training and development"

Theme 5: Grow Volume of Business

Growth is essential to attract and retain A players, to cover for inevitable setbacks, and to win in the marketplace. Flat performance is unsustainable.

Strategic Flywheel cog examples:

- High-end e-commerce service: "Attract sweet-spot customers"

- Imaging software developer: "Customer community attracts new labs onto our platform"

- Property management and brokerage firm: "Develop new markets, segments, and services"

Theme 6: Innovate Offerings

Again, it is critical for a business to innovate regularly to differentiate itself in the marketplace and garner profitable growth.

Strategic Flywheel cog examples:

- Real estate investment company: "Design better client experiences"

- High-end e-commerce service: "Build vision and plan for next-level customer impact"

- Imaging software developer: "Develop adjacent solutions for users"

Theme 7: Deepen Customer Engagement

Deepening customer engagement with your business is helpful to building a low-churn business with recurring customers who engage with a growing portfolio of your products—a critical ingredient for the SaaS business model.

Strategic Flywheel cog examples:

- Imaging software developer: "Customers engage with and contribute to our community"

- Precision instrument distributor: "Sell more services, consumables, and accessories"

- High-end e-commerce service: "Delivering on promises makes clients recurring"

Theme 8: Upgrade Service Delivery

Upgrading service delivery relates to improving the technical quality of service delivery rather than its relationship aspect.

Strategic Flywheel cog examples:

- Imaging software developer: "Invest in improving core services"

- Home energy-efficiency contractor: "Deliver innovative, quality, customer-focused services"

- High-end e-commerce service: "Define and execute precise scope engagements"

Theme 9: Increase Productivity

Productivity improvement allows your business to improve profitability as it grows.

Strategic Flywheel cog examples:

- Online retailer: "Grow revenue while controlling fixed costs"

- Custom homebuilder: "Increased home values and lower construction cycle time"

- Real estate investment company: "Drive economies of scale"

Two Common Strategic Flywheel Structures

The most frequently used flywheel combination is what I call the *output-driven business*. In an output-driven business, the leadership focuses on pushing capacity growth and strengthening the brand. The Strategic Flywheel in Figure 11.4 is typical for businesses that strive to succeed in established industries.

Figure 11.4 Strategic Flywheel: output-driven business

Improve
Profitability

Expand
Production
Capacity

Increase
Productivity

**OUTPUT
DRIVEN
BUSINESS**

Create
Customer
Success

Grow Volume
of Business

Strenghten
Brand

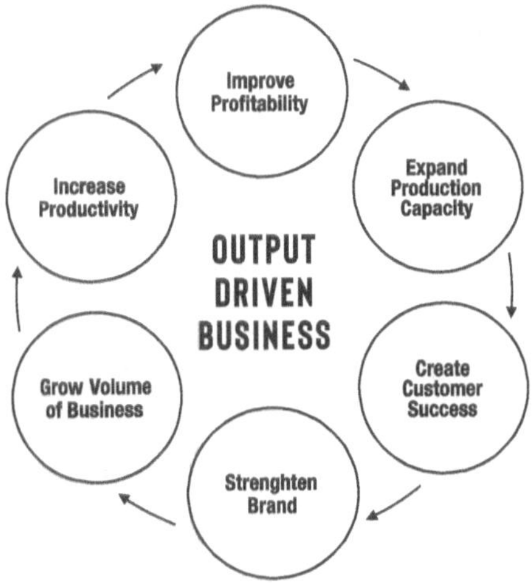

A less frequently trodden path, but still a very common one, is that of the *innovation-driven business*. In organizations driven by innovation, leaders drive growth through innovating and through deepening customer engagement. Figure 11.5 shows the typical flywheel pattern for innovative, tech-enabled businesses and SaaS companies.

Figure 11.5 Strategic Flywheel: innovation-driven business

Improve
Profitability

Innovate
Offerings

Increase
Productivity

**INNOVATION
DRIVEN
BUSINESS**

Create
Customer
Success

Grow Volume
of Business

Deepen
Customer
Engagement

Key takeaways from Chapter 11

- Building a Strategic Flywheel for your business allows you to understand the major themes in your business that help you create and sustain growth momentum.

- Start by identifying the main constraint in your business and then find the Advanced Profit per X metric that helps you leverage it. Make it the first cog at the top of the clockface of your Strategic Flywheel.

- Consider the nine essential themes in constructing your Strategic Flywheel and pick four to six cogs from among them that your business needs to build profitable growth momentum.

- Review the most common Strategic Flywheel models of output-driven businesses and innovation-driven businesses. Which one is more like your organization?

Now that you have a flywheel to spin, read the next chapter to learn what further Unique Activities will help you turn the wheel faster.

CHAPTER TWELVE

Ideate Unique Activities

The best way to have a good idea is to have lots of ideas.

—Linus Pauling

In his seminal book, *On Competition*, Michael Porter talks about how "competing to be the best" is a trap for unwary business owners. By imitating the "best practices" of others, you end up looking like them, and too much sameness leads to commoditization.

Instead, you should strive to provide differentiated value to your Core Market customers. You can do that not by marketing yourself as unique but by actually performing Unique Activities.

In earlier chapters, we discussed how IKEA, Ryanair, and MB Partners turned the Business Constraints their businesses were facing into brand promises and how each brand promise was manifested in Unique Activities.

IKEA evolved its mail-order business into a unique catalog, eventually printing 300 million copies; it turned a manufacturers' boycott into an Eastern European supply chain and dreamed up the modular, self-assembled furniture concept based on a broken table leg.

Ryanair responded to its near bankruptcy by one-upping Southwest Airlines and down-stripping its commercial flying services to the bone—charging extra for airport check-in, moving life vests overhead, and removing seat pockets to make more room for passengers and less room for trash. Outrageous publicity stunts replaced ad spend.

MB Partners compensated for its lack of experience and its strong balance sheet with innovative buyer research, promotion of hard-to-sell companies to buy-in investors, and slashing the time it took to take companies to market.

Now that we have figured out your flywheel, we can ideate further Unique Activities for *your* business around the cogs of the wheel. The ultimate objective is to build a stack of these Unique Activities—what I call the *Strategy Stack*. Having a Strategy Stack digs a moat around your business by creating and cementing sustainable competitive advantage. (We talk more about that in Step 5.)

In the previous chapter, you picked five to seven themes to construct your unique flywheel.

As the next step, we will use the Unique Activity Generator tool to contrast them with Six Business Leverage Concepts and I will ask you questions to trigger potential ideas on what other Unique Activities could accelerate *your* business.

Subsequently, we'll review the five technology trends of the early 2020s and, again, I will ask you questions to see which ones could be useful tools to power Unique Activities that can create differentiated value for your customers. (See Figure 12.1.)

Figure 12.1 Unique Activity Generator

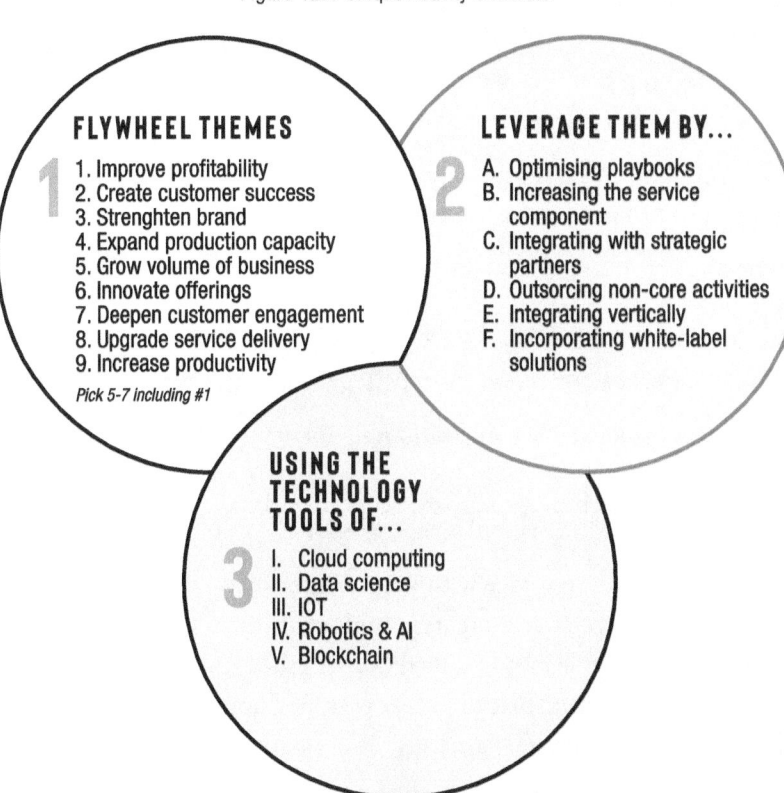

The Six Business Leverage Concepts

Let's dive into each of these business leverage concepts in turn to consider which ones could be used to push one or more cogs in your flywheel.

Optimizing Playbooks

A playbook is high-level process documentation that creates consistency and scalability in your business.[1] You can optimize your playbooks to create higher value by enriching them with value-add steps or by eliminating wasteful steps. The ultimate in playbook optimization is automation, which removes the human element and reduces to near zero the marginal costs of executing processes.

A popular way of optimizing playbooks is to apply workflow management software such as Tallyfy, Mavenlink, or Process Street. These applications keep track of workflow progress, prompt team members to execute steps when due, and send email alerts to inform supervisors.

You can read more on this topic in *Pinnacle: Five Principles that Take Your Business to the Top of the Mountain.*

Questions

- *Have you documented all your playbooks?*

- *Which playbooks represent the top 20 percent impact in your business?*

- *How could you optimize and automate them?*

Increasing the Service Component

Bundling a high-value service with your product can help you differentiate and de-commoditize it and create a high-margin-producing, recurring-revenue offering. Apple bundled its iPod with the iTunes download service and created a premium-priced category-killer application in the highly commoditized MP3 player segment.

Bundling services with your product can also be beneficial when your customer has a complex problem. Amazon Web Services (AWS) serves tech start-ups with a pay-as-you-go cloud infrastructure, which eliminates their need to invest in servers and application programming interfaces (APIs).

Bundling also helps where the quality of the service needs to be improved, such as when Xerox copiers were bundled with peace-of-mind service contracts to eliminate business disruptions.[2]

Another example, Clear Impact, a SaaS company offering a results-based accountability software service to nonprofits, offers its clients implementation services as an optional bundle. The services remove any implementation concerns clients may have while they position Clear Impact as a premium provider and create an additional revenue stream for the company.

Questions

- *Do you have a commoditized product that could be differentiated with an add-on service?*

- *Do your customers have a complex problem that you could solve by bundling your own or a third party's white-label service?*

- *Do you offer a service that could be improved further by adding a professional service layer onto it?*

Integrating with Strategic Partners

Strategic partnerships allow two businesses to pool their resources in a mutually beneficial way while staying independent. Their goals may include increasing market share, expanding into new markets, or strengthening their brands.

An example of a prominent strategic partnership is the collaboration of Uber and Spotify. Riders can access their Spotify playlists, thus enabling Uber to provide an enriched driving experience, while Spotify gains free advertising and increased sign-ups to its service.

Another example is Starbucks coffee shops nestled inside Barnes & Noble (B&N) bookstores. B&N attracts more buyers who love to sip a cup of coffee while browsing a book, and Starbucks gains a captive audience in its Core Market of middle-class shoppers.

Questions

- *Is there a market that you could reach by partnering with a company that has access to it?*

- *Which company would you like to be affiliated with to enhance your brand? Can you offer that company a hard-to-refuse advantage?*

Outsourcing Noncore Activities

Both IKEA and Apple have fully outsourced their supply chains. These companies are in the business of innovation, design, marketing, and retailing and they do best by focusing on these areas and leaving manufacturing to specialists.

As a more modest example, I personally outsource all administrative, media production, design, and technology work to experts so that I can focus on client engagements, research, writing, speaking, and podcasting.

Questions

- *What are the activities outside your Core Business activities, as defined in Chapter 1, that you have not outsourced yet?*

- *What are the low-hanging fruits that you could outsource immediately?*

- *What activities should you plan to get rid of in the next twelve months?*

Integrating Vertically and Horizontally

Integrating is the opposite of outsourcing. You may have a part of your supply chain that represents high added value and which you would prefer to control. Or perhaps bringing it in-house could enhance your brand and/ or your profitability.

Apple decided to vertically integrate its retail channel to create a differentiated customer experience. Establishing Apple Stores enhanced the company's brand and allowed it to bundle a high-touch customer service offering through its Genius Bar. The Apple Store also allows the company to sell high-margin add-ons with its hardware products, dramatically increasing profitability.

Apple products are also horizontally integrated. Steve Jobs expressed the belief that hardware and software should be combined for a seamless performance. Apple products are almost unique in relying on their own Apple operating system, and the company sets high standards in helping its customers control their privacy better than with competing products.

Questions

- *What part of your supply chain or sales channel would you like to control?*

- *What opportunities do you have to take over a part of your value chain that is controlled by third parties, or to develop your own integrated hardware-with-software product?*

Incorporating White-Label Solutions

White-labeling means selling a product or service offered by a third party under your own brand. Software companies such as HubSpot and WordPress offer white-label versions of their products to users who want to include these services as part of their own offering.

Questions

- *What software or other service would make sense bundled with your offering under your own brand?*

- *How could you offer more value to your clients?*

- *What services are your customers buying elsewhere that you could bundle with your own and make your customers' lives easier and your relationship with them stickier?*

Five Technology Trends

We are living through a technology revolution where disruption is continuous. New technologies are becoming part of our everyday lives, including artificial intelligence, Internet of Things (IOT), data science, robotics, blockchain, and others.

The options are overwhelming, but you cannot ignore new technologies if you want to stay ahead of the game. I have selected the five most-talked-about technologies of the early 2020s for your top consideration. After you gain familiarity, I ask you questions to help stimulate your imagination about their potential use.

Please remember that you don't need to deeply understand these technologies to use them. You need only to understand their potential and to develop an approach for identifying and vetting people who can help you implement solutions using them. As business coach Dan Sullivan likes to say, it's the WHO, not the HOW, that you need to figure out.

Cloud Computing

Cloud computing is the on-demand availability of computer system resources, especially data storage and computing power, without direct, active management by the user.[3] Cloud computing allows you to access technology applications as needed without having to invest time and money in buying and customizing hardware and software.

The beauty of cloud applications is that you can experiment with them without any significant commitments. I try many applications on a month-to-month basis, keep the 20 percent that I like, and cancel the rest of my subscriptions after a few weeks or months of experimentation.

Questions

- *What part of your business would you like to simplify or automate by using a cloud-based application? (Chances are there is an app for it.)*

- *What repetitive tasks are you doing? (These are all candidates for being "cloudified.")*

Data Science

Data science is about analyzing data for actionable insights. Retailers are known to be analyzing terabytes of data collected on the internet gathered from our smartphones, desktops, IOT devices, and media and credit card companies. They glean insights into our shopping habits, interests, and desires in order to better market to us and influence our thinking to their advantage.

We can argue about the ethics of data use, but the fact that the data is out there and is being used, in most cases legally, is undeniable. You may not have access to as much data as Facebook does, but chances are you are currently using less information than you could or that you already collect.

Questions

- *What information do you already have access to that would be worth analyzing to understand your customers better?*

- *What information that you don't yet possess could you acquire from other companies to help you reach your Core Market better?*

- *What information would you love to have? Who can you hire to research where to get it?*

Internet of Things

The Internet of Things (IOT) describes physical objects that contain sensors, processing ability, software, and other technologies that connect and exchange data with other devices and systems over the internet or other communications networks.[4]

Examples include wearable technologies, such as heart rate monitors, and home security and comfort appliances that can be controlled by an app or the spoken word, such as Amazon's Alexa speakers.

Questions

- *What existing IOT device could you bundle with your current products or services?*

- *What kind of IOT device can you imagine revolutionizing how your customers access your services? Who might help you develop it?*

Robotics and Artificial Intelligence

Robotics is an interdisciplinary branch of computer science and engineering. Robotics involves design, construction, operation, and use of robots. The goal of robotics is to design machines that can assist humans.[5]

One of the most easily accessible fields of robotics is robotic process automation (RPA) that creates automatic workflows that are sometimes enhanced by artificial intelligence (AI). AI can perform tasks that normally require human intelligence, such as visual perception, speech recognition, decision-making, and language translation.[6]

Questions

- *What repetitive tasks exist in your business that require minimal human judgment and that could be robotized?*

- *Who could you hire to analyze your business for the potential of automation with robotics, including RPA?*

Blockchain

A blockchain is a decentralized, distributed, and public digital ledger. It is used to record transactions across many computers so that the record cannot be altered retroactively without the alteration of all subsequent blocks and the consensus of the network.[7]

Distributed Ledger Technology (DLT), such as blockchain, is already being used in a wide variety of industries that have nothing to do with cryptocurrencies. Blockchains facilitate efficient and secure international payments in major currencies, settlement of capital markets and real estate transactions, and management of health records, among many other uses. Global spending on blockchain is projected to approach $18 billion by 2024.[8]

Question

- *Where could your business use DLT to make multiparty transactions more secure, efficient, and transparent?*

Key takeaways from Chapter 12

- In addition to the Unique Activities that you came up with in Chapter 9, you can ideate more Unique Activities for your chosen Flywheel Themes.

- Brainstorm flywheel-spinning Unique Activities using the Six Business Leverage Concepts.

- Review the top five technology trends of the 2020s and consider how you could use them to create differentiated value for your customers.

Now that you are clear on who you are (Core Business), what you do (Strategic Position), what you offer (brand promises) for whom (Core Market) and how your unique flywheel can be accelerated by the Six Business Leverage Concepts and the five new technologies, it's time to weave your Unique Activities into a consistent, mutually reinforcing, and optimized Strategy Stack.

A Strategy Stack allows you to dig a moat around your business and make it virtually unassailable by your competitors. We will look at how to build one now in Step 5.

STRATEGIZE A STACK

If the cards are stacked against you, reshuffle the deck.

—John D. MacDonald

In the year 2000, a fifty-nine-year-old family business located in a small Lichtenstein municipality of 6,000 people decided to reinvent its business.[1] The company's CEO proposed a brand-new way of approaching its market: the construction and mining companies who bought the power tools, including pneumatic drills, that his company was famous for. He proposed that the company stop marketing the drills and start selling the holes.

The CEO of HILTI, Dr. Pius Baschera, realized that good enough Asian manufacturers had started chipping away at HILTI's market share, and the company had to change its ways.[2] Fast.

HILTI approached the top management of its most loyal customers and offered to buy back its tools only to lease them back on subscription instead. This would allow customers to always use the latest version of any tool they needed, without having to worry about its availability, maintenance, or repair.

Many of the tools were used sparingly anyway, and customers leasing them only when needed would actually cost them less. HILTI could manage the idle tools and lend them out to other customers.

What started as a simple change in approach turned out to be a complete reinvention of how the company operated. HILTI transitioned from a manufacturing firm to a service and consulting business that sold long-term contracts to CEOs rather than individual tools to builders and miners.

The company had to reinvent its IT systems to keep track of and optimize its decentralized tool fleets around the world. It replaced or retrained its salespeople into high-powered consultants who could grasp customers' business goals and offer tailored solutions to achieve them. HILTI's account managers didn't just advise but also became the sponge soaking up unmet customer needs and feeding them back to the company's innovation lab.

HILTI has been growing by double digits in a mature market, with its sales exceeding $5.5 billion in 2021. Curiously, however, none of its major competitors has copied its approach. This is because the company has built a Strategy Stack of more than a dozen Unique Activities that, in combination, are almost impossible to emulate.

HILTI's Strategy Stack

1. Service-focused Sales and Marketing	2. Leasing vs. Selling of Power Tools and Drills	3. Fleet Management	4. IT & Logistical Infrastructure
5. Technology and Consulting Services	6. Financing Inventory of Tool Fleets	7. Selling to Top Management Not Workers	8. Direct, Consultative Sales Force
9. Any Tool at Any Time at Any Location	10. Premium Quality, Long-lasting Tools	11. 6% of Budget Invested in Innovation	12. Family Ownership Allows Long-term Thinking
13. No Middlemen Between the Company and its Customers	14. 24/7 Customer Care Service	15. Dedicated Account Managers	16. Tool Park Optimization

In our earlier example, IKEA monopolized its own Strategy Stack; for over sixty years, it has not been copied. Its largest competitor, JYSK, has only grown to one-tenth of IKEA's size.

In this Step 5, we drill down into how you can multiply and forge *your* Unique Activities into a Strategy Stack that makes your business unassailable as well.

- In Chapter 13, we discuss how you can improve the fit of your Unique Activities with your strategy and with each other, thereby amplifying their impact.

- In Chapter 14, we discuss how you can innovate more Unique Activities in the prime value areas of your business and how you can expand from your initial niche into adjacent markets, products, geographies, sales channels, and industries.

- Finally, in Chapter 15, we review how you can utilize network effects to further entrench your leadership and accelerate your growth.

Now let's dive in and examine how a company's Unique Activities should fit with its overall strategy.

CHAPTER THIRTEEN

Ensure Activity Fit

What sets you apart can sometimes feel like a burden and it's not. And a lot of the time it's what makes you great.

—Emma Stone

German sports car manufacturer Porsche was founded by an engineer named Ferdinand Porsche, his lawyer and son-in-law, and a race car driver and businessman friend of Ferdinand. The company started as a consultancy and, early on, was hired by Hitler's government to design a "people's car," which became the Volkswagen Beetle. The first Porsche automobile, the Type 64, was developed using many components from the Beetle.[1]

During World War II, Porsche designed a military Beetle and two tanks for the German army, and for it, Ferdinand Porsche received a twenty-month prison sentence from the Allies after V-Day. During the principal founder's hiatus from the company, his son Ferry saved the business and built himself a sports car—the Porsche 356. This car was the precursor of the Porsche 911, which is to this day the company's most popular model.

The extreme longevity of the 911 allowed Porsche to experiment and refine the design and develop a set of Unique Activities that have made Porsche the most profitable mass market luxury carmaker in the world.[2]

So, what makes Porsche cars unique? And how do the company's Unique Activities fit with its Strategic Position as "An exclusive sports car brand designed for everyday journeys"?[3] (See Figure 13.1.)

Porter's Three Elements That Increase Fit

Michael Porter, in *On Competition*, talks about the three components that increase the fit of your Unique Activities. Such fit is desirable because it makes your Unique Activities more powerful and creates chain-linked systems that accentuate your business's differentiation in the marketplace.

These three elements are the following:

A **Consistency:** Do your Unique Activities *communicate, amplify,* or *support* your Strategic Position?

B **Reinforcement:** Do your Unique Activities *amplify* the positive impact of *another Unique Activity* on your Strategic Position?

C **Optimization:** Have you developed tactics that would make multiple Unique Activities more impactful, efficient, or cheaper?

Figure 13.1 Porsche's Strategy Stack

1. Focus on Driving Experience vs. Speed & Aesthetics	2. Perfected Aerodynamics with Attractive, Uniform Look	3. Precision Driving, Near-Perfect Control and Responsiveness	4. Well-Organized Ergonomic Cockpit
5. Perfect Driving Position, Snug Like a Glove	6. Spacious and Classic Interior	7. Luxuriously Appointed, but not Ostentatious	8. Welcoming, Hugging and Supremely Comfortable Seats
9. Owners can Infinitely Customize & Improve Cars	10. Well-Engineered Flat-Six Boxer Engine	11. Rear-Engine Layout	12. Excellent Fuel Economy
13. Rear-Wheel Steering and Front-Axle Lift System	14. Vehicles are Easy to Drive, Park and Maintain	15. Technologies Evolved from Decades of Racing	16. Lineup Includes Sporty SUVs and Sedans

Let's examine Porsche's Unique Activities through the lens of Porter's fit-powering elements.

Fit Element A: Consistency

Do Porsche's Unique Activities communicate, amplify, or support its Strategic Position of being "An exclusive sports car brand designed for everyday journeys"?

As you can see in Figure 13.2, all of Porsche's Unique Activities that I could identify are consistent with the company's stated Strategic Position.

The three legs of the "Porsche stool," which are "exclusive," "sports car," and "for everyday journeys," resonate with each of the company's sixteen Unique Activities.

Figure 13.2 The consistency of Porsche's Unique Activities

#	Unique Activities	Reinforcing?	Consistent With...
1	Focus on driving experience more than speed and aesthetics	YES	"For everyday journeys"
2	Perfected aerodynamics with attractive, uniform look	YES	"Exclusive sports car"
3	Owners can infinitely customize and improve cars	YES	"Exclusive" and "for everyday journeys." Users can personalize their car
4	Well-organized, ergonomic cockpit	YES	"Sports car"
5	Spacious and classic interior	YES	"Exclusive" and "for everyday journeys"
6	Perfect driving position, snug like a glove	YES	"Sports car"
7	Luxuriously appointed, but not ostentatious	YES	"Exclusive"
8	Welcoming, hugging, and supremely comfortable	YES	"Exclusive"
9	Precision driving: near-perfect control and responsiveness to driver inputs	YES	"Sports car"
10	Well-engineered flat-six "boxer" engine	YES	"Sports car"
11	Rear engine layout	YES	"Sports car." Improves steering and control
12	Rear-wheel steering and front axle lift system	YES	"Sports car." Improves steering and control. Lift system improves reverse driving
13	Excellent fuel economy	YES	"For everyday journeys"
14	Easy to maintain and easy to drive and park	YES	"For everyday journeys"
15	Technologies evolved from decades of racing	YES	"Sports car"
16	Lineup includes sporty SUVs and sedans	YES	"Sports car" and "for everyday journeys"

Fit Element B: Reinforcement

Do Porsche's Unique Activities *amplify* the positive impact of *another Unique Activity* in its Strategic Position of being "An exclusive sports car brand designed for everyday journeys"?

As you can see in Figure 13.3, over 90 percent of the Unique Activities reinforce each other.

For example, by focusing on the driving experience (Unique Activity 1), vehicles have to be made comfortable (UA8) and with more precise control (UA9), which is helped by the flat-six, better air-cooled engine (UA10) and the rear engine layout, which allows improved balance and steering (UA11) as does the rear-wheel steering (UA12).

The notable exception is UA16, having a lineup of sporty SUVs and sedans, which doesn't reinforce other Unique Activities. However, this lineup has been added for another reason—to reduce the cyclicality of the sporting car business. During recessionary years, sales of 911s declines, but family SUVs and sedan sales continue to hold up, keeping the company profitable.

Figure 13.3 Are Porsche's Unique Activities reinforcing each other?

#	Unique Activities	Amplifies Another Ua?	Which One?
1.	Focus on driving experience more than speed and aesthetics	YES	8, 9, 10, 11, 12, 15
2.	Perfected aerodynamics with attractive, uniform look	YES	7, 15, 16
3.	Owners can infinitely customize and improve cars	YES	8
4.	Well-organized, ergonomic cockpit	YES	5, 6, 7, 8, 9, 14, 15
5.	Spacious and classic interior	YES	4, 6, 7, 8
6.	Perfect driving position, snug like a glove	YES	4, 5, 8, 9, 15
7.	Luxuriously appointed, but not ostentatious	YES	2, 4, 5, 8
8.	Welcoming, hugging, and supremely comfortable	YES	1, 3, 4, 5, 6, 7, 14
9.	Precision driving: near-perfect control and responsiveness to driver inputs	YES	1, 4, 6, 11, 12, 14, 15
10.	Well-engineered flat-six "boxer" engine	YES	1, 9, 14, 15
11.	Rear engine layout	YES	1, 9, 12
12.	Rear-wheel steering and front axle lift system	YES	1, 9, 11, 15
13.	Excellent fuel economy	YES	14, 15
14.	Easy to maintain and easy to drive and park	YES	4, 8, 9, 10, 13
15.	Technologies evolved from decades of racing	YES	1, 2, 4, 6, 9, 10, 12, 13
16.	Lineup includes sporty SUVs and sedans	NO	In the lineup to keep company profitable during downturns

Fit Element C: Optimization

Has Porsche developed tactics that make multiple Unique Activities more impactful, efficient, or cheaper? (See Figure 13.4.)

Porsche has developed several tactics in recent years that optimize its Unique Activities. Read about some of these below.

Making the 911 the Reference for All New Designs

All research begins with the 911, originally designed in 1963, as the standard-bearer. The round instruments with the rev counter in the middle is an indispensable element of the interior of any new Porsche.

The Four-Point Headlight

Porsche reimagined the headlights of all its models to a four-point design. This tactic reinforces several Unique Activities. The new design

- strengthens brand identity by allowing people to recognize a Porsche from afar;

- saves money because it no longer requires expensive rippled glass;

- saves energy because new LED lights convert 20 percent of energy into light compared to 3 percent for traditional lights;

- helps drivers navigate in rainy weather and in heavy oncoming traffic; and

- allows safer driving because it doesn't blind other drivers and helps them get out of the way.

Porsche Product Line Principle

Since 1999, product line leaders who report directly to the CEO make all product-related decisions. These include new model development, variants, production support, and model updates.

This approach makes product line leaders personally accountable for building fascinating, attractive, and high-quality vehicles using an efficient and economical manufacturing approach. The company attributes its financial success in part to reorganizing around this principle.

Distraction-Free Driving

To reduce distraction, Porsche follows two principles:

1. **Less is more:** How can engineers create more options with fewer buttons? Designers observe what people do, and what they do not do, in their cars and augment and simplify controls accordingly.

2. **Order:** Order creates space for new things, like augmented reality, which is the insertion of virtual elements into the driver's field of vision. Every moment drivers look at the road and not at the display of a smartphone means more security and speed.

Increasing Driving Pleasure

Interior designers consider both the structure and the visual appeal of displays to enhance the driving experience.

Another focus is to help drivers improve their driving skills on the race track or when parking in tight spaces. Designers isolate recurring situations and brainstorm to design helpful improvements.

Figure 13.4 Are Porsche's Unique Activities being optimized?

Porsche Tactics	Which Unique Activities Benefited?
911 is the reference for all new designs[4]	2, 3, 4, 5, 6, 7, 8, 9, 11, 13, 16
Four-point headlights[5]	1, 2, 14, 15
Porsche product line principle[6]	2, 3, 13, 14, 15, 16
Distraction-free operation	1, 3, 4, 7, 14
Increasing driving pleasure	1, 3, 4, 9, 14

How to Develop Reinforcing Unique Activities and Optimizing Tactics

To develop new Unique Activities, use your existing UAs to ideate other UAs that will reinforce them. Use the brainstorming approaches described in Chapter 5 to generate these ideas.

The Unique Activity Generator will also come in handy here. Use your flywheel cogs, the Six Business Leverage Concepts, and the five new technologies discussed in Chapter 12 to generate ideas.

As is visible in the Porsche example, once you have designed Unique Activities, it is simple to generate tactics that optimize several.

In fact, the existence of defined Unique Activities drives the ideation process, just as it did for Porsche's four-point headlight project. The project had to improve the driving experience while fitting in with the classic 911 design and strengthening the brand. It was also meant to be practical and helpful in contributing to successful races.

Everything ultimately derives from the evolutionary constraints on your business and the brand promises they catalyze along the way. Consider rereading Step 3: Capitalize on Constraints to see how this works.

Key takeaways from Chapter 13

- Analyze your Unique Activities to make sure they are consistent with your positioning. Tweak them to enhance consistency.

- Make sure your activities reinforce each other, and develop new ones that do.

- Brainstorm tactics that make your Unique Activities more impactful, more efficient, and less expensive to deliver.

Now you have Unique Activities that derive from your brand promises and others that you designed to accelerate your Flywheel Themes. You also have ensured that these Unique Activities are rock solid and consistent with your Strategic Position. Further, they *reinforce* each other and you have developed tactics to *optimize* them.

Chances are that your business is gaining the momentum needed to dominate your niche. It is now time to raise your sights and spread your business tentacles.

Next, we will explore how to expand your business to other products, geographies, markets, channels, and industries.

CHAPTER FOURTEEN

Spread Your Tentacles

It's better to be an octopus than a fish. If an octopus loses a tentacle to a predator, the octopus will survive with seven tentacles left for itself.

—Gene Simmons

After Independence Day in 1994, a thirty-year-old New York hedge fund manager quit his job to launch a website selling books on the internet from his garage. He called it the "Earth's Largest Bookstore" and used a technical loophole to pose as a retailer and get book distributors to sell him individual books to fulfill internet orders.

Initially, the founder rang a bell every time an order came in, and his small staff ran to check whether they knew the customer. These days did not last, however. Within a month, the company, Amazon.com, was selling books in all fifty states and forty-five countries, and its founder, Jeff Bezos, had to switch off the bell.[1]

Bezos, however, did not leave a high-six-figure New York job to become a bookseller. A book published in 2013, *The Everything Store*, relays how Bezos had a vision to build a dominant retailer from the start, and fittingly he named his company after the largest river in the world.

Amazon started small, built momentum in a niche, and then used it to decisively penetrate other product categories, geographies, markets, and industries. In the past two decades, Amazon has become a dominant technology company in e-commerce, cloud computing, online advertising, digital streaming, and artificial intelligence. It has become an influential economic and cultural force in the world and one of the world's most valuable brands.[2]

But it all happened from a focused, small start. From Seattle, Amazon developed Unique Activities in the book business, and then spread its tentacles. By 1998, it was selling music and videos, and it started acquiring online booksellers in the United Kingdom. From 1999, Amazon offered video games, consumer electronics, home improvement items, software, games, and toys. And by 2002, it had launched Amazon Web Services, the first of many other industries Bezos has come to dominate since.

So, what does it take to create this kind of expansion? Let's consider the Six Dimensions of Expansion and how Amazon leveraged its Unique Activities to succeed in other businesses it's entered. See Figure 14.1.

Read the following section with your own business in mind to pick up lessons that *you,* too, could apply in *your* business.

The Six Dimensions of Expansion

You can think of expanding your business as spreading your tentacles in six directions:

o   Adjacent markets

o   Other geographies

o   New products

o   Additional channels

o   Different industries

o   Spawned businesses

Figure 14.1 The Six Dimensions of Expansion

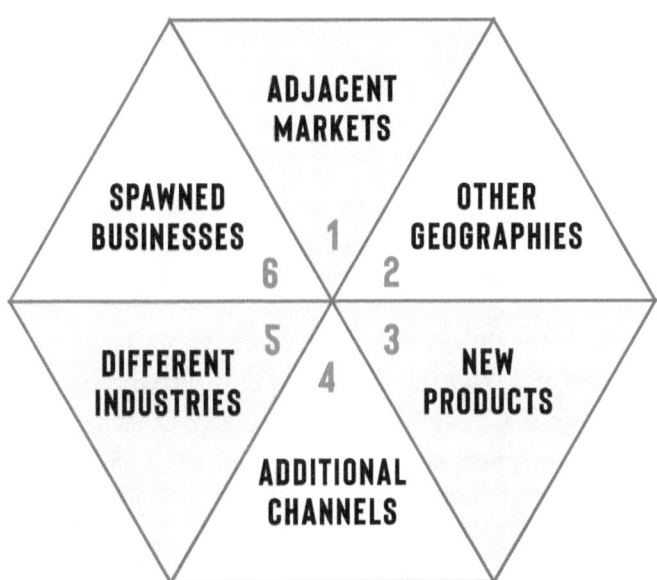

Dimension 1: Adjacent Markets

After its initial public offering (IPO), Jeff Bezos raised his sights to launch other product categories on Amazon.com.

Books were flying off warehouse shelves, and the most logical next step was to offer additional media products. CDs and videos were similarly low price point and nonperishable with a wide selection of potential products that no brick-and-mortar retailer had a chance to stock.

I have personal experience related to this situation, having spent a good part of the 1990s in London as an avid collector of jazz CDs. I regularly browsed the largest retailers there, such as Virgin Music, Tower Records, and HMV, and it struck me how limited their selections were. Even in major categories, such as 1960s bebop jazz, my area of interest at the time.

The more obscure albums were only published in Japan and had to be imported by British record stores at exorbitant prices. Online retailers, such as Amazon, were in a prime position to solve this problem. They could catalog and source titles on demand without having to hold inventory.

Unique Activities at Play

Jeff Bezos openly talks about his company's Unique Activities at Amazon's annual shareholder meetings, which he calls the company's "14 Principles."[3] (See Figure 14.2.) These are more strategic than the Unique Activities of IKEA, HILTI, or Porsche because Amazon has grown into a Strategic Position of Variety on the Positioning Matrix (see Chapter 3).

To Bezos's 14 Principles I added two more approaches: "Wide selection with low prices" and "Getting closer and closer to the customer." These latter two UAs developed as the company entered other service areas such as web services, book publishing, and media distribution and production.

Figure 14.2 Amazon's Strategy Stack

1. Encourage Successful Failure	2. Bet on Big Ideas	3. Practice Dynamic Invention & Innovation	4. Obsess Over Customers
5. Apply Long-Term Thinking	6. Understand Your Flywheel	7. Generate High-velocity Decisions	8. Make Complexity Simple
9. Accelerate Time with Technology	10. Promote Ownership	11. Maintain Your Culture	12. Focus on High Standards
13. Question What's Measured & Trust Your Gut	14. Believe it's Always Day 1	15. Wide Selection, Low Prices	16. Getting Closer & Closer to Customers

As a bookseller, the company's Strategic Position was in the Focus quadrant in a narrow niche: "online book retailing." As it quickly grew to become the dominant online book retailer, Amazon started branching out to other products.

By the year 2000, the company had shifted its Strategic Position to a larger niche that included books, music, and video that we may label "online consumer media retailing."

It is hard to know all the principles that influenced Amazon's expansion to new product lines. However, some of the elements of Amazon's Strategy Stack were clearly in play.

Unique Activities at Play in Amazon's Expansion to Adjacent Markets

- **Encourage Successful Failure (UA1):** Getting into new products that Amazon knew little about involved risk.

- **Bet on Big Ideas (UA3):** Expanding from a niche to becoming a broader-line retailer was a very big idea, especially against stiff competition from record stores, video rental companies, major offline retailers, and pre-internet-bubble e-tailers.

- **Obsess Over Customers (UA4):** Without making existing customers happy, the expansion would not have made sense. This put Amazon staffers under immense stress, many routinely working sixty-hour weeks or longer, especially around the holiday season.

- **Apply Long-Term Thinking (UA5):** The expansion burned cash at a time when Amazon was yet to turn a profit, and its share price stopped growing. However, Bezos was confident that his long-term plan would work and Amazon would turn a profit before it ran out of cash.

- **Wide Selection, Low Prices (UA15):** Amazon applied the same playbook that had worked so well for books, in music and video retailing and other product areas.

After the year 2000, Amazon continued to add product categories, including software, apparel, baby products, consumer electronics, beauty products, gourmet food, groceries, health and personal care products, industrial and scientific supplies, kitchen items, jewelry, watches, lawn and garden items, musical instruments, sporting goods, tools, automotive items, toys and games, and farm supplies.

By the end of the 2000s, Amazon's Strategic Position widened and shifted from the Focus to the Variety quadrant as it became "The Everything Store." See Figure 14.3.

Figure 14.3 Amazon's shift in Strategic Position in the 2000s

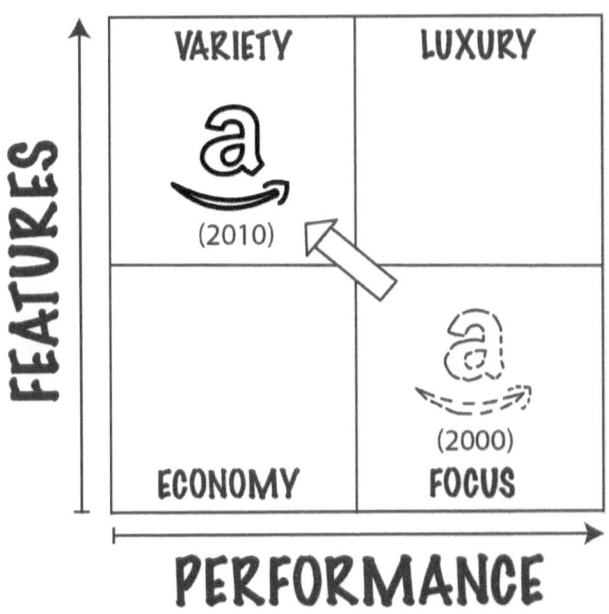

Dimension 2: Other Geographies

In October 1998, Amazon opened online stores in the United Kingdom (amazon.co.uk) and Germany (amazon.de), followed by France and Japan in the year 2000. Through the rest of the decade, Amazon expanded only to Canada, and China by default, after acquiring the online book retailer Jojo.

Jeff Bezos's first foreign forays, into the UK, Germany, France, and Canada, were successful because the company was an early mover there and offered significantly better shopping experiences and generous refund policies that local competitors could not match.

However, Amazon struggled to gain traction in China because a major competitor, Alibaba, was already well established. Alibaba understood price-sensitive Chinese shoppers, communicated in their language, and offered to transact on low-cost local payment services that Amazon was slow to adopt.[4]

The challenges in China slowed Amazon's geographical expansion until the company "cracked the code" on how to tackle linguistic, regulatory, and cultural challenges in its international markets. After 2010, the expansion momentum revived, and Amazon has since expanded to fifteen more countries. However, the group has been making losses in its international operations and may not attain dominance in many of its markets without access to similar logistical infrastructure that the U.S. operation enjoys.

Unique Activities at Play in Amazon's Geographic Expansion

- **Encourage Successful Failure (UA1):** Following its early setbacks in China, Amazon slowed down its international expansion and focused on low-hanging fruits, such as AWS. Its further expansion challenges may lead to it quitting markets with existing entrenched competitors, in the future.

- **Obsess Over Customers (UA4):** The company has been successful with its customer obsession in its core geographies. However, it may quit marginal markets where it cannot deliver an exceptional experience.

- **Apply Long-Term Thinking (UA5):** Amazon demonstrated a long-term commitment to international expansion when it returned to this strategy in 2010. It's since been financing quarterly losses in its international markets,[5] and Bezos may be banking on beating expectations like he did in the 2000s when the stock price stagnated through the decade.

- **Accelerate Time with Technology (UA9):** This is critical for the company's success in countries where it has to catch up to early entrants.

- **Wide Selection, Low Prices (UA15):** This is Amazon's trump card, but it requires the ability to scale the business in remote markets as well. Easier said than done without the logistical infrastructure Amazon enjoys in the United States.

- **Getting Closer and Closer to Customers (UA16):** Another activity that plays into Amazon's hands is approaching customers from multiple directions, such as offering AWS's services and media production and distribution with Amazon Prime.

Dimension 3: New Products

Amazon has developed a number of services and products. Some grew organically out of its core consumer retail business.

One of these is the Amazon Prime subscription service launched in 2005, which offers free two-day shipping for a flat annual subscription fee. Amazon later bundled other services such as video and music streaming into Prime. By 2022, the number of Prime subscribers exceeded 200 million people.

Another organically created product was Fulfillment by Amazon (FBA), which is offered to third-party sellers on the Amazon retail platform. Sellers can send their products to Amazon fulfillment centers that take care of picking, packing, and delivering online orders on behalf of sellers.

Amazon has created physical products as well, including the groundbreaking Kindle e-reader, the Amazon Fire TV stick, and Alexa, an artificial intelligence–powered voice assistant. The development of Alexa has also led to the creation of a household robot called Astro that can be controlled through instructions spoken to Alexa.

Unique Activities at Play in Amazon's Product Expansion

- **Encourage Successful Failure (UA1), Practice Dynamic Invention and Innovation (UA2),** and **Bet on Big Ideas (UA3):** New products require experimentation and the willingness to fail. Amazon went in big on its new inventions and experienced its share of failures, such as the Fire Phone and Local Register, which unsuccessfully tried to compete with the Square payment terminal.[6]

- **Obsess Over Customers (UA4):** This principle paid off with several products that anticipated and addressed unmet customer needs. Few would have imagined that people would prepay for free Prime shipping and that Kindle tablets would replace physical books and magazines. The futuristic Alexa also became a major hit with consumers.

- **Make Complexity Simple (UA8):** Prime was a major simplifier because, with free shipping and offline-equivalent prices, online ordering became a no-brainer. This principle also helped with the design of the Kindle e-reader, a stripped-down tablet that doesn't distract users with a backlit screen or apps.

Dimension 4: Additional Channels

Amazon's reason for existence was online retailing, but over time the company developed its business through brick-and-mortar and hybrid distribution channels as well.

Its first foray back in 1996 was to launch an affiliate program that allowed content creators, bloggers, and marketers to monetize their website visitors by promoting Amazon's products.[7]

For example, the host of a philosophy podcast I used to listen to requested listeners fund the show by visiting Amazon through his website. I never bothered to do this but felt guilty enough to become a paid subscriber to the show.

Amazon also launched the "aStore," which allowed affiliates to have a white-label Amazon storefront that they could promote to their customers for a commission. In 2017, Amazon discontinued this channel because it became a distraction for the company to maintain outside of its main platform.[8]

Amazon experimented with physical bookstores and with pop-up locations where it sold its highly reviewed books. However, these stores made no return and were later shuttered.

The company eventually opened three other physical store brands: the Amazon Go checkout-free stores, Amazon Fresh grocery stores (more on these later), and Amazon Style, a store brand that sells apparel and accessories for both sexes.[9] Amazon Go and Amazon Style are still fledgling concepts, but Amazon Fresh operates over forty locations in late 2022.

Unique Activities at Play in Amazon's Channel Expansion

- **Encourage Successful Failure (UA1):** Clearly, Amazon has been experimenting and was apparently okay with the failures of aStore and the offline bookstore concepts.

- **Bet on Big Ideas (UA3):** Amazon Go's Just Walk Out convenience store concept is a big idea and it can revolutionize shopping if it works on a larger scale.

- **Accelerate Time with Technology (UA9):** All the additional channel concepts are new-technology-driven, and the Just Walk Out shopping concept can become a major timesaver to customers and Amazon alike.

- **Focus on High Standards (UA12):** Making the new low-staff shopping concepts work requires highly engineered human-free systems that set the bar high.

- **Getting Closer and Closer to Customers (UA16):** Amazon's drive to be a force in offline retail is in tune with its attempt to be ubiquitous in its customers' lives.

Dimension 5: Different Industries

In parallel with developing new products, Amazon has created new services to go with them, to increase recurring revenues so well loved by investors. In 2007, the launch of the Kindle and the Kindle Direct Publishing (KDP) platform started a self-publishing revolution, disrupting the professional publishing industry.

In the past, authors needed an agent to even get their work in front of a publisher. When a publisher finally liked a concept, the book had to be written under its guidance, and it often took two years for the book to get to market. In the meantime, authors lost creative and distribution control of their work and rarely saw royalties other than the advance.

Using KDP, authors produce their book at their own pace, keep creative control, and collect up to 70 percent of the royalties, with 30 percent going to Amazon. Amazon also sells author copies for a few dollars plus shipping.

Publishers don't have crystal balls anyway, and ultimately the market dictates whether a book is a success.

Amazon also acquired Audible, a publishing platform for audiobooks, which has since become the dominant audiobook platform.

Another industry Amazon entered early is on-demand movie distribution and production. The Prime Video streaming service started as a free add-on for Prime subscribers and was later expanded to offer highly rated movies for rent or purchase on demand.

In 2010, Amazon Studios started creating original content for Prime Video. In 2018, the studio won two Golden Globe awards for the period comedy-drama television series *The Marvelous Mrs. Maisel.*

Unique Activities at Play in Amazon's Expansion to Other Industries

- **Apply Long-Term Thinking (UA5):** Prime Video was a long-term play, requiring Amazon to invest for years into a free service while it built up its subscriber base. The Kindle and reimagining the book publishing business were also long-term plays initially received with skepticism by the public.

- **Understand Your Flywheel (UA6):** Fulfillment by Amazon was a real flywheel spinner because it allowed Amazon to scale its retail platform to serve other industries, monetizing a logistical infrastructure it had already built for its own distribution.

- **Make Complexity Simpler (UA8):** Kindle, KDP, and Audible make the production and consumption of books simpler and more effective. Kindle offers instant gratification with immediate access to purchases. Audible allows people with little inactive time to reconnect with books while driving, exercising, or working around the house.

- **Getting Closer and Closer to Customers (UA16):** By entering the media and publishing businesses, Amazon strengthened its brand further by associating with the learning and entertainment industries. According to Statista, between 2006 and 2022, Amazon's brand value skyrocketed from $6 billion to over $700 billion.[10]

Dimension 6: Spawned Businesses

Along the way of growing its retail platform, Amazon spawned completely new businesses. The most successful of these is Amazon Web Services (AWS), the world's most comprehensive and broadly adopted cloud platform that offers more than 200 technology services.

Amazon created AWS to run its own technology efficiently and securely in the cloud and later decided to leverage it for third-party customers, the same way it did with its online marketplace. AWS's top four users are LinkedIn, Facebook, CNN, and the BBC.

Another successful Amazon-spawned business is Amazon Fresh, which started in 2007 as a grocery delivery service for Amazon Prime members. The service is available in most major U.S. cities and in Berlin, Hamburg, London, Milan, Munich, Rome, Tokyo, and in some locations in Singapore and India. The strength of Amazon Fresh is its extraordinary selection, in some cases ten times more than a leading physical supermarket chain.[11]

Unique Activities at Play in Businesses Spawned by Amazon

- **Bet on Big Ideas (UA1)**: AWS was a gigantic idea, and in 2021 that business generated 74 percent of Amazon's profit.[12]

- **Understand Your Flywheel (UA6)**: AWS is a real flywheel pusher because it leverages existing infrastructure to generate a high-margin, scalable product in an exploding market.

- **Accelerate Time with Technology (UA9)**: AWS was created by driving the scalability and operating effectiveness of Amazon's own technology platform.

- **Focus on High Standards (UA12)**: AWS is the standard-bearer in its industry, with 34 percent market share globally, ahead of Microsoft Azure (21%) and Google Cloud (11%).[13]

Key takeaways from Chapter 14

- Having outgrown your niche market, you may spread your tentacles by expanding in six dimensions:
  - To adjacent markets
  - In other geographies
  - Into new products
  - Through additional channels
  - To Different industries
  - By spawning new businesses
- Take gradual and organic steps and consider leveraging competencies that you have developed in-house for third parties, as Amazon did for third-party retailers and AWS users.
- Leverage your Unique Activities when expanding to adjacent markets, developing new products, entering additional sales channels, or entering new industries.

Having expanded your business into new dimensions, let's pull on another lever: network effects, in the next chapter.

CHAPTER FIFTEEN

Exploit Network Effects

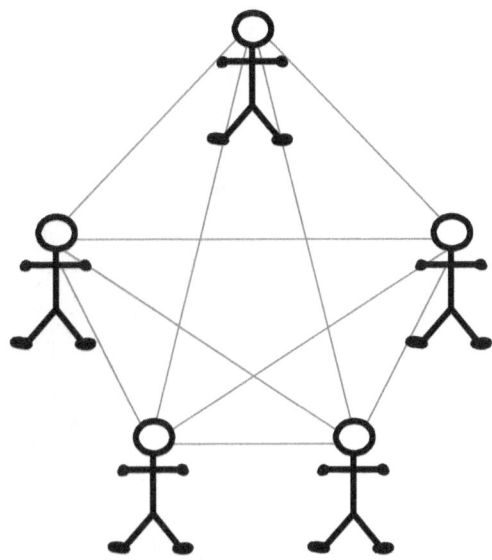

*Doing your best is not the answer. Having a network that allows
you to be your best is far better.*

—Rich Simmonds

What Are Network Effects?

Network effects exist when the growth in the usage of a product increases
the value of the product to all other users. The more your friends are on
Instagram, the more likely you want to join too. The more properties are
listed on Airbnb, the more motivated you will be to look for accommodation
there.

If you find a way to catalyze network effects for your product or service, your business can start growing exponentially. According to the Network Effects Bible, network effects have been responsible for 70 percent of all the value created in technology since 1994.[1]

Theodore Vail, the chairman of AT&T, noticed network effects first. In his company's 1908 annual report, he pointed out that people won't need a new telephone if they can already reach the people who own the old one.[2] In other words, the value of the telephone network was bigger than that of the hardware.

Figure 15.1 Network effects

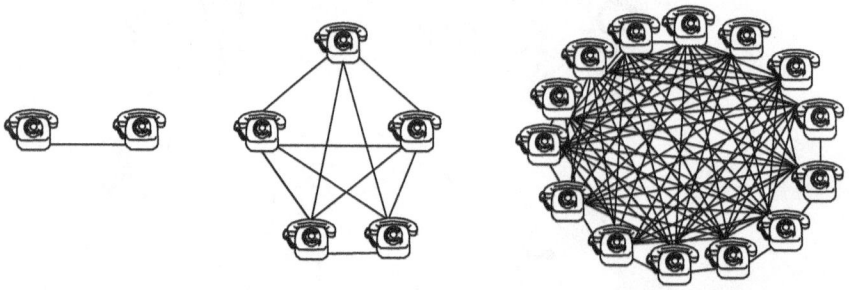

Like telephone networks, the first recognized networks were all physical and included roads, railways, and utility infrastructure such as water, gas, and sewage systems.

Subsequent network generation examples included protocols, such as VHS for videotapes and Ethernet for computing. Later came Skype for long-distance telephony and Bitcoin for cryptocurrencies. When one such technology became dominant, people adopted it en masse to gain access to a built-in user base.

Then, in the late 1990s, personal utility networks started to proliferate, such as SMS and ICQ messaging, and later Skype and WhatsApp. These utilities allowed one-to-one communication based on personal identities. Personal networks like Facebook and LinkedIn proliferated in the 2000s, allowing people to connect and network with each other in a public forum using their public identities.

Two-Sided Network Effects

Two-sided network effects arise when both sides of a network, for example, buyers and sellers, benefit from the growth of the other side of the network.

The early 2000s witnessed the advent of the first marketplaces like eBay and Amazon that allowed buyers and sellers to find each other. Marketplaces created two-sided network effects because the more buyers signed on to the network, the more attractive it became to sellers.

Initially, as a bookseller, Amazon was a one-sided network. Its value grew linearly in line with the growth in number of customers that frequented its site. After Amazon invited third-party sellers onto its platform, the company tapped into exponential growth.

Figure 15.2 Two-sided network effects

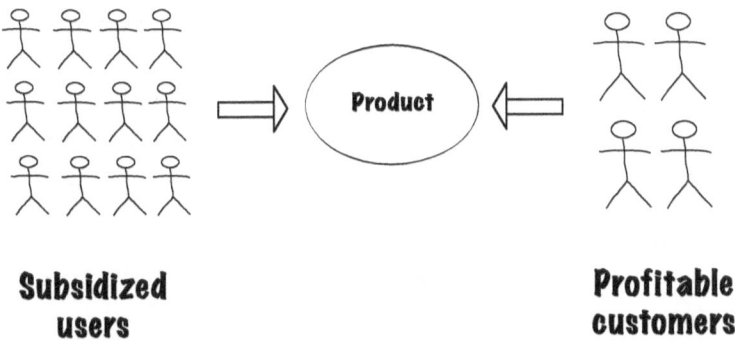

**Subsidized
users**

**Profitable
customers**

Another example of a two-sided network is a platform where users and developers create value for each other, such as the Microsoft OS, the Android operating system, and gaming consoles like Xbox and PlayStation.

The beauty of creating a platform is that, after it has gained traction, the participants take over from the initiator in doing the heavy lifting of creating value. Platforms are also called three sided network effects, as three distinct, interdependent groups of users create value for each other. The needs of these users must be balanced for a sustainable ecosystem.

Figure 15.3 Three-sided network effect or "platform"

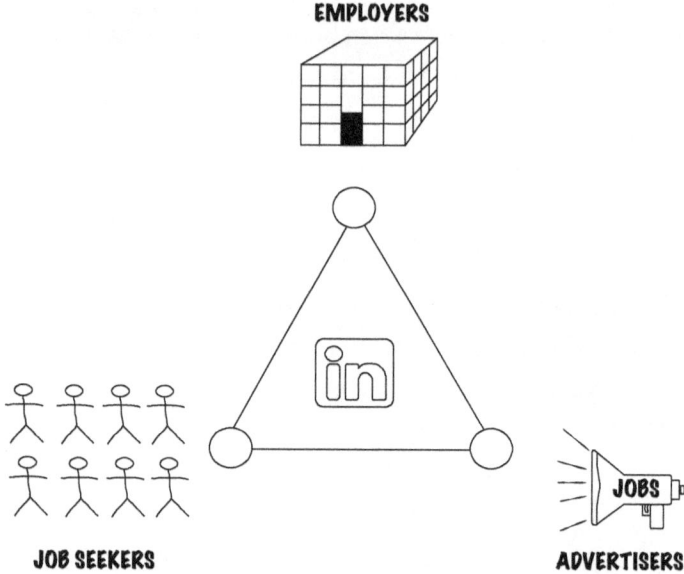

Depending on the marketplace, such value creation may grow linearly with demand, such as in the case of Craigslist or eBay. The more suppliers populate these platforms, the more transactions and value created.

Other marketplaces grow very slowly first and accelerate as numbers on the supply side or the demand side build up. This is what happened with the OpenTable restaurant reservation app. A critical mass of restaurants had to enroll on the app before the platform became useful for diners to book tables.

The inverse of the delayed growth effect is an asymptotic marketplace, such the Uber and Lyft ride-sharing apps, where the increase in passenger demand for rides can cause congestion and longer wait times.

Having to wait can cause passengers to cancel rides and prompt drivers to head home in frustration. Such situations can lead to a decline in the use of a platform.

Similar to congestion, network effects can also turn negative owing to network "pollution." A network becomes polluted when, for example, you build up too many marginal connections on LinkedIn and your feed gets polluted by irrelevant posts.

Businesses That Create Strong Network Effects

If you have read this far, I assume that you are not a start-up founder but a leader of an established business. Therefore, the question is not what kind of company to launch but rather how your existing business might tap into the benefits of network effects. Let's consider a few examples of business strategies that can produce network effects.

Launch a Free Service

Is there a free service that you could launch in your Core Market? If the service is valuable and targeted to your prospects or referral sources, it could create buzz and go viral when users invite other Core Market customers to sign up.

Then you have an opportunity to engage these customers by creating valuable content, building trust, and eventually offering them premium paid services. Zillow allows homebuyers to browse its listings for free and to estimate financing and mortgage rates. The company builds a community of users and makes money by offering leads to real estate agents and property management companies and by selling advertising space.

Connect Buyers and Sellers

Find a niche where you can connect buyers and sellers. Axial, launched in 2010, connects middle-market business owners and investment banks with buyers and investors through a step-by-step confidential process.

All Axial members pay a monthly fee, and sellers, investors, and lenders pay an additional per transaction success fee for deals originated by Axial.

Bring Your Business Community Together

Are you a thought leader in a niche where you have an audience ready to be engaged? Tech and consulting companies, such as Cisco, Gartner, and investment bank Jeffries, organize annual conferences for their clients. Gathering like-minded people fosters a community and helps clients engage with your people, your products, and each other. This makes your business stickier and reinforces your reputation with your clients and any guests they bring along.

> Question: What topic could you take ownership of and host an in-person, virtual, or hybrid conference on?

Create a Platform for Thematic Social Connection

By analyzing the behavior of its customers, Twitch discovered that gamers were the most avid users of its IRL platform. The platform allowed niche audiences to play their favorite video games together and engage with master gamers.

> Question: Is there an opportunity around your business to create a thematized social connection between the customers or users of your product?

Curate Content around a Niche Topic

Curate a website, blog, or podcast around a niche topic connected to your business. Monetize it by engaging your target audience, build trust, and offer paid products or services. According to content curation specialist Robin Good, there are twelve different ways to curate information, including aggregating, synthesizing, distilling, mapping, trendspotting, and investigating.[3]

> Question: What topic could your business become a thought leader on to attract your Core Market customers and intermediaries to engage and gain trust in you?

Launch a Minimum Viable SaaS Product, App, or API

Is there a solution developed for your company that you could productize for others? Amazon leveraged the cloud platform it had created to run its own e-commerce operation into AWS, which over time became the dominant market leader in cloud computing.

NASA spun off a variety of consumer innovations that became blockbuster products. These include memory foam, scratch-resistant sunglasses, cordless vacuums, the Global Positioning System (GPS), and LED lights that keep people awake.[4]

Question: Is there an in-house solution that you've developed that could solve the same problem for others?

Turn Your Product into a Platform

Salesforce, which started out as cloud-based customer relationship management (CRM) software, and Shopify, an e-commerce application, both turned their businesses into a platform.

Salesforce's platform, AppExchange, offers free and paid apps organized into categories and industry solutions covering the subject areas of small business, customer service, education, manufacturing, and real estate.

Shopify is a user-friendly sales platform that allows sellers to build an online store and add sales channels such as brick-and-mortar stores and in-person mobile sales or to use Facebook, Instagram, and Amazon as sales channels.

Question: Are there any software packages that could enhance your offering and that you could bundle as a branded or white-label add-on solution for your customers?

Scaling Your Network-Effect-Potential Product

So now that you have found a potentially network-effect-inducing product, how can you grow it?

Andrew Chen, a former marketing executive of Uber and the author of *The Cold Start Problem*, suggests dissecting revenue growth into its elements and creating "loops" that will help scale them.[5] Chen suggests creating two types of such loops and using both:

- Acquisition loops to acquire new revenue

- Engagement loops to cement existing customers and reactivate inactive users

Acquisition Loops

According to Chen, most tech companies use three types of scalable customer acquisition loops.

Acquisition Loop Type 1: User-Generated Content Loops

Here is how user-generated loops work. Users search for content and sign up to access it. They then add their own content to the site, which is indexed by Google and which drives more traffic to the platform. Examples are Yelp, Wikipedia, Reddit, and Glassdoor.

Figure 15.4 User-generated content loop

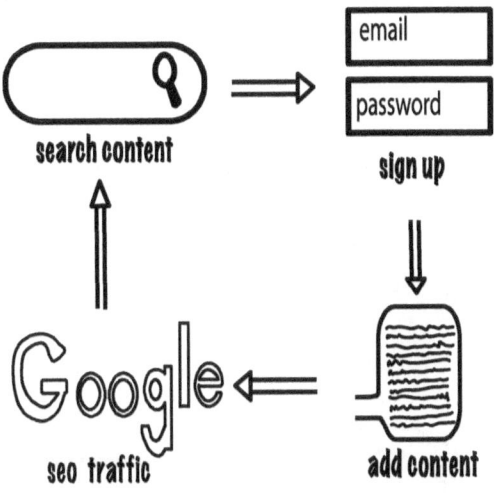

Acquisition Loop Type 2: Paid Marketing Loops

Here, new users click on an ad and sign up to try a product such as Blue Apron, Uber, or Casper. A percentage of these users will buy the product, the proceeds of which are reinvested into buying more ads.

Figure 15.5 Paid marketing loop

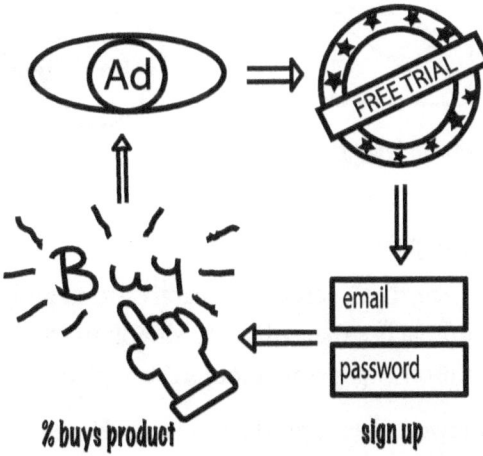

Acquisition Loop Type 3: Viral Loops

New users sign up for a service such as Dropbox, LinkedIn, or Instagram. They invite their friends, who engage with the product, and some of them sign up. The viral loop repeats with further invites and sign-ups.

To improve the effectiveness of these customer acquisition loops, dissect each step of the process into a dozen sub-steps, and then individually optimize each sub-step. For example, reduce the number of uncompleted sign-ups or remove friction for users who have forgotten their password and are trying to sign back in.

Figure 15.6 Viral loops

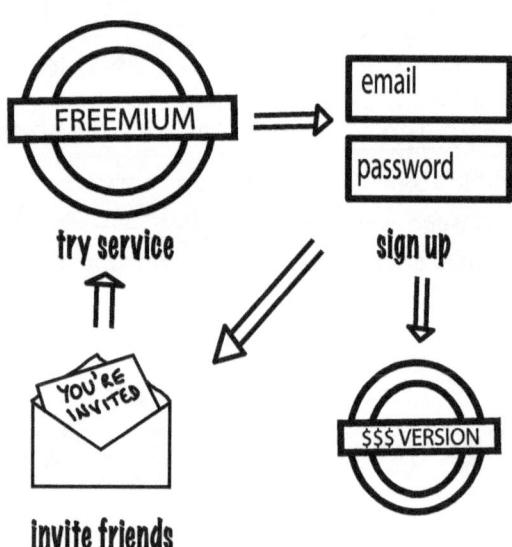

Engagement Loops

Chen makes the case that increasing reactivations and reducing churn require different approaches than what you should use to acquire customers. The two most common engagement loops are explained below.

If you have a network-based product, your goal is to have your customers engage with each other to create positive network effects.

If you have a utility-type product that users use on their own, then you want to structure it so that actions taken in one time period trigger actions at a later time period.

Engagement Loop Type 1: Social Feedback Loops

After a user creates content on apps like Instagram, LinkedIn, or Gmail, other users respond to it and the app sends a notification to the original user. The more "dense" the network with engaged users and the easier it is to create content, the more effective this feedback loop will be.

Figure 15.7 Social feedback loop

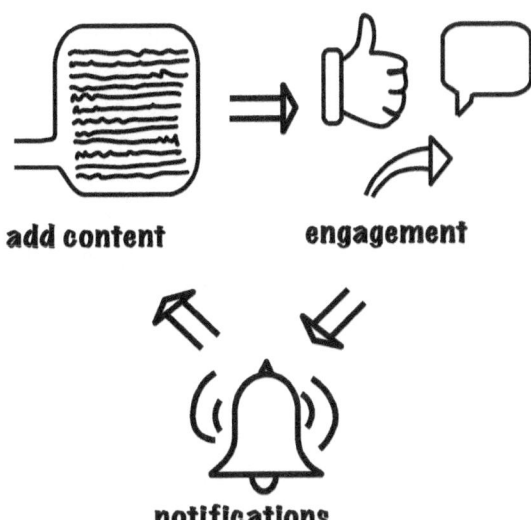

add content   **engagement**

notifications

Engagement Loop Type 2: Personalized Content Loops

Personalized loops work for utility apps like Zillow, Credit Karma, and Uber. When you sign up to Zillow with your home address, you will receive notices of local listings, mortgage rates, and changes in the value of your house. Credit Karma notifies you of credit changes. Uber notifies you when a driver has confirmed the trip and when they have arrived to pick you up.

Figure 15.8 Personalized content loop

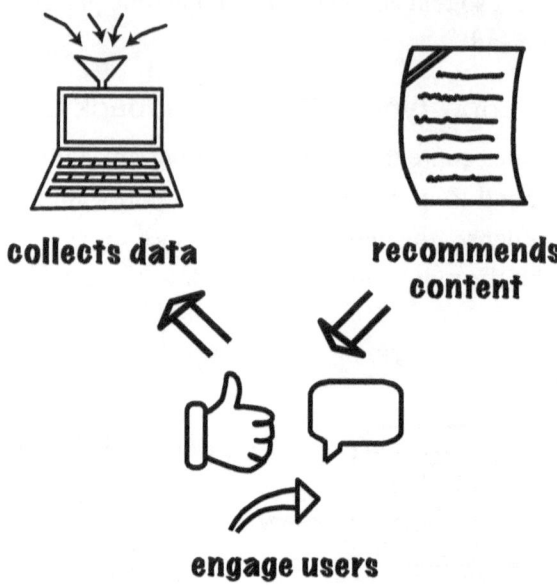

collects data   **recommends**
                        content

engage users

Other engagement triggers include Uber's sign at the airport reminding you to use the app or getting lost and remembering to check your Waze app.

Engagement loops can be improved similarly to how acquisition loops are improved: by breaking down each loop into its elements and optimizing each one.

Making content creation easy, such as allowing likes, hearts, or easy photo uploads and commenting, is often the biggest lever.

Linear Marketing Activities

Content marketing, conferences, partnerships, and public relations activities in themselves are not scalable. But you should use them to drive traffic to your loops to amplify them.

Traps That Diminish Network Effects

As mentioned, network effects can turn negative. Thus, it is essential to build networks by minimizing impacts that can lead to disengagement and churn.

The Cold Start Problem

The cold start problem is often the trickiest challenge to overcome because networks are hard to start without users. Some applications such as Zoom or Slack need only a handful of initial users to make the product useful.

On the other hand, rideshare apps need a concentration of riders and drivers to be meaningful. Uber solved this challenge by launching in what Andrew Chen calls atomic markets, such as in downtown San Francisco.

Figure 15.9 The cold start problem

Bank of America launched its first credit card by mailing no-application cards to 60,000 Fresno residents. The demand this created allowed the bank to sign up downtown shops to accept these cards.[6]

Switching Costs

Avoid competing with products that have high switching costs. For example, Android struggles to attract Apple's customers who, if they switch to Android, could no longer easily sync their phone with their computer, would have to use a different calendar application, and would no longer have access to their iMessages and Facetiming apps.

Figure 15.10 Switching costs

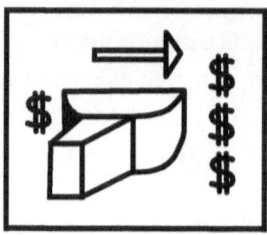

Multi-Tenanting

Multi-tenanting occurs when there are low costs or no costs to simultaneously participating in competing networks.

Uber and Lyft share many riders and drivers, who switch platforms if prices are uncompetitive or if wait times or dropped reservations are high. The same goes for property owners who can list on both Airbnb and VRBO.

Figure 15.11 Multi-tenanting

Ultimately, the greater network that offers more functionality and depth usually wins out. The smaller platform may get only residual traffic and will not be able to compete for advertising space.

Disintermediation

Disintermediation can become a threat when users of a marketplace platform take their subsequent transactions offline, depriving the platform of repeat revenues.

Figure 15.12 Disintermediation

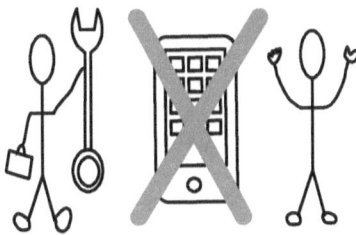

To combat this in the freelancing marketplace, Upwork promises customers performance guarantees and holds 50 percent of customer payments in escrow until completion of the project. Customers can also monitor screenshots to make sure that contractors are not charging more time than they actually use on time-based contracts.

User Retention

User retention depends on how often users come back to use your product. Without high usage, it is difficult to reap network effects because network effects are created by usage, not customer count.

Figure 15.13 User retention

Cloud-based data storage, processing, and analytic platform Snowflake employs consultants whose job is to continuously explore ways that major clients can increase the usage of their products.

Key takeaways from Chapter 15

- Network effects exist when the growth in the usage of a product increases the value of the product to all other users.

- Networks include physical networks, protocols, communication systems, direct utility tools, networking applications, marketplaces, and platforms.

- Explore how your business could take advantage of network effects by offering a free service, connecting people, building a community, or turning your product into a platform.

- To scale a network, you must implement acquisition loops and engagement loops and continually analyze and optimize their components.

- Creating networks is fraught with challenges, the greatest being the cold start problem.

Now that you have strategized your Strategy Stack by ensuring your Unique Activities fit; spread your tentacles to adjacent markets, products, services, geographies, verticals, and industries and spawned new businesses; and explored the use of network effects, it is time to build a perpetual expansion engine for your conglomerate.

We look at how to do that next.

PERPETUATE
PROGRESS

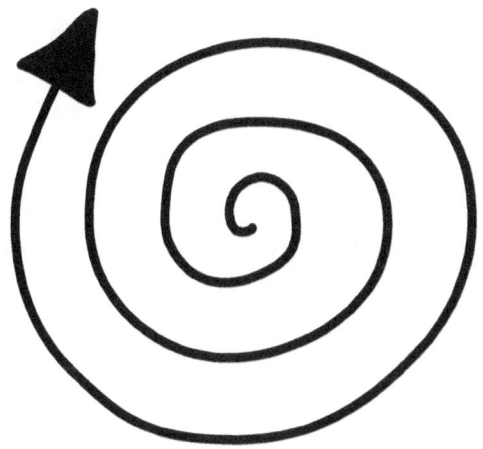

Success is not arriving at the summit of a mountain as a final destination. It is a continuing upward spiral of progress. It is perpetual growth.

—Wilferd Peterson

In 1981, a forty-six-year-old chemical engineer was appointed CEO of General Electric (GE), an institution of American business formed in 1889 in New York by JP Morgan, by merging the different business ventures of Thomas Edison. In its first ninety years of operation, General Electric became a sprawling conglomerate composed of a variety of businesses, from manufacturers of light bulbs, toasters, and household equipment to radio and TV stations, defense contractors, and computer manufacturers.[1]

The new CEO was Jack Welch the son of an Irish railway conductor. In the ensuing twenty years, Welch quadrupled GE's sales and grew its market value from $12 billion to $417 billion.

Upon taking the helm of the company, Welch announced a policy to reevaluate all of GE's businesses and to only keep those that could reach the number one or two positions in their respective markets. Companies that had no path to market leadership were fixed, sold, or closed down.

Many of these businesses had no future with the emergence of cheap manufacturing competition from the Far East, and Welch decided to take radical steps to disrupt the entrenched bureaucracy of the company which kept them alive.

He actively pruned and rebuilt the conglomerate's portfolio with future-oriented businesses and ultimately reinvented GE by divesting its mining and houseware activities and adding new services, including financial services, to the group's portfolio.

Whereas in 1980 GE derived 85 percent of its revenues from the sale of products, by the year 2000, 70 percent of its sales came from services.[2]

Jack Welch also introduced significant management innovations. He turned GE into a "boundaryless organization" to break down silos. He launched "Work-Out," a series of structured and facilitated forums that brought people together across levels, functions, and geographies so they could share best practices, solve problems, and make decisions.

In 1995, he adopted the Motorola Six Sigma quality program as a way to identify and eliminate defects in the production process throughout the GE group,[3] and he tied bonuses to reaching quality improvement targets.

Welch also upleveled GE's executive training center in Crotonville, New York. He booked time each year on his calendar to teach, challenge, and inspire the company's executives.[4]

Jack Welch emphasized the importance of culture and encouraged his managers to fire productive employees who didn't embrace GE's core values. He would tolerate culture fits who struggled to hit their numbers a while longer.

Welch was later criticized for his aggressive management approaches and for reorienting GE toward financial services, which led to huge losses after the 2008 financial crisis under his successor, Jeff Immelt. However, during Welch's time, GE demonstrated all three approaches to keeping a mature business performing: innovation, mergers and acquisitions, and reinvention.

Step 6 of the Strategy OS is about turning your already successful business into a perpetually thriving organization:

- In Chapter 16, we talk about how you can foster innovation, feed the spirit of curiosity, and make invention vibrant in your business.

- Then in Chapter 17, we discuss how to leverage Smart M&A to sell underperforming and ill-fitting businesses and acquire ones that can rejuvenate your company.

- In Chapter 18, we address how, when small fixes are no longer enough, you can reinvent your business, as many of your entrepreneurial forebears have done in the past.

Now, let's look at innovation first in the next chapter.

CHAPTER SIXTEEN

Foster Innovation

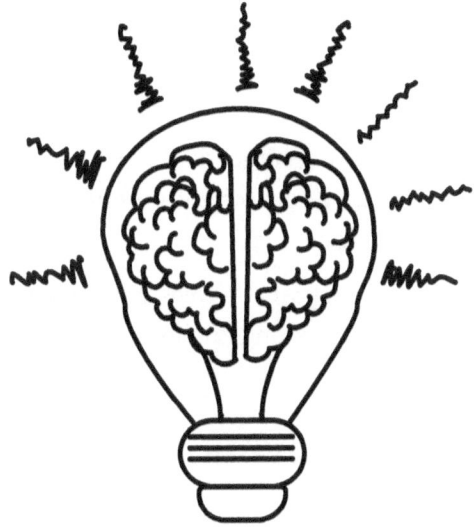

Innovation distinguishes between a leader and a follower.

—Steve Jobs

During the outbreak of the Covid-19 pandemic, a new word appeared in the business lexicon. This word fast became a synonym for remote meetings worldwide, and the eponymous company grew its number of daily users from 10 million to 300 million in the first four months of 2020.[1]

No doubt, you have already figured out that this company is Zoom, an innovator in a business that has been around since the 1970s.[2] Between 2004 and 2020, Zoom's market was dominated by GoToMeeting and later by Cisco Webex. Zoom wasn't launched until 2011, by Cisco Webex alumnus Eric Yuan and a group of engineers he persuaded to jump ship with him.

So, how could a latecomer in a mature market completely disrupt it seemingly overnight?

The pandemic certainly helped, but it only accelerated a growth trend that already existed. Zoom overtook its market by articulating and focusing on a simple mission: "Make video communications frictionless."[3]

Zoom's competitors required users to download software and suffer through elaborate registration and security protocols, whereas you could jump on a Zoom call by simply clicking a link.

While the other apps' new users got confused and were late to meetings, Zoomers just had to show up. Zoom screens were also much clearer, intuitive to operate, and easy to navigate.

In this chapter, we dissect what allows companies to maintain their growth by nurturing a culture of ongoing innovation.

What's Innovation, Anyway?

After analyzing more than sixty definitions of innovation, Canadian research professor Anahita Baragheh concluded:

> *Innovation is the multi-stage process whereby organizations transform ideas into new or improved products, services or processes, in order to advance, compete and differentiate themselves successfully in their marketplace.[4]*

An innovation can be new to the world or just new to an industry or market. Innovation may also create a new product or service or innovate a process to create or deliver one.

Austrian American management guru Peter Drucker saw innovation as a function of entrepreneurship by which the entrepreneur creates or improves wealth-producing resources.

Up until World War II, *innovation* carried a mixed, mainly negative connotation of trying to mess with something that works. However, in the

1930s, when another Austrian American, economist Joseph Schumpeter, popularized the concept of creative disruption, people started seeing product innovation as a positive force that created economic growth and competitive advantage.

Schumpeter argued that industries should continuously look for better products, processes, and distribution methods to produce better ways to satisfy consumers with improved quality, durability, service, and price.

Clayton Christensen, author of *The Innovator's Dilemma*, claims that innovation can be either sustaining or disrupting.[5]

Sustaining innovations produce improvements in products or services where customer needs are already known; for example, multicamera smartphones and faster broadband service.

On the other hand, **innovation is disruptive** when new products or services create new markets and eventually displace existing competitors. For example, the iPhone disrupted physical type-pad phones, and on-demand video streaming disrupted the DVD rental and movie theater businesses.

Innovation Hubs

Innovation often spreads when smart people get frustrated with the status quo and leave organizations to make improvements elsewhere.

Silicon Valley was initiated in 1957 by eight disgruntled employees who left Nobel Laureate transistor coinventor William Shockley's company to form Fairchild Semiconductor. Eventually, Fairchild's founders left to start Intel and another sixty-four different, mainly information technology–related enterprises.[6]

Governments routinely try to re-create this knowledge-dispersion effect by creating incubation hubs for tech businesses attached to universities and think tanks. By providing business infrastructure, mentors, and funding, governments hope to catalyze the birth of start-up businesses that convert the research from these institutions into marketable products.

According to the International Business Innovation Association, a global nonprofit, there are 1,400 business incubators in the United States alone, and statistics show that incubation doubles the survival rate of start-ups to 87 percent in their first five years.[7]

Models of Innovation

There are three main ways innovation is catalyzed.

In the Industrial Age, the conventional approach was the **linear model of innovation**. Here, the catalyst was pure scientific research the results of which were channeled into applied research and development (R&D).

Companies that invested in R&D expected to generate inventions with the intention of creating sellable products. The linear model of innovation is also called "push innovation" because business leadership can bring it about by establishing R&D spending budgets.

The opposite, the **pull approach to innovation**, is called the chain-linked model, where the recognition of unmet market needs triggers research and product design and development.

This is followed by an iterative redesign and production process, followed by the marketing of the new product.

A third approach to innovation is **user-initiated innovation**, when an end user innovates a product that solves their unmet needs.

Recall from Chapter 13 the early years of the Porsche car company, when Ferdinand Porsche's son Ferry designed himself the Porsche 356, the car he wanted to drive. The 356 became the inspiration for the 911, which became the most successful production sports car of all time.

The latest innovation trend is **open innovation**. The term implies that firms should source ideas and information to innovate products and go-to-market strategies from everywhere, including from inside and outside their business, from competitors, and from creative users and consumers.

The open-source movement is a manifestation of the open innovation approach. The most famous example is Linux, a software operating system created by Finnish engineer Linus Torvalds in 1991.

The Amazon Kindle, the Android, Instagram, Google's self-driving cars, the world's 500 top supercomputers, and NASA, among many others, use Linux.[8]

Another example is the Mozilla Firefox internet browser. After Microsoft squeezed Netscape out of the browser market, Netscape made its source code available license-free to developers.

Because of its lightning-fast load speed and numerous innovations, by the year 2010, Firefox had over a billion users and became the most popular browser in Europe. (Since then, however, with the resources of two tech heavyweights behind them, Google Chrome and Apple Safari have eclipsed Firefox.[9])

How to Facilitate Innovation

Now that we know what innovation is, where it comes from, and its different contexts—being R&D-driven, market-induced, user-initiated, or community-enhanced—let's discuss how you can facilitate one or more of these types of innovation in *your* business.

Create an Innovation-Friendly Work Environment

Innovation requires risk-taking, and if you want your business to generate innovations, you need a culture that fosters experimentation and allows for failure and learning. Innovation-friendly organizations can be intentionally created by applying some of the following design principles.

Keep Your Organization Flat

We all know that sprawling bureaucracies don't produce much innovation. By implication, you should avoid building one or de-layer it if it's already present. Consider how Jack Welch eliminated layers of management to accelerate information flows and decisions while improving coordination and productivity.

When you remove the middle management layer in your organization, you must empower the remaining executives to make more decisions themselves. This will motivate your A players to take initiative to grow the business. This smaller leadership group will get to know each other better, which will improve communication and your company culture.

Encourage Risk-Taking

Innovation requires experimenting with things that have not been done before, which carries inherent risk. Your people will only be willing to try new things if they are allowed to make mistakes. "The fastest way to succeed," IBM's Thomas Watson Sr. once said, "is to double your failure rate."[10]

A culture of willingness to fail is easier said than created. No one likes to fail and employees are worried about losing a promotion or a bonus by missing the mark. Robert Shapiro, Monsanto's CEO, explained to his employees that product development required experiments and they would only be seen to fail if they made a half-hearted, sloppy effort—well-thought-out failed experiments were welcome.[11]

Early in his career, Jack Welch suffered a giant setback when he accidentally blew up a chemical plant. Fortunately, no one was hurt, but Welch was summoned to New York to see a senior vice president of the company, Charles Reed. Welch thought he would be fired. However, Reed gently coached him, instead, about what he should have done. Welch recognized this event as a turning point in his career and how it informed his approach to leadership.[12]

Evaluate and Empower

If you want an innovative culture, your people need to come up with answers. Encourage them by listening to their ideas with an open mind. You will find that people have no trouble buying in to their own ideas and will work twice as hard to implement them. Err on the side of approving a project when you see someone with the energy to execute it.

Encourage Moon Shots and Celebrate 70 Percent

Incremental goals are not motivating. The excitement comes with the challenge of big goals that are difficult to accomplish. Encourage your people to set some stretch goals, even moon shots, and celebrate when they accomplish 70 percent or more. If only 100 percent success is acceptable, people will sandbag goals and A players will get bored and leave.

In a 2013 *Wired* article, Larry Page explained why he prefers 10X goals to 10 percent improvements. Shooting for 1,000 percent improvements requires people to completely rethink problems and explore the edges of what is technically possible. This approach attracts the best people to join your company, those who want to be part of creating epoch-changing products, like self-driving cars.[13]

Foster Diversity

If you'd like your people to generate diverse ideas, choose a diversity of people, from all creeds, colors, and orientations, including foreign nationals who come from far-flung cultures with divergent experiences.

Fifteen years ago, while living in Hungary, I asked my friend Craig Butcher why he had moved his private equity firm from Budapest to London. It puzzled me, because he still lived in the hills of Budapest with his family and had to commute to the UK weekly while his firm's target region was Hungary and its neighboring countries.

Craig explained that London attracted the best and brightest from all over Central and Eastern Europe and he wanted to hire them. Flying back and forth and maintaining an expensive London office was the price he was willing to pay for being able to assemble the best team possible.

Encourage User Innovation

Innovation will only happen if you surround yourself with self-starters and telegraph to your people that their ideas and inventions are welcome and will be rewarded. Below are a handful of approaches to choose from.

Grant Side-Project Time

Invest in innovation. Your people with the ideas and the energy to innovate are already the busiest, so give them some of the company's time to come up with inventions. Google instituted the 20% Project, an initiative with which its employees could spend one day a week on their pet initiatives. This is how AdSense was invented and how the Gmail email service was born, which reached 1.5 billion active users by the end of 2019.

Other companies offering side-project time include the BBC, Apple, Australian software firm Atlassian, and LinkedIn.[14]

Find Evangelists

An evangelist is a person marked by extreme enthusiasm. Such people are excited by ideas and will mobilize much-higher-than-usual energy to implement their ideas. Evangelists are hard to manage, but you can channel their zeal if your business has a compelling purpose.

Hiring and unleashing even a single evangelist can shift your business's self-image and will signal to your talented employees that you are serious about building an Innovation Culture.

Incubate and Spin Off Start-Ups

However dynamic your culture, large companies can't help themselves in enforcing a level of conformity. To encourage innovation, consider incubating ideas for new offerings, products, or business models by isolating a small team from the company as if they were a start-up.

If they evolve toward a viable business, you may choose to spin them off, offer the team stock grants or options, and let them grow as an autonomous business. Save them from corporate constraints and policies and let them innovate on a lean budget that will force them to remain creative.

SAP.io, the venture studio of the software giant, helps its employees nurture ideas and concepts into new products and businesses by providing funding and coaching.

Ericsson One, the incubator-accelerator of Ericsson, the global network communication company, encourages intrapreneurs to test and validate their prototypes, build minimum viable products, and scale their ventures with the help of in-house support and mentoring.[15]

Encourage Community Contributions

Tapping into the innovative contributions of your community of users is a blue ocean opportunity for your business.

Wikipedia, which by November 2021 had accumulated 6.6 million articles, is written exclusively by a community of volunteer editors. The most prolific is Steven Pruitt, currently a records manager of the Defense Health Agency, who has personally made 4.4 million edits and has written 33,000 articles for the online encyclopedia.[16] Pruitt's mother grew up in the Soviet Union and Pruitt is motivated by the idea of providing free, credible information.

Lego Ideas, an online platform, sources toy kit designs from LEGO fans from all over the world. Users can submit their ideas for a LEGO set, complete with a model, photos, and a detailed description. Once a fan gets 10,000 supporters to back their set, the idea is evaluated by the Lego Review Board, which selects successful ideas for production. A user's set can end up on store shelves and LEGO will pay the person designer royalties.[17]

Pursue Systematic Programs

You can also spur innovation by setting specific targets for your company. Nothing fosters ideas better than a specific goal to push against.

Goals could include extending the product range of your business. Mature consumer goods companies often fulfill organic growth targets by creating product extensions.

A marketing executive of Philip Morris, owner of Marlboro and other tobacco brands, told me that each year his company introduces a new tobacco product. The multiple benefits for the company include expanding its Core Market and capturing some revenue growth while limiting the shelf space available for competitors' products.

Other innovation-fostering programs could target the improvement of quality, as Jack Welch did when introducing Six Sigma at GE. Enhancing production processes can help increase efficiency and flexibility, streamlining future production runs.

If your business competes on price, then you might consider how you can streamline processes to reduce material, labor, and energy costs.

General Innovation Approaches

The most measurable and traditional approach to fostering innovation is to *increase your R&D budget.* Push more investment into research and development programs in the hope that you will reap a commensurate growth in output. Many mature industrial companies still budget innovation that way.

Another approach is to work with *lead users and early adopters* of your product to improve it. The equipment for new sports, including skateboarding, mountain biking, and windsurfing, was developed with the help of lead users who could guide manufacturers to tailor products to the community of users' needs. Similarly, the first personal computers and 3-D printers were also developed by early users.[18]

With the *agile collaboration* of a subject matter expert and an analyst, promising user innovations can be found in any consumer product or service fields using artificial intelligence and assisted analytic and modeling techniques.[19]

Testing many solutions is another viable approach to innovation. Edison famously invented the incandescent electric light bulb by trying out more than 3,000 theories.[20]

Drug research firms also innovate by testing thousands of compounds to see whether they have any activity against a disease-inducing molecule. Promising compounds are analyzed and modified to reduce side effects and to make their manufacture cost-effective.

Facebook, Netflix, and Google use *A/B testing* to optimize design of websites and mobile apps. This approach involves testing two slightly different designs, and then the one favored by consumers is selected for further tests until the optimal design is found.[21]

On the online site PickFu, you can test product designs, book covers, and marketing slogans with a paid group of fifty or more reviewers who, for a few cents' pay, choose one of the designs and provide a short explanation to support their decision. I used that site for testing different covers for my two earlier books.

The S Curve

The adoption of new innovations, also called diffusion, is illustrated by a so-called S curve, as shown in Figure 16.1.

Figure 16.1 The S curve

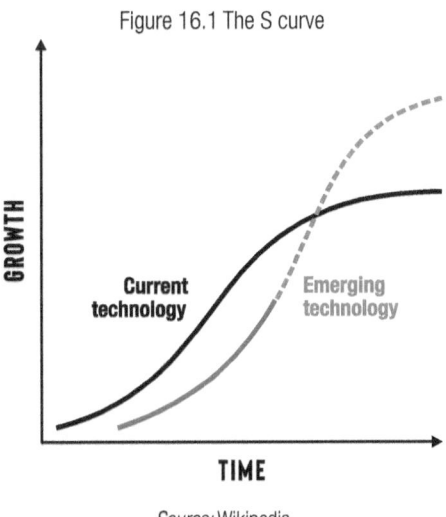

Source: Wikipedia

In the early stages of an innovation, growth (adoption) is slow as the new product establishes itself. As customers start to demand it, product growth picks up and is further fueled by incremental innovations. Eventually, the product matures, growth slows, and the curve tails off or even starts to decline as demand falls for an outdated product.

Innovative companies always work on new innovations to replace maturing, slow-selling products with ones on the upswing.

Key takeaways from Chapter 16

- Innovation is how you transform ideas into new products or processes in order to differentiate your business in the marketplace. Innovations may be sustaining, may improve existing products, or may be disruptive, creating new markets.

- Innovation may be linear, chain-linked, user-led, or open, depending on whether the organization pushes or the market or users pull it along.

- You can facilitate innovation by:
  - Creating an innovation-friendly work environment
  - Encouraging user innovation
  - Fostering community contribution
  - Pursuing systematic programs
  - Using other general approaches

- The S curve describes the shape of demand for innovations. It tends to start slow, rises fast, and tails off as products mature. Innovative companies have a pipeline of new innovations to sustain their growth over time.

Now that we've explored the ways you can innovate, let's discuss how to use mergers and acquisitions to grow your business even further.

CHAPTER SEVENTEEN

Use Smart M&A

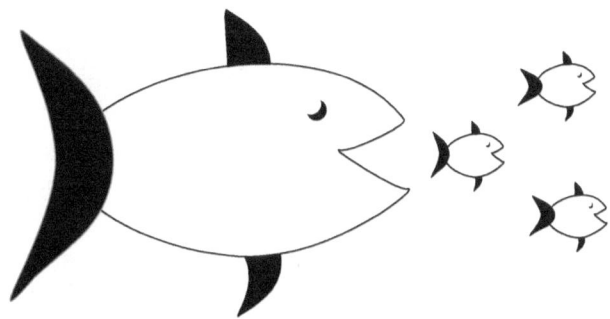

Capital isn't scarce. Vision is.

—Sam Walton

In April 2012, weeks before going public, Facebook (now Meta) made a shocking announcement. In a social media post, the CEO shared the news that his company just paid a billion dollars for a year-old start-up with thirteen employees.

This start-up was Instagram, which just a few days earlier had completed a $50 million investment round with a group of venture capital investors who valued it at $500 million.

"Is Zuckerberg out of his mind?" I wondered, along with many others who could not fathom how a group of kids with a photo-sharing app could have created the GDP of the British Virgin Islands in the course of a year.[1]

It turns out he wasn't. Buying Instagram was a brilliant idea that cemented Facebook's leadership in the social media landscape and injected a growth business into the company just when the Facebook app started to mature.

By 2021, Instagram's share of Meta's revenue surpassed 44 percent and it is projected to trump Facebook's by the year 2024.[2]

As of this writing, Meta's stock has declined 65 percent off its peak, but Instagram is still worth more than $100 billion, giving Zuckerberg a 100X return in ten years. A Smart M&A deal if there ever was one.

What is more mind-boggling is that Facebook's purchase was not an anomaly. Just four years earlier, Google (now Alphabet) purchased a two-year-old YouTube for $1.65 billion. As of 2021, YouTube has generated 11 percent of Google's overall revenue and it was valued at $180 billion in 2022.[3] That's a 110X return over the past sixteen years.

Another example is Twitch, an IRL platform discussed earlier in Step 4. Amazon acquired Twitch in 2014, with sales revenues of about $16 million.[4] By 2022, Twitch's revenues had grown to approximately $4 billion.[5] A 250X increase!

So, how do these acquisitions happen? How can a company increase its value by over a hundred times in the hands of an acquirer?

I call this "Smart M&A," and it's what this chapter is all about. Let's look at how you can use acquisitions and sell-offs to augment, reorient, or restructure your business in order to keep it growing.

The Wrong Reasons to Buy a Business

You probably have heard the statistics that about 80 percent of acquisitions fail.[6] The quoted reason for failure is almost always "integration." However, acquiring for the wrong reason is an even bigger cause of failures. The wrong acquired business will not integrate well because there is no organic reason for the buyer and the acquiree to be combined in the first place.

Let's look at some of the wrong reasons for acquiring another business.

Empire Building

Public company CEOs often acquire to grow their personal power. The bigger your ship, the better your status on the golf course and in the media. CEOs of larger companies travel on private jets, and the compensation committee benchmarks them to a better-paid peer group.

Pressure to Grow

Stock valuations are based on future earnings growth; therefore, public companies are under immense pressure to keep growing. The same is true for private equity–backed businesses: Financial sponsors have promised their own investors a doubling of their monies every three to five years, so they pressure investee companies to continue growing at least 10–20 percent each year, depending on the sector.

The growth imperative even applies to owner-managed businesses. These, too, face the expectations of shareholders, who push for the company to generate debt payments, and owners, who demand a risk-commensurate return on their entrepreneurial effort that will pay for their lifestyles and retirement.

And let's not forget about employees who want their bonuses and are watchful for career prospects inside the business, both of which compel growth. Flat performance is unsustainable for most companies.

However, ill-fitting acquisitions can kill growth, whether ill-chosen or poorly executed. Acquiree company employees will leave if the cultures of the two businesses are incompatible, and customers often depart with them.

Boredom

Richard Rumelt, author of *The Crux*, talks about the tedium *Fortune*-ranked company CEOs often feel at the top. All the exciting stuff of innovation, engineering, marketing, and customer acquisition strategies happen at lower levels in the organization.

The CEO is a glorified administrator who makes sure the leadership, the employees, the customers, and the media are happy and who puts out any fires as rapidly as possible. The boring business-as-usual.

A CEO's only chance for adventure is a major acquisition: It involves a lot of money, secret high-profile meetings, dealmaking, and strategizing with the board. Acquisitions shake CEOs from their slumber and give them something fun to do for a while.

Therefore, they will be tempted to make sexy acquisitions, even if these don't make strategic sense for their company.

FOMO

Fear of missing out is another strong motivator for action. What if one of your peers buys this exciting company that just came on the market? How does it feel when they are in the limelight, not you? Isn't it better to be involved than to look on from the sidelines?

Maybe not, actually.

The Smart Rationales for Acquiring a Company

So, the above-mentioned examples are some of the wrong reasons to make an acquisition. However, M&As can make sense in many cases. Let's look at these situations next.

Leverage Existing Channels

Companies that have a large customer base or a well-established sales channel can benefit by acquiring businesses that offer products that can be sold through the buyer's sales channels.

IBM, for example, acquired forty-three businesses in the early 2010s to expand its software business's offerings. Big Blue paid an average of $350 million each for these acquisitions and has managed to increase the sales of the acquired products by about 40 percent within two years of these transactions.

Health care is an active space for acquisitions that provide market access to acquirers.

In 2021, Swiss pharmaceutical company Roche acquired molecular testing company GenMark Diagnostics for $1.8 billion to increase its diagnostics business. Similarly, the publicly traded Irish biotech company Jazz Pharma acquired the British multiple sclerosis treatment company GW Pharmaceuticals in order to offer cannabis-based treatments to its customers.[7]

Both these transactions made strategic sense, although the integration may still go sideways.

Acquire a New Market

The acquisitions of Instagram, YouTube, and Twitch, as discussed earlier, are all examples of *market* acquisitions.

By buying Instagram, Meta tapped into a younger and more visually oriented demographic than Facebook's dominant audiences. YouTube allowed Alphabet to storm into the video streaming ad space, while Amazon gained a foothold in the IRL and, specifically, video gaming markets by buying Twitch.

In 2014, Meta also bought the virtual reality headset company Oculus for $2 billion to enter the gaming market. Since then, the acquisition has evolved into a cornerstone of Meta's strategy of becoming a leading player in the Metaverse market.[8]

These market-driven acquisitions overlap with the strategy of acquiring new technologies, so let's look at that M&A strategy next.

Gain New Technology

Some buyers initiate an acquisition when the target business owns proprietary technology that can be strategically integrated into the buyer's business as a way of enhancing existing applications or initiatives.

Alphabet has made several such acquisitions over the years.[9] In 2013, it acquired satellite navigation system Waze for just under $1 billion. Although Waze was kept as a standalone product, Alphabet integrated its crowdsourced location platform into the Google Maps product.

Subsequently, in 2014, Alphabet acquired DeepMind Technologies, a British AI company that built learning algorithms using machine learning and neuroscience techniques. This acquisition supported Alphabet's initiatives to grow its AI and robotics business.

As another example, in 2018 Amazon acquired video doorbell maker Ring in a $1 billion deal.[10]

The goal of the transaction was to acquire Ring's technology to augment Amazon's voice-controlled digital assistant, Alexa. Users would be able to request Alexa to show them around their homes via Ring cameras. The service could also help customers monitor received packages and security around their homes.

Enter a New Geography

In certain industries, such as consumer products, geographical expansion is the prime motivator of acquisition activity. In a Deloitte study of 8,000 consumer acquisitions between 2010 and 2017, 56 percent of acquisitions were driven by geographic expansion.

An example is Vibrant Credit Union in Moline, Illinois, which grew its assets from $400 million to more than $1 billion over a three-and-a-half-year period by acquiring six other community banks, from Des Moines, Iowa, to Covington, Indiana.[11]

In the $100 billion merger in 2016 of two of the largest beer companies—AB InBev and SABMiller—the main motivation was AB InBev's desire to be present in the fast-growing African and Latin American markets.[12]

Acquire Management

In many cases, the acquisition of an up-and-coming business is at least partially motivated by the buyer's desire to acquire management talent.

In 2009, Meta CEO Mark Zuckerberg posted a query on Quora asking which start-ups would be good acquisition targets for his company. In a follow-up talk in 2010, he stated:

> We have not once bought a company for the company. We buy companies to get excellent people... In order to have a really entrepreneurial culture, one of the key things is to make sure we're recruiting the best people. One of the ways to do this is to focus on acquiring great companies with great founders.[13,14]

Arguably, this was the case when Apple acquired NeXT Computer. The deal was ostensibly about the NeXT Operating System, which Apple needed because it had failed to develop an OS in-house and had only a few options to choose from. The company's board supported the idea that, as part of the acquisition, Steve Jobs would join Apple as an advisor to the CEO.

Those who knew Jobs from his earlier tenure as Apple's cofounder and those who had read his biography (most likely all the board members) must have known that he would not be content to stay on the sidelines.[15] As it happened, Jobs ascended to interim and then permanent CEO of the company within nine months of the NeXT deal closing.

However, there is an even more astonishing story of reverse takeovers, where the acquiree ends up running the acquirers' businesses instead. In her highly readable book *Tearing Down the Walls*, about former Travelers Group chairman Sandy Weill, Monica Langley tells the fascinating story of how a small fish can eat bigger ones.[16]

After building up the second-largest brokerage firm on Wall Street organically and through acquisitions, Weill and his partners sold it to American Express for $915 million. Weill stayed on to run different subsidiaries of Amex for another three years until it became clear that he would not be promoted to president of American Express.

Soon after he left Amex, in 1985, Weill and his protégé, Jamie Dimon, the future CEO of JPMorgan Chase, acquired an ailing consumer finance business called Commercial Credit for $7 million. While turning around Commercial Credit, Weill and Dimon built a cohesive team that worked hard and played hard together around the clock.

Then, using the company as a Trojan horse, Weill started acquiring bigger and bigger insurance companies that he, Dimon, and their team took charge of. Eventually, he acquired a 27 percent stake in the struggling Travelers Insurance and bought back his old brokerage firm from Amex, since renamed Shearson Lehman.

In 1993, Weill combined all his holdings into Travelers Group of which he became chairman. By 1997, Travelers Group had acquired control of Aetna Life & Casualty and Salomon Smith Barney, as well, for a combined $13 billion!

As his crowning achievement, the following year, Weill convinced John Reed, the CEO of Citicorp, to agree to a merger with Travelers to form Citigroup in a $70 billion transaction.[17] Two years later, instead of retiring together and handing the baton to Jamie Dimon, as had been agreed, Weill ousted Reed in a management shake-up and became the CEO of Citigroup.

So, be careful when acquiring management talent as they might want to eventually replace you in the CEO seat.

Neutralize Future Competitors

"Instagram can hurt us," wrote Mark Zuckerberg, the CEO of Facebook, six weeks before his company acquired Instagram.

In this and other emails revealed at a 2020 hearing before the House Antitrust Committee, it became clear that part of the rationale behind Facebook's acquisition of Instagram was fear of disruption. In an answer to Facebook's chief financial officer, Zuckerberg alluded to the necessity of neutralizing Instagram and integrating its social mechanics to win time against similar competitors.[18]

Another example of this is Google's 2011 purchase of Motorola Mobility, the iPhone-disrupted phone maker, for $12.5 billion that was so well publicized at the time.

The acquirer's apparent rationale was buying Motorola's mobile phone and wireless technology patents as a way to fend off Apple's patent infringement lawsuits against the company. This was effectively a defensive move so that Google would avoid being left behind by Apple in the touchscreen smartphone market.

Sow the Seeds of Future Growth

Most acquisitions are made to take advantage of future growth opportunities. Some, however, are more visionary and long term than others, such as Amazon's purchase of autonomous mobility start-up Zoox.

Zoox's mission is "to make personal transportation safer, cleaner, and more enjoyable for everyone,"[19] and it will extend Amazon the options to offer ride-hailing services and use Zoox's vehicles in its delivery network.[20]

Integrate versus Keep Separate

When should you integrate and when should you keep acquired businesses separate? The following various considerations can help you decide:

- **Does the product have a strong brand?** If the acquired product is already established with happy users, then you might want to keep the original brand and company separate. On the other hand, if the acquired business is pre-revenue or early revenue, then you can rebrand the product. This is what Meta did with the Oculus VR handset.

- **Is the company's culture valuable?** Mergers often fail when the acquired company's employees sense a loss of their culture and corporate identity. Keeping the business separate may help alleviate this loss, at least in the short to medium term, until the two businesses cross-fertilize.

- **Do you want to keep the acquiree's management?** Maintaining autonomy of the acquired business often helps because entrepreneurs find it difficult to adjust to reporting lines. The founders of the acquiree may have agreed to contingent purchase price payments that can only be enforced if the founders keep control of the day-to-day management of the business.

- **Are there strategic reasons to keep the brand?** The acquired brand is sometimes seen as a rival to the acquirer. You may want to keep it separate to keep the loyal customers of each brand. This is the approach used by the three car rental companies that own 95 percent of the market: Enterprise owns both National and Alamo. Avis owns Budget, Payless, and Zipcar; and Hertz owns Dollar and Thrifty.[21]

Amazon uses both the integration and the keep-separate strategies. In late 2022, Amazon acquired warehouse machinery and robotics company Cloostermans and announced that it would be integrated into the Amazon Robotics arm.[22]

Amazon approached its acquisition of Whole Foods in 2017 differently. Whole Foods was a nationwide premium brand already, and Amazon decided to keep it as a standalone business. However, in the following five years, the retail giant substantially reengineered its health food retailing subsidiary.

Under new ownership, Whole Foods lowered prices, embedded self-checkout technology at 500 locations, and opened 60 new locations, including a "dark store" dedicated to fulfilling online orders.

Amazon also centralized store operations at Whole Foods' headquarters in Austin, Texas, and added 3,000 local brands customized to stores, which represented a 30 percent increase.[23]

Manage Your Portfolio

For keeping your large business growing and vibrant, acquisitions can help but are insufficient. From time to time, you need to prune from your portfolio businesses that no longer make sense to keep.

Some legacy activities may no longer fit your Core Business, and they are going nowhere while sucking up management time and administrative resources. They may still be profitable, but if a business does not contribute to your vision, it makes no sense to hold onto it. Sell these businesses early while they are still growing and can fetch top dollar from a strategically aligned buyer.

The Growth-Share Matrix designed and published by the Boston Consulting Group in 1970 is a tool that allows business leadership to understand the maturity of its product lines and manage its investment in different products and businesses accordingly. The matrix is shown in Figure 17.1.

Figure 17.1 The Growth-Share Matrix created by the Boston Consulting Group

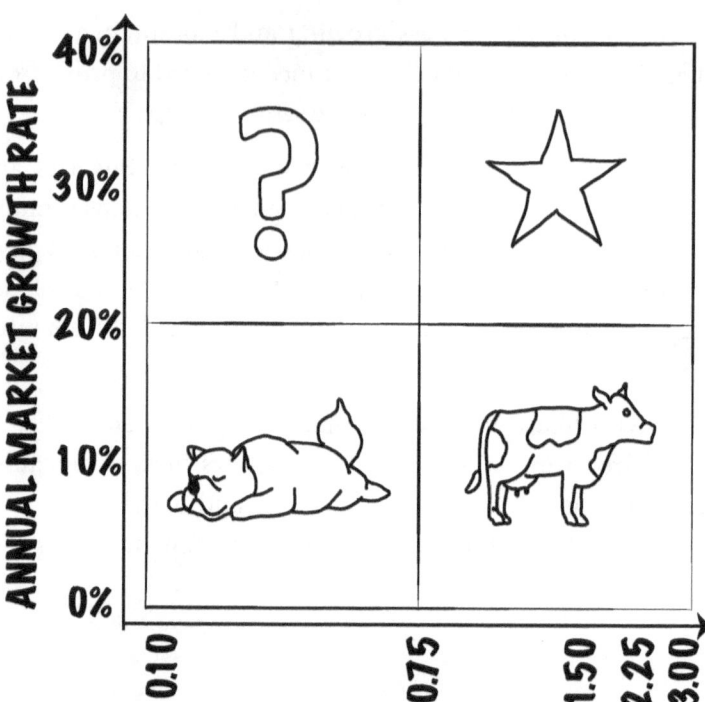

Products and businesses are plotted on a four-square matrix. The horizontal axis represents the relative market shares of these products and businesses compared to their leading competitor, and the vertical axis depicts the annual revenue growth of these items.

In the figure, the square below the Star is for products that have high market share but that are not growing fast anymore. These are your Cash Cows that don't have a bright future but throw off most of your profits. Carefully consider how much you want to invest in them.

The bottom left quadrant represents your Dogs. These are low-relative-market-share and low-growth products. Are these still profitable? Are they worth keeping or should you sell them or close them down?

In the top left quadrant are your Question Marks. These are businesses with high growth but low market share. Gaining substantial market share would turn them into Stars, while falling growth could condemn them to Dog status.

Your Stars in the top right quadrant are products with high growth and high market share. They may or may not generate cash, depending on your investment. Your goal is to grow these products into your future Cash Cows.

The Growth-Share Matrix is not a panacea, but it gives you a visual framework to use in considering where different businesses are in their respective life cycles and can help you make investment decisions. Ideally, you always need Cash Cows that help you turn Question Marks into Stars and keep your Stars growing.[24,25]

Key takeaways from Chapter 17

- Smartly selected, executed, and integrated M&A deals can help maintain your business's growth even as a mature company.

- Don't make acquisitions for the wrong reasons, such as to build your empire, to succumb to undue growth pressures, to allay boredom, or for fear of missing out.

- Smart acquisitions are transacted for the following reasons:
  - Leverage existing channels
  - Acquire a new Core Market
  - Gain new technology
  - Enter a new geography
  - Acquire management
  - Neutralize future competitors
  - Sow the seeds of future growth

- You can integrate acquired companies or keep them separate depending on their brand, culture, and necessary autonomy.

- Don't neglect managing your portfolio and culling businesses that no longer contribute to your mission or are no longer the right strategic fit.

- Check out my earlier book *Buyable*,[26] for a more detailed discussion of the M&A process and how to optimize you success both as a buyer and seller of companies.

Having considered M&A as a source of growth and corporate renewal, let's consider the nuclear option: When you need to reinvent your business to stay viable in the future. Turn to Chapter 18 to learn how.

CHAPTER EIGHTEEN

Reinvent Yourself

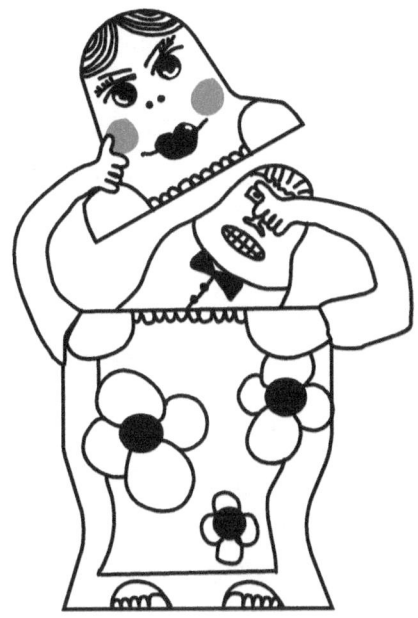

When things are bad, it's the best time to reinvent yourself.

—George Lopez

When Lou Gerstner was hired to turn IBM around, it was clear that something had to give. The easy answers had already been tried and failed.

The personal computer (PC) was winning the war against mainframe machines, the bread and butter of IBMs business. Big Blue, which had initially trumped the PC market, lost its dominance as IBM-clone machines with Intel chips inside and running DOS undercut Big Blue's prices.

Gerstner's predecessor, John Akers, activated Plan B to restructure and decentralize IBM, but even that did not stem the losses, which in 1993 reached $8 billion.[1]

The situation looked so bleak, that IBM's board could not attract any major tech executive to run the business. The company whose name had been a synonym for stability for decades—"no one was ever fired for choosing IBM"—was seen by insiders as hopeless. Consultants suggested breaking it up.

IBM's board was ready to use the nuclear option and brought in outsider Lou Gerstner, hoping he could take a fresh look and discover a viable way forward. He did, and he started a renaissance at IBM, as discussed in Chapter 6.

Something similar played out at GE when Jack Welch took over in 1982. The company was a sprawling conglomerate with a vast number of businesses, such as household appliance manufacturing, in which it no longer had a competitive advantage.

Conglomerates were going out of vogue anyway: After the steep rise in interest rates in the seventies, the resulting high debt payments eroded conglomerate profitability, exposing the strategic weakness of acquiring diverse businesses.

Jack Welch responded by aggressively selling off GE's portfolio companies that did not hold future potential. "Neutron Jack" applied the same approach to the conglomerate's human capital, administratively forcing out the lowest performers and handing stock options and bonuses to A players.

Effectively reinventing the American conglomerate, Welch quadrupled GE's sales revenue over a twenty-year period.

In this final chapter, we will examine how successful businesses have responded in the face of existential crises. Businesses with longevity tend to see their industries commoditized or disrupted over time, and sooner or later they reach a moment when they must reinvent themselves to survive.

By studying the most successful reinvention stories, I have identified eleven distinct approaches to business renaissances. Let's look at each one with examples.

Deepen Your Expertise

Corning Inc. is a multinational technology company that focuses on the industrial application of glass and ceramics. One of the company's most iconic products is Gorilla Glass, which is used for many of the leading smartphone brands, including the iPhone.[2]

Corning has come a long way in deepening its glass expertise. (See Figure 18.1.) Founded as Corning Glass Works in 1851, it initially focused on manufacturing the flint glass used in prisms and lenses.

In 1870, Thomas Edison approached Corning for help developing bulbs for electric light, which by 1908 became half of the company's business.[3] In the same year of 1870, Corning set up an industrial research department.

Figure 18.1 Deepen your expertise

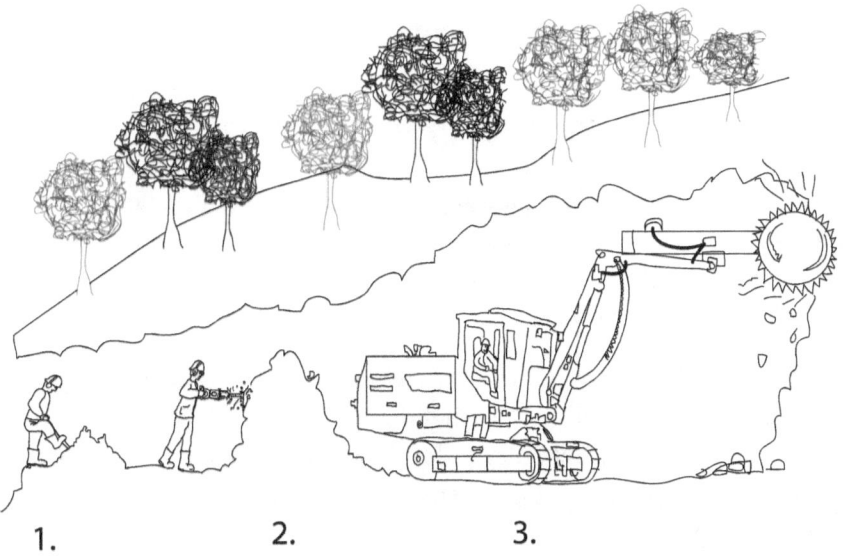

1.   2.   3.

The research started to pay off in the early 1910s, when Corning developed a heat-resistant signal lantern for the railways and heat-resistant cookware under the Pyrex brand.

Over the next two decades, the company continued to invent. Its radio lamps allowed the mass production and dispersion of radio technology, and Corning technology was used in oscilloscopes and experimental television sets. The company also designed a pure silica compound that would later be used in spacecraft windows, optical lenses, optical fiber, and telescope mirrors.

By the 1930s, Corning glass was used in telescope technology and radar technology during World War II, and it enabled the mass production of TV screens and TV tubes. These innovations were followed by glass ceramics in the 1950s and flat glass in the 1960s, foreshadowing the invention of the liquid crystal display used in consumer electronics such as flat TVs and smartphones.

One of Corning's greatest achievements was the invention of low-loss fiber optics in 1970, which helped launch the age of optical communications.

Corning continues to reinvent itself by ever deepening its expertise in glass technologies.

Rescue a Dying Product

Play-Doh, a nontoxic, non-staining modeling compound, is one of the most successful toys sold by Hasbro. The original use of the product, however, was very different. It was invented in the 1930s by a Cincinnati-based soap manufacturer, Kutol Products, to clean coal residue from wallpaper.

But after World War II, washable vinyl wallpaper was introduced, and heating homes with coal and the resulting soot declined. These developments made wallpaper-cleaning putty redundant, pushing Kutol Products to the brink of bankruptcy. (See Figure 18.2.)

Around the same time, the spouse of a Kutol employee, a nursery school teacher, learned that the putty could be used for art projects. She suggested the product be manufactured as a kids' toy and be called Play-Doh.

The product took off. By the late 1950s, Macy's of New York and Marshall Field's of Chicago were selling it, generating $3 million in revenue for the company now called Rainbow Crafts. Rainbow Crafts patented and started exporting Play-Doh in the 1960s, and after multiple mergers, Hasbro became the owner of Play-Doh in 1991.

Figure 18.2 Rescue a dying product

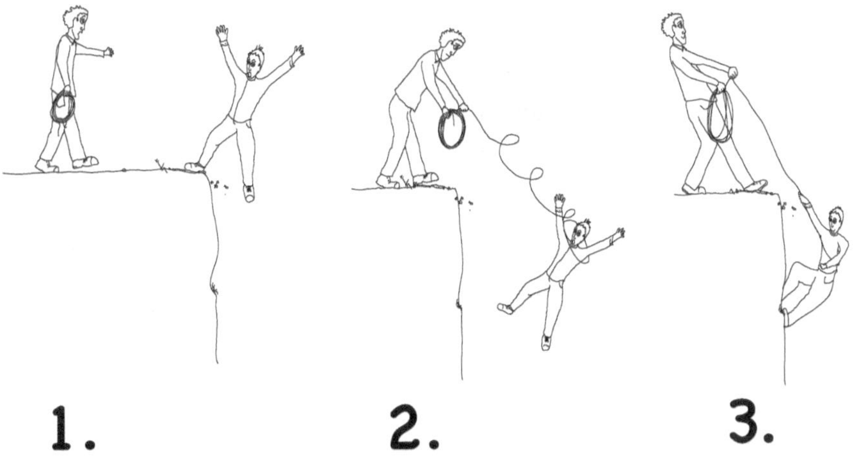

1.   **2.**   **3.**

By finding a new application for a practically defunct product, the business hit a new growth trajectory. By the year 2022, Play-Doh had become one of Hasbro's leading products of which over 3 billion cans have been sold.[4]

Expand to a Conglomerate (or Refocus to a Niche)

In the United States, the age of the conglomerate ended with the 1970s, but in other parts of the world this organizational form remains successful.

The biggest examples are in South Korea, where the family-controlled conglomerate, the *chaebol,* continues to reign supreme. Chaebols are the remnants of Japanese colonial rule and the crony capitalism of the 1950s under Syngman Rhee's First Republic.

Following efforts to reform the system in South Korea, later administrations realized that it was better to cooperate rather than to fight with the country's powerful entrepreneurs. Under the guise of "guided capitalism," the government selected companies to undertake projects, channeled funds from foreign loans, and provided bank guarantees.[5]

Chaebols such as LG have taken advantage of this economic climate and opportunistically grew in multiple industries. Starting in 1952 in chemicals, LG was the first Korean company to engage in the plastics industry and it produced its first radio. Gradually, the company expanded to consumer electronics and toiletries, cosmetics, textiles, batteries, beverage bottling, and management consulting.[6] (See Figure 18.3.)

By the early twenty-first century, LG became a leading global player in electronic and digital home appliances, LCDs, and semiconductors, as well, generating group revenue of more than $65 billion.[7]

Figure 18.3 LG's expansion to a conglomerate

1.   **2.**   **3.**   **4**

Sometimes conglomerate growth reverses course and the company slims down to focus on a niche.

One example is Finnish Nokia, which started in 1865 as a pulp mill and manufacturer of paper products. Later, it entered a diverse array of manufacturing industries, including forestry, cables, rubber, electronics, electricity generation, respirators, and, more recently, typewriters, minicomputers, and PCs.

In the 1990s, the conglomerate Nokia acquired an edge in mobile telecommunications and developed car phones, mobile phones, smartphones, set-top boxes, speakers, wireless LANs, camera phones, mobile games, internet-enabled tablets, and the operating systems to run them. By 2007, Nokia became the giant of the mobile phone market, with a 49 percent global share.[8]

However, the iPhone and an ill-fated partnership with Microsoft disrupted Nokia's leadership in the phone industry. To save itself, the company abandoned its conglomerate strategy and narrowed its focus to its telecommunications infrastructure business and Internet of Things technologies.

After collapsing from its $110 billion peak to a low of $6 billion, Nokia's market capitalization regained some of its lost ground and stabilized around $20 billion.[9]

Expand from a Niche to a Become a Universal Player

Ally Financial, formerly known as General Motors Acceptance Corporation (GMAC), was founded in 1919 by General Motors to provide financing for car purchases.

Twenty years later, the company founded Motors Insurance Corporation and started offering car insurance. The next expansion step took forty-five years. In 1981, in an effort to diversify, the company formed GMAC Mortgage and acquired an $11 billion mortgage portfolio. In the following decade, the company started a real estate brokerage operation and a direct bank, GMAC Bank.

Following ownership changes, mortgage losses, and a government capital injection, GMAC Bank rebranded as Ally Financial in 2010. Four years later it went public. Two further acquisitions followed, launching the company as a player in patient financing and credit cards.

After a hundred years in business, Ally Financial has gradually expanded to become a top 25 U.S. bank by assets and was top-rated by Time.com for overall customer service, range of products, interest rates, and online banking.[10,11]

Escape Commoditization

At the start of this chapter, we talked about how Lou Gerstner reinvented IBM. The company's traditional strength—mainframe computers—was disrupted by the PC revolution. This trend accelerated in the 2000s with the advent of cloud computing and giant data centers that made most framework-based proprietary data centers obsolete.

In the early 1980s, IBM switched to manufacturing PCs, but its early advantage was squandered because it did not acquire exclusive rights on the DOS operating system or Intel's chips. By the mid-1990s, Microsoft and chipmaker Intel were raking in the PC industry's profits, and IBM was left out in the cold.

Lou Gerstner's strategy was to reinvent IBM by escaping the commoditized PC manufacturing business. He refocused Big Blue on its core competencies of client relationships and engineering expertise. This allowed the company to advise clients on choosing and integrating complex software solutions and to service clients' ongoing technology needs. (See Figure 18.4.)

Figure 18.4 How IBM escaped the disruption of mainframes and commoditization of the PC

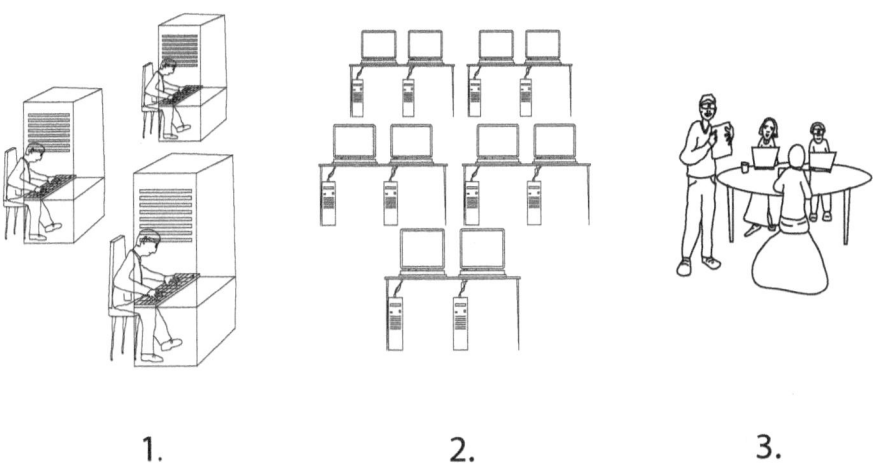

1.   2.   3.

Intel, which won the chip wars in the 1990s, was itself a product of escaping commoditization. Its CEO, Andy Grove, engineered the company's exit from the commoditized computer memory market and went all in on developing and manufacturing microchips. After two years of losses, Intel rebounded and grew to dominate the PC chip business for the next two decades.

Flee from Industry Disruption

American Express is one of the most valuable financial services firms in the world and a leader in payment cards.

However, the company started from humble beginnings. It was founded as an express mail business in 1850 in Buffalo, New York, when the businesses of Henry Wells and William Fargo merged. Two years later, the two founders departed to fund Wells Fargo & Co. after the board vetoed their proposal to extend operations to California.

Initially, Amex enjoyed a virtual monopoly in moving goods, mail, and currencies across New York State, and gradually it expanded nationwide by affiliating with other express companies, railroads, and steamship enterprises.[12]

However, in 1917, during World War I, Woodrow Wilson nationalized American Express, depriving Amex of its Core Business in which it had a 40 percent market share nationwide.

Fortunately, by that time Amex had invented the Travelers Cheque and built a stellar reputation internationally. The company acted as the British government's agent, and by the end of the war was delivering 150 tons of parcels a day to British prisoners in six countries. Amex also had become a strong player in the money order business, competing with the United States Postal Service.

In 1958, American Express was the second bank to issue a charge card and the first to launch a plastic card. This was the company's first innovation, which was followed by a segmenting of users with gold and platinum cards and the introduction of a credit card product in 1987.

The company also innovated by offering other services, such as free insurance to cardholders. In 2013, Amex launched a series of airport lounges for its platinum and centurion cardholders. (See Figure 18.5.)

Figure 18.5 Flee from industry disruption

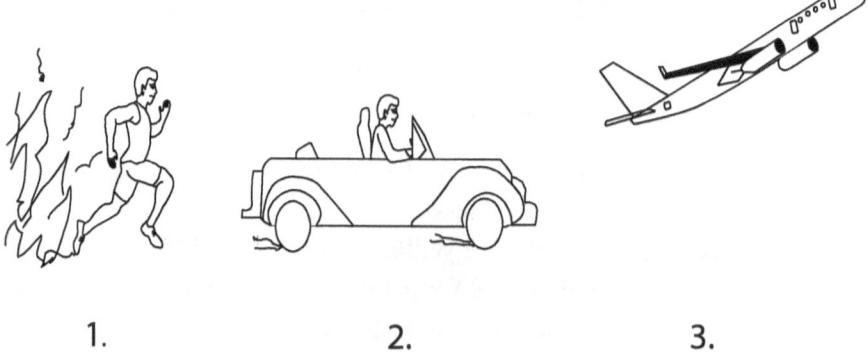

1.   2.   3.

Another example of fleeing industry disruption is streaming service Netflix. Netflix was a leader in online video rentals from the mid-1990s, disrupting the business of Blockbuster. After witnessing the success of YouTube's video upload service, Netflix began to offer its most popular videos through a streaming subscription service.

Instead of fleeing disruption, Netflix got ahead of the curve and disrupted its own business—and preempted any upstart competitors that might have considered doing the same.

Penetrate Retail and Expand Worldwide

Starbucks started in Seattle in 1971 as a roaster and wholesaler of coffee beans, inspired by San Francisco's Peet's Coffee & Tea.

The company was slowly building a following until, in 1982, the general manager of a Swedish housewares company, Howard Schultz, showed up and asked to be hired as a marketing executive. After a product sourcing trip to Italy, Schultz developed a vision to turn Starbucks into a retail chain that brought the Italian coffee experience to the American public.

Starbucks's founders initially refused to support his plan, but in 1986 they agreed to sell Schultz the business while they, in turn, took over and focused on running Peet's Coffee. In the coming years, Starbucks expanded rapidly, and by the time of its IPO in 1992, it had 140 stores.[13]

After the IPO, Starbucks continued rapid expansion, both organically and through the acquisition of other chains. The company also developed its wholesale business and established stores in Barnes & Noble and Target stores. The company had grown to 35,700 coffee stores worldwide by 2022.[14] (See Figure 18.6.)

Figure 18.6 Starbucks's vertical integration and global retail expansion

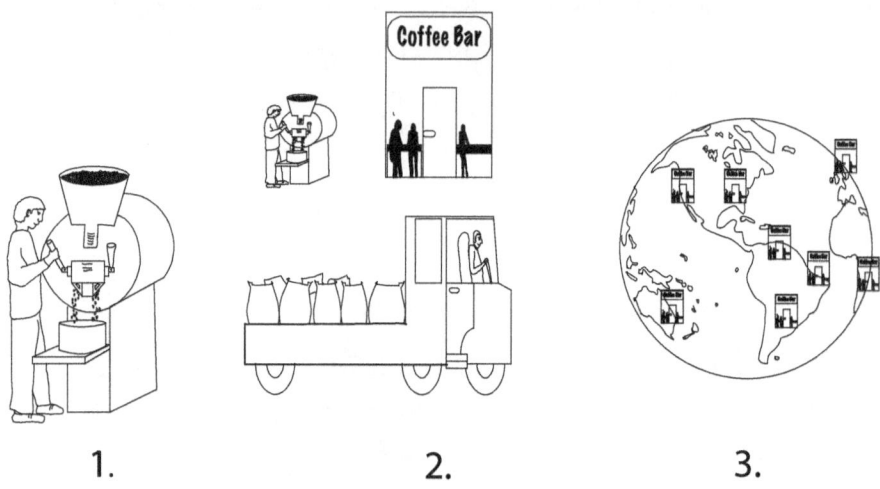

By establishing a differentiated retail vision and brand, Starbucks reinvented itself from a processor of coffee beans to a global lifestyle brand. A customized cup of Starbucks coffee fetches three to seven times more than what coffee drinkers would pay for a cup in a convenience store.

Apple also successfully executed a retail penetration strategy with the Apple Store concept. The stores allow Apple to create a different customer experience from what any of its competitors can offer and enable the company to position itself as the retailer of a premium product.

Further, Apple redefined the shopping experience as one of discovery and entertainment—I must admit to have succumbed to the hype myself when the first iPad came out, and I queued up in the wee hours near a Central Park store to get my tablet.

Mutate Your Product into a Multimedia Franchise

LEGO (which means "play well") was started in 1932 by a Danish carpenter, Ole Kirk Christiansen, who made wooden toys, including interlocking ones he called Automatic Binding Bricks. However, it wasn't until 1958 that LEGO developed a modern version of the interlocking blocks that could be built into a toy system.

After patenting the system in multiple countries, the blocks started spreading. In 1969, the company came out with Duplo, larger bricks for smaller kids, and the first minifigures in 1978. From there, LEGO developed thematic kits such as LEGO robots, pirates, trains, and castles and after the year 2000 started selling Star Wars, Batman, Harry Potter, and other branded kits.

LEGO minifigures began starring in animated movies and TV shows, and the company opened a number of theme parks around the world, including replicas of famous places.

In 2015, Brand Finance, a consulting company, ranked LEGO as the "world's most powerful brand," ahead of Ferrari. LEGO has become a global cultural icon. (See Figure 18.7.)

Figure 18.7 How LEGO turned into a global cultural icon

1.   2.   3.   4.

Another example is Marvel, which evolved from a ten-cent comic book series about superheroes through books and movies to TV shows, digital comics, augmented reality, and a comic book retail chain. The company was acquired by Disney for $4 billion in 2019.[15]

Disney itself ran much the same course. The business was started by the Disney brothers as a cartoon, animation, and merchandising operation, which gradually evolved into film studios, television, broadcasting, streaming media, theme park resorts, consumer products, publishing, and a global brand. At its 2021 peak, Disney's market capitalization exceeded $360 billion.

Evolve Integrated Consumer Technology Products

Nintendo was founded in 1889 and in its first sixty years hand-produced traditional Japanese hanafuda playing cards. When the family company's third-generation owner, Hiroshi Yamauchi, saw that the leading card manufacturer in the world, the United States Playing Card Company (USPCC), was run from a small office, he realized that he had to reinvent the business.

He introduced plastic cards and licensed Disney characters to position cards as a game safe for kids, not a device for gambling. Subsequently, Nintendo's sales grew rapidly, allowing the company to go public and raise growth capital. Soon after, though, the card market was saturated and Nintendo had to look elsewhere.

Luckily, Nintendo had a talented maintenance engineer, Gunpei Yokoi, who started developing quirky toys, such as an extended plastic arm, a batting toy, a programmable drum machine, and an electronic toy called the Love Tester, which allowed young couples to measure the electricity in their relationship by holding spherical metal sensors.

Another toy Nintendo developed was a solar-powered plastic gun that could be used for the then-fledgling arcade games that Nintendo started to distribute under license. Soon Yokoi jumped in the fray and, in the early 1980s, started developing Nintendo's arcade games, including Donkey Kong and later the Mario and Super Mario games, which became blockbusters.

From that point, Nintendo jumped ahead of the pack and developed video consoles, the Game Boy, GameCube, and Wii and the latest console called the Switch.[16]

The other company that cornered the consumer electronics market was, of course, Apple. Steve Jobs and Steve Wozniak founded the company in Los Altos, California, to produce one of the first personal computers. The company had a great initial run, but Jobs was too green and abrasive and was forced out by the then public company's board in 1985, only to return in 1997.

Figure 18.8 Apple's evolution from computers to a consumer electronics company

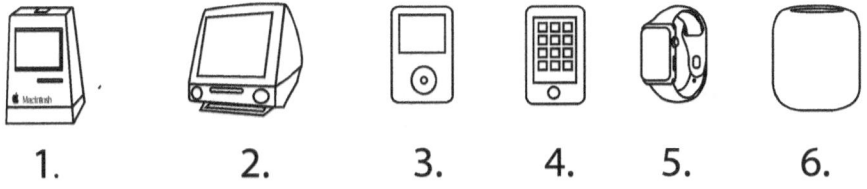

1.   2.   3.   4.   5.   6.

By the time Jobs returned to Apple, the company had 350 different product varieties. Jobs cut them down to four principal product groups to refocus engineering and marketing onto the company's Core Business. Reportedly, he was ready to wait for the "next big thing" to emerge before making a move.

That revolutionary product was the iPod, followed by a string of successful launches, including the iPhone, the iPad, the Apple Watch, and the HomePod. (See Figure 18.8.) It was a gradual metamorphosis that made Apple the most valuable company over the next twenty years. Many, including this book's author, doubted that Apple would continue to thrive after Jobs's death, but he proved us all wrong.

Bundle Your Software into a Subscription Platform

Adobe Inc. was founded by John Warnock and Charles Geschke, two alumni of Xerox PARC, the research and development arm of Xerox Corporation. Warnock and Geschke left Xerox to develop and sell the PostScript page description language, which allowed computer-generated pages to be translated into high-definition instruction sets for top-quality printing.

Steve Jobs wanted to buy control of Adobe, but he was only allowed to buy a 19 percent stake, which together with a five-year up-front license purchase made Adobe instantly profitable.

Over the following forty years, Adobe gradually developed and acquired killer apps such as Adobe Photoshop and Adobe Acrobat and Reader. These initially targeted graphic designers but over time expanded to audio and video editing and other creative activities.[17]

In February 2012, Adobe made a courageous decision to switch its license holders to a subscription model.[18] From that point on, customers could not purchase lifelong licenses for individual products but instead had to purchase a monthly subscription to the Adobe Creative Cloud, which bundled all Adobe's creative products. (See Figure 18.9.)

Following this switch, Adobe's stock price rose from $32 to peak at over $650 in 2021.[19]

Figure 18.9 Bundle your software into a subscription platform

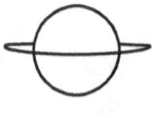
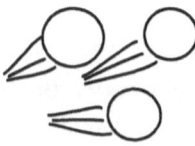
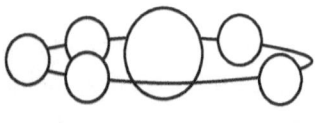

1.   2.   3.

Reinventing Adobe Inc. as a Software-as-a-Service company contributed to a 20x growth-multiple in a ten-year period.

Pivot the Subfunction of a Failed Application into a New Product

Sometimes a failed product has a silver lining.

Three PayPal refugees, Steve Chen, Chad Hurley, and Jawed Karim, founded YouTube in 2005 as a video-enhanced online dating service. They posted ads on Craigslist offering $100 to attractive women if they uploaded a video. The service went nowhere, but the video uploading feature proved popular, so the founding trio decided to relaunch it as a standalone product. We all know the rest of the story.

The founding of Slack followed a similar pattern. Slack, which originally stood for "Searchable Log of All Conversation and Knowledge," was developed by Stewart Butterfield as an internal tool for a social video game called Glitch. Butterfield started developing Glitch in 2002 but got distracted by a photo hosting side project that later became Flickr.[20]

Glitch finally launched in September 2011, but the appropriately named application had to be taken down to correct technical issues.

Glitch never resurfaced, but Butterfield ended up launching Slack as a standalone product two years later. Slack grew rapidly and in 2021 was acquired by Salesforce for $27.7 billion. (See Figure 18.10.)

Could there be a minimum viable product hidden in your business too?

Figure 18.10 Pivot the subfunction of a failed application into a new product

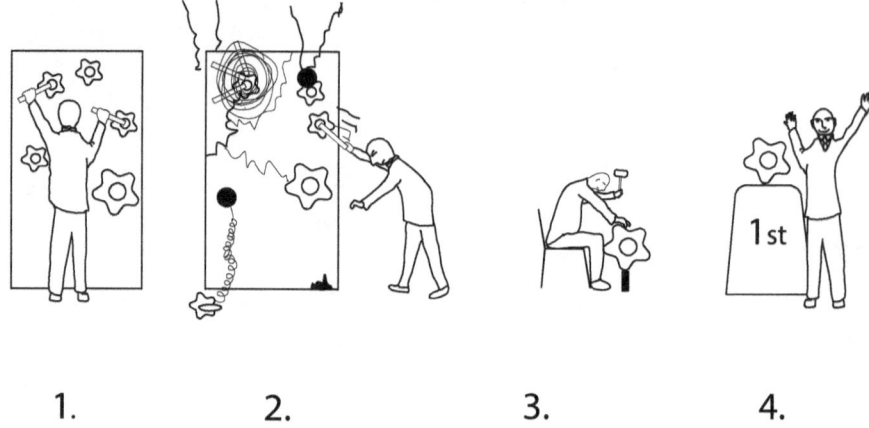

1.   2.   3.   4.

Key takeaways from Chapter 18

In certain cases, incremental changes don't allow you to save or grow your business. In such situations, you will have to throw in the towel *or* reinvent your business. There are at least eleven approaches to execute a reinvention:

- Deepen your expertise

- Rescue a dying product

- Expand to a conglomerate (or refocus to a niche)

- Expand from a niche to a universal player

- Escape commoditization

- Flee from industry disruption

- Penetrate retail and expand worldwide

- Mutate your product into a multimedia franchise

- Evolve integrated consumer technology products

- Bundle your software into a subscription platform

- Pivot the subfunction of a failed application into a new product

Perpetuating growth requires fostering innovation, acquiring selectively, and regularly pruning your portfolio of suboptimal businesses. If innovation and M&A are not enough to keep your business growing, consider reinventing your business.

You can keep your strategic activities coherent with your culture and vision and execute them well by following a business operating system such as EOS, Scaling Up, or Pinnacle. Strategy OS is your toolkit to take your business from solid execution to differentiated growth.

Whether you are aggressive, like Welch's GE, or aspirational, like Google's empire-building founders, now you have a philosophy and a complete strategic system for perpetuating growth.

Let's zoom out and review how your Strategy Operating System works from A to Z.

Conclusion

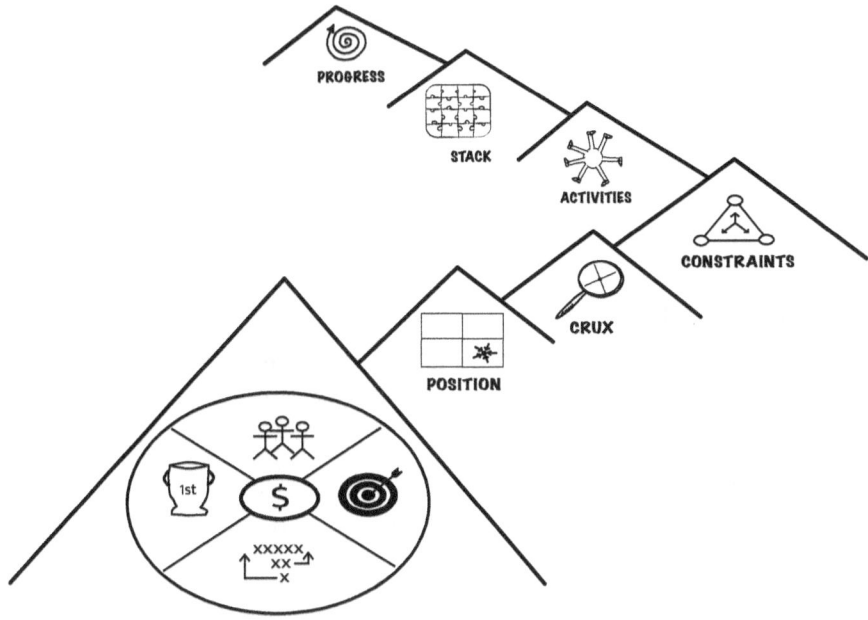

Start where you are. Use what you have. Do what you can.

—Arthur Ashe

In the conclusion of *Pinnacle: Five Principles*, I share a story about a friend of mine and I trekking in the mountains of the Greek island of Crete twenty-five years ago. How we struggled up to the top of a rocky cliff in our flip-flops, facing gusting winds, hoping to reach what we thought was the pinnacle of the island. Our disappointment was tremendous when we discovered that it was a "false peak" with a yet higher mountain rising behind.

Turns out *Pinnacle: Five Principles* was one of these false peaks, which my coauthor Greg and I knew it would be all along. As Greg likes to say, "No one has the market cornered for good ideas," him and I included.

My goal with this book was to discover the next peak beyond the Pinnacle "mountain." To explore how to conceptualize, dissect, and make digestible the heavy fare that the giants of strategy—Michael Porter, Bruce Henderson, Martin Bower, Jim Collins, Richard Rumelt, and many others—have cooked up.

Take, for example, the concepts of positioning and brand promises. I wanted to understand how these really worked and then refine the process so that they could be determined with a more scientific approach than just relying on gut feels. In particular, Porter's existing framework for positioning seemed too limited and somewhat confusing to be practically useful.

As to Jim Collins's flywheel, Michael Porter's differentiating activities, and the idea of the Strategy Stack, my goal was to dig a layer or two deeper to discover how these tools could be built logically, with intention, from first principles.

I also wanted to string these concepts into a sequential system so that CEOs, business owners, and leadership teams could develop them organically. Building a solid strategy takes time, and it is not always the first priority.

Having a Strategy Operating System allows you to develop your whole strategy over a multiday workshop or to weave these concepts piecemeal into the agenda of your quarterly strategic leadership meetings.

The concepts contained in the Strategy OS are particularly useful for companies that have already implemented EOS, Scaling Up, Pinnacle, or another business operating system.

The Strategy OS enables any organization that already executes well to scale to new heights. If your business already has a vision, accountability, a meeting structure, quarterly objective setting, scoreboard metrics, and documented playbooks, Strategy OS will help you take your game to the next level.

Next Steps

If you would like to implement the Strategy Operating System™, you can do it in various ways:

1. Follow along with the chapters in this book and use them to guide your thinking or to facilitate your leadership team's journey through the process. Use the concepts and questions to figure out your Core Business, Strategic Position, Crux Challenge, Business Constraints, Strategic Implications, Unique Activities, Core Market, and Strategy Stack and progress from there to spread your Business Tentacles and eventually build a perpetually progressing empire.

2. Learn how to implement Strategy OS™ for your own business, or for other companies as a Steve Preda Business Growth Guide™ (or SPBG Guide for short) by signing up to the Strategy OS App™ self-coaching portal at: **https://StrategyOS.app**.

3. Visit https://StevePreda.com for free downloadable tools for growing your business, to test drive the Summit OS™ self-coaching portal, or get matched with an SPBG Guide™ to help take your business to the top of the mountain.

I wish you a fun and fulfilling climb to your strategy peaks.

About the Author

STEVE PREDA'S "Why" is to help entrepreneurs reach their ideal lives while creating a positive impact. He believes that with the right tools and coaching we can eradicate "Business Covid" in America, and save 185,000 companies each year from disappearing.

Steve built and sold an investment banking firm in Europe before moving to the United States in 2012. Since then, he has helped thousands of businesses grow their teams, revenues, and profits as an author, speaker, coach, and as the founder of Steve Preda Business Growth (SPBG).

Steve explores business-growth shortcuts on the Management Blueprint podcast, and he and his fellow SPBG Guides love helping growth-minded entrepreneurs and their leadership teams reach their business-pinnacles.

Steve lives with his wife and their two teenage sons in Virginia.

Review Request

Thanks for reading!

If you enjoyed this book or found it useful, I'd love to receive a short review from you on Amazon. Your support makes a difference, and your feedback will make possible future editions of this book even better.

You can leave your review at: https://www.amazon.com/dp/B0C12X9JL4/

With gratitude,

Steve Preda

Further Resources

Strategy OS App™ self-coaching portal: **https://StrategyOS.app**

Streve Preda Business Growth Home Page: **https://StevePreda.com**

Steve Preda, *Buyable: How to Build a Self-Managing, Fast-Growing and High-Profit Business* (Glen Allen, VA: Amershire Publishing, 2021)

Steve Preda and Gregory Cleary, *Pinnacle: Five Principles that Take Your Business to the Top of the Mountain* (Glen Allen, VA: Amershire Publishing, 2022)

Business Buyability Assessment: **https://BuyabilityAssessment.com**

Management Blueprint Podcast: **https://bit.ly/MBPpodcast**

Succession Secrets Podcast: **https://apple.co/39RBsah**

Acknowledgments

This book has been the hardest to write out of the five, but I have received tremendous support. Without it, I could not have succeeded.

Firstly, I am standing on the shoulders of giants, strategy thinkers and practitioners, including Michael Porter, Richard Rumelt, Jim Colins, Henry Mintzberg, Joan Magretta, Carl Stern, Michael Deimler, Bruce Henderson, Marvin Bower, Andrew Chen, and many others.

I am deeply grateful to my resilient wife, Dora, who put up with my absences and absent-mindedness through the long winter nights while I was barricaded in my writing "dungeon." She has been very supportive through this process, putting aside her natural aversion to harebrained projects and patiently listening to my excited ramblings about Strategy OS during our walks together, without once criticizing it. Our youngest child, Sandor, offered encouraging words, proposed occasional critiques, and showed interest in the project along the way, which motivated me to keep going. Thank you to both of you!

My friend and collaborator of more than twenty years, Zoltan Ember, helped create many of the graphics and charts in the book, and he worked tirelessly to help design over a hundred pages of coaching tools for the accompanying Strategy OS App portal. Thanks, Zoli, for being such a selfless partner and an invaluable resource over the past two decades, even when I could barely pay you.

I'd like to thank my UK-based graphic design team: Jason Anscomb, Will Sargent, and Andy Meaden, for translating my ideas into a design I find top-notch. Hopefully, you, the reader, agree.

Christina Palaia, my editor extraordinaire, has been a great champion of my work, offering insightful suggestions and encouragement from the early days. Thanks for allaying my fears and trepidations about whether the initial draft would turn out to be the system I wanted to create. I am also grateful to Toni Culley, who has once again produced a high-quality index for the book. Thanks Rajendra Singh for accurately and quickly converting the pdf manuscript into an ebook.

I also owe a debt of gratitude to Ghada Sleiman, my incomparable tech expert; Alejandro Martinez, my enterprising copywriter; and my indispensable assistant, Victoria McKinley, who have endured and lived up to my often-unreasonable expectations. Thanks, Peter Santry, for jumping on a plane and coming down to Richmond to help shoot the videos for the accompanying Strategy OS App portal.

My friends Arvin Delgado and Patrick Burke have selflessly invested many hours poring over the advance version of the book, pointing out errors and suggesting improvements. Adam Zatik and Ian Price also gave me valuable feedback. Thank you, guys, for helping to make this book better!

My long-time coach Dave Quick helped clarify my thinking around the book's concept and how I approached it. Thanks, Dave, for always having my back and challenging me, even when I don't want to hear it. You are a true friend!

My parents, Beata and Istvan, offered valuable encouragement on our weekly Skype calls. More importantly, they have always encouraged me to find my own path and never imposed their career preferences. Thank you for trusting me with my journey. I am still a work in progress, but finally making some.

Not least, I would like to thank my friends and fans who read an early version of this book and provided invaluable input, encouragement, and support: Mfon Akpan, Burak Ali Gul, James Ashcroft, Darryl Bates-Brownsword, Tommy Battle, Nick Beavers, Dave Beeler, Jeff Berkowitz, Brad Betson, Doug Bloom, Gary Breininger, Douglas Brown, Michael Brown, Chris Burger, Patrick Burke, Susanna Calvert, Gordon Caudle, Srikant Chellappa, Kyle Christensen, Gregory Cleary, Allison Conners, Krista Crawford, Matt Curry, Steven Dalley, April Dumas, Joyce Durst, Mike Eckert, Michael Episcope, Sal Filardi, Charles Fry, John Fulwider, John Gaudet, Andrew Gorter, Chris Grandpre, Robin Green, R. J. Grimshaw,

Doug Hall, Armin Hartmann, Forth Heffner, Rob Hirschfeld, George Hodges-Fulton, Craig Huston, Gus Iurillo, Scott J. Medeiros, David Jenyns, Tanya Kabuya, Mike Kaeding, Ryan Kalmbach, Charlene Krassoi, Deanna Kuempel, Glenn Kurtz, Ron Levene, Mitch Lewandowski, Kevin Lingg, Reed MacNaughton, Susan Mann, Duane Marshall, Alejandro Martinez, Kent McKown, Joshua McMahon, Lisa Miller, Wayne Mullins, Leann Murphy, Eric Negron, Clyde Northrop, Denis O'Shea, Stephen Ogburn, Jim Padilla, Richard Palmer Smith, Jim Palzewicz, Andres Pedraza, Christy Pennison, Gary Perkins, Kristi Piehl, Freddie Price II, Tip Quilter, Wanina Rae, Linda Ratner, Vikram Raya, Christopher Reckord, Harlan Reichle, Adam Rhoads, Zsolt Rieder, Luigi Rosabianca, Jason Rothfuss, Richard Rumrill, Chris Rutkai, Michael Sanjek, Ben Santelman, Tyler Sickmeyer, Sergiu Simmel, Bill Smith, Samuel Smith, Russ Sorrell, Carol Steinberg, Andrew Stewart, Aaron Stone, Mate Szeles, Abe Tatosian, Mike Taylor, Paul Tetreault, Michael Trautman, Chandresh Trivedi, Keith Trost, Jon Tsourakis, Chris Tully, Debbie Tyler, Peter Van Nest, Rob Van Vely, Mike Wittenstein, Darya Yegorina, Adam Zatik, and Jing Zhou. Thank you all very much!

Writing these acknowledgments made me realize how many people have supported this effort. I am blessed to have been surrounded by family, colleagues and friends that made this endeavor worthwhile, and who have helped it to hopefully become a useful toolkit for entrepreneurs everywhere.

Endnotes

STEP 1

1   Simon Bigouette, "Where Does Volvo's Reputation for Safety Come From?" Wyant Group, https://wyantgroup.com/where-does-volvos-reputation-for-safety-come-from/.

2   Wikipedia, s.v. "Airbag," last modified February 1, 2023, https://en.wikipedia.org/wiki/Airbag.

3   Michael Porter, *On Competition* (Boston: Harvard Business Review Books, 2008).

Chapter One

1   Collins Dictionary, s.v. "Core Business," https://www.collinsdictionary.com/us/dictionary/english/core-business.

2   Ross Freedman, "If the Computer Is 'a Bicycle for Our Minds,' Artificial Intelligence Is a Harley Davidson," Customer Think, October 24, 2017, https://customerthink.com/if-the-computer-is-a-bicycle-for-our-minds-artificial-intelligence-is-a-harley-davidson/.

Chapter Two

1   Joan Magretta: Understanding Michael Porter p. 54 (Harvard Business Review Press, Boston, 2012)

Chapter Three

1   Dollar General, "About Us," https://www.dollargeneral.com/about-us.html.

2   Austin Irwin, "10 Cheapest New Cars for 2021," *Car and Driver*, December 23, 2020, https://www.caranddriver.com/features/g34908888/10-cheapest-new-cars-for-2021/.

3   "Walmart Brand Guides," Walmart, https://studioazura.com/storage/app/media/pdf/Walmart-brand-guidelines.pdf.

4   "2021 (Full Year) Global: Toyota Worldwide Car Sales, Production, and Exports," Car Sales Statistics, January 31, 2022, https://www.best-selling-cars.com/brands/2021-full-year-global-toyota-worldwide-car-sales-production-and-exports/.

5   Aditya Shastri, "Comprehensive Porsche Marketing Strategy," IIDE, September 2, 2021, https://iide.co/case-studies/porsche-marketing-strategy/.

6   "2023 Bentley Flying Spur at Bentley Austin," Bentley, https://www.bentleyaustin.com/bentley-model-research/new-flying-spur-model-research/.

STEP 2

1   Richard P. Rumelt, *The Crux: How Leaders Become Strategists* (New York: PublicAffairs, 2022).

2   Rich M, "Free Solo: The Crux," YouTube video, 2:40, March 1, 2019, https://www.youtube.com/watch?v=DKOtBYzDy-Y&t=50s.

3   "Aircraft Production During the Battle of Britain," Battle of Britain Historical Society, 2007, https://www.battleofbritain1940.net/document-42.html.

Chapter Four

1   Anthony Smoak, "Andy Grove and Intel's Move from Memory to Microprocessors," *Smoak Signals* (blog), March 27, 2016, https://anthonysmoak.com/2016/03/27/andy-grove-and-intels-move-from-memory-to-microprocessors/.

2   Richard S. Tedlow, *Andy Grove: The Life and Times of an American Business Icon* (New York: Portfolio, 2006).

3   Leander Kahney, "The Inside Story of the Iconic 'Rubber Band' Effect That Launched the iPhone," Cult of Mac, June 29, 2017, https://www.cultofmac.com/489256/bas-ording-rubber-band-effect-iphone/.

Chapter Five

1   Allen Packwood and Stuart Roberts, "How Churchill Waged War," University of Cambridge, https://www.cam.ac.uk/ChurchillAtWar.

2   Wikipedia, s.v. "Timeline of the Battle of France," last modified December 23, 2022, https://en.wikipedia.org/wiki/Timeline_of_the_Battle_of_France.

3   "How Roger Federer Upgraded His Game," *New York Times*, August 24, 2017, https://www.nytimes.com/interactive/2017/08/24/magazine/usopen-federer-nadal-backhand-wonder-year.html.

4   Wikipedia, s.v. "Brainstorming," last modified January 23, 2023, https://en.wikipedia.org/wiki/Brainstorming.

5   Wikipedia, "40 Principles of TRIZ Method," infographic, https://upload.wikimedia.org/wikipedia/commons/2/2e/40_principles_of_TRIZ_method_960dpi.jpg.

Chapter Six

1   Isaacson, Walter. Steve Jobs (pp. 337-338). Simon & Schuster. Kindle Edition.

2   Wikipedia, s.v. "Apple Newton," last modified November 25, 2022, https://en.wikipedia.org/wiki/Apple_Newton.

3   "Apple Is Worth $1,000,000,000,000. Two Decades Ago, It Was Almost Bankrupt," *New York Times*, August 2, 2018, https://www.nytimes.com/2018/08/02/technology/apple-stock-1-trillion-market-cap.html.

4   Jeremy Reimer, "Total Share: 30 Years of Personal Computer Market Share Figures," ARS Technica, December 14, 2005, https://arstechnica.com/features/2005/12/total-share/.

5   Wikipedia, s.v. "Lou Gerstner," last modified January 23, 2023, https://en.wikipedia.org/wiki/Lou_Gerstner.

6   "How Lou Gerstner Got IBM to Dance," Forbes, November 11, 2002, https://www.forbes.com/2002/11/11/cx_ld_1112gerstner.html?sh=1b3e96194257.

STEP 3

1   "The Story of IKEA," IKEA Museum, https://ikeamuseum.com/en/digital/the-story-of-ikea/.

2   "The IKEA Story: Innovation Begins at Home," Paperflite, June 12, 2020, https://www.paperflite.com/blogs/ikea-story.

3   Wikipedia, s.v. "IKEA," last modified January 31, 2023, https://en.wikipedia.org/wiki/IKEA.

Chapter Seven

1   Harold Marcuse, "Historical Dollar-to-Marks Currency Conversion Page," UC Santa Barbara, August 19, 2005, last updated October 7, 2018, https://marcuse.faculty.history.ucsb.edu/projects/currency.htm.

2   Joanna Bailey, "How Southwest Inspired the Ryanair We Know Today," Simple Flying, November 24, 2020, https://simpleflying.com/how-southwest-inspired-the-ryanair-we-know-today/.

3   Wikipedia, s.v. "Ryanair," last modified January 31, 2023, https://en.wikipedia.org/wiki/Ryanair.

4   Damian Corrigan, "9 Ryanair Fees and How to Avoid Them," TripSavvy, last updated on January 25, 2023, https://www.tripsavvy.com/ryanair-charges-fees-1644055.

Chapter Eight

1   Tim Higgins and Susan Pulliam, "Elon Musk Races to Exit Tesla's 'Production Hell,'" *Wall Street Journal*, June 27, 2018, https://www.wsj.com/articles/elon-musk-races-to-exit-teslas-production-hell-1530149814?mod=searchresults&page=1&pos=4.

Chapter Nine

1   Steve Preda and Gregory Cleary, *Pinnacle: Five Principles that Take Your Business to the Top of the Mountain* (Glen Allen, VA: Amershire Publishing, 2022).

2   "IKEA Catalog 2022," The Nordroom, last modified August 15, 2022, https://www.thenordroom.com/ikea-catalog-2022/.

3   "Bathroom," IKEA, https://www.ikea.com/us/en/rooms/bathroom/.

4   "Where Is IKEA Furniture Made? (Sweden or China?)," HomeCareZen, https://homecarezen.com/where-is-ikea-furniture-made/.

5   "How IKEA Saves Millions through Packaging Optimization," Chainalytics, https://www.chainalytics.com/ikea-save-millions-packaging-optimization/.

6   Noah Friedman and Lamar Salter, "The Meaning behind All Those Obscure IKEA Product Names," Insider, February 15, 2019, https://www.businessinsider.com/ikea-product-naming-system-meaning-2017-10.

7   "Fees," Ryanair, https://www.ryanair.com/us/en/useful-info/help-centre/fees.

8   Wikipedia, s.v. "Ryanair: No Frills," last modified January 31, 2023, https://en.wikipedia.org/wiki/Ryanair#No-frills.

9   Tom Boon, "How Ryanair Manages Super Tight Turn Arounds," Simple Flying, October 22, 2019, https://simpleflying.com/ryanair-25-minute-turnaround/.

10   Wikipedia, s.v. "List of Ryanair Destinations: Top Airports by Destinations," last modified January 26, 2023, https://en.wikipedia.org/wiki/List_of_Ryanair_destinations#Top_airports_by_destinations.

STEP 4

1   Wikipedia, s.v. "Justin.tv," last modified January 11, 2023, https://en.wikipedia.org/wiki/Justin.tv.

2   Wikipedia, s.v. "Twitch (service)," last modified February 1, 2023, https://en.wikipedia.org/wiki/Twitch_(service).

3   Kevin Morris, "Inside Twitch, the Site Powering the Esports Revolution," Dot Esports, November 10, 2013, https://dotesports.com/culture/news/twitch-tv-esports-future-livestreaming-32.

Chapter Ten

1   "Lab Startup Equipment List and Average Costs," Charter Capital, June 10, 2021, https://charteraz.com/2021/06/10/lab-startup-equipment-list-average-costs/.

2   "Microsoft Segmentation, Targeting, and Positioning," Wondershare EdrawMind, https://www.edrawmind.com/article/microsoft-segmentation-targeting-and-positioning.html.

Chapter Eleven

1   Jim Collins, *Turning the Flywheel: A Monograph to Accompany Good to Great* (New York: Harper Business, 2019).

2   Verne Harnish, Scaling Up: *How a Few Companies Make It...and the Rest Don't* (Miami: Gazelles, 2014).

3   Jim Collins, Good to Great: *Why Some Companies Make the Leap...and Others Don't* (New York: HarperBusiness, 2001).

4   More examples of flywheels are shown in Steve Preda and Gregory Cleary, Pinnacle: *Five Principles that Take Your Business to the Top of the Mountain* (Glen Allen, VA: Amershire Publishing, 2022).

Chapter Twelve

1   See Steve Preda and Gregory Cleary, *Pinnacle: Five Principles that Take Your Business to the Top of the Mountain* (Glen Allen, VA: Amershire Publishing, 2022), 89–126.

2   Venkatesh Shankar, Leonard L. Berry, and Thomas Dotzel, "A Practical Guide to Combining Products and Services," *Harvard Business Review*, November 2009, https://hbr.org/2009/11/a-practical-guide-to-combining-products-and-services.

3   Wikipedia, s.v. "Cloud Computing," last modified January 31, 2023, https://en.wikipedia.org/wiki/Cloud_computing.

4   Wikipedia, s.v. "Internet of Things," last modified January 31, 2023, https://en.wikipedia.org/wiki/Internet_of_things.

5   Wikipedia, s.v. "Robotics," last modified January 25, 2023, https://en.wikipedia.org/wiki/Robotics.

6   Wikipedia, s.v. "*Oxford English Dictionary*," last modified January 28, 2023, https://en.wikipedia.org/wiki/Oxford_English_Dictionary.

7   "Blockchain," Synopsys, https://www.synopsys.com/glossary/what-is-blockchain.html.

8   Insider Intelligence, "The Growing List of Applications and Use Cases of Blockchain Technology in Business and Life," Insider Intelligence, January 24, 2023, https://www.insiderintelligence.com/insights/blockchain-technology-applications-use-cases/.

STEP 5

1   Ramon Casadesus-Masanell, Oliver Gassmann, and Roman Sauer, "Hilti Fleet Management (A): Turning a Successful Business Model on Its Head," Harvard Business School, HBS Case Collection, May 2017, last revised September 2018, https://www.hbs.edu/faculty/Pages/item.aspx?num=52550.

2   "Prof. em. Dr. Pius Baschera," https://ethz.ch/en/the-eth-zurich/organisation/who-is-who/retired-professors/details.Nzk1NDQ=.TGlzdC80MDEsMTk1NzY4MzcwOQ==.html.

Chapter Thirteen

1   Wikipedia, s.v. "Porsche," last modified January 15, 2023, https://en.wikipedia.org/wiki/Porsche.

2   Lawrence Ulrich, "Why Porsche Is the World's Most Profitable Mass-Market Luxury Auto Brand," *Worth*, December 17, 2019, https://www.worth.com/why-porsche-is-the-worlds-most-profitable-mass-market-luxury-auto-brand/.

3   "Porsche Brand Strategy/Positioning Case Study," BrandStruck, https://brandstruck.co/porsche/.

4   "Design: The Porsche DNA," Porsche, https://www.porsche.com/international/aboutporsche/innovation/innovation-porschedna/.

5   Jo Clahsen, "Light is one…," Porsche, https://www.porsche.com/usa/aboutporsche/christophorusmagazine/archive/367/articleoverview/article09/.

6   Hermann-Josef Stappen, "The Porsche Product Line Principle: For 20 Years a Role Model for the Industry," Porsche Newsroom, March 30, 2019, https://newsroom.porsche.com/en/2019/company/porsche-product-line-principle-20-years-organisation.html.

Chapter Fourteen

1   Avery Hartmans, "Jeff Bezos Originally Wanted to Name Amazon 'Cadabra,' and 14 Other Little-Known Facts About the Early Days of the E-commerce Giant," *Insider*, July 2, 2021, https://www.businessinsider.com/jeff-bezos-amazon-history-facts-2017-4.

2   Wikipedia, s.v. "Amazon (company)," last modified January 30, 2023, https://en.wikipedia.org/wiki/Amazon_(company).

3   Steve Anderson, *The Bezos Letters: 14 Principles to Grow Your Business Like Amazon* (Newport News, VA: Morgan James Publishing, 2019).

4   Aaron, "Amazon International Expansion and What We Can Learn," DayTranslations Blog, May 18, 2020, https://www.daytranslations.com/blog/amazon-international-expansion/.

5   Jeremy Bowman, "Don't Be Fooled. Amazon's International Business Is More Profitable Than You Think," Motley Fool, November 14, 2022, https://www.fool.com/investing/2022/11/14/dont-be-fooled-amazons-international-business-is-m/.

6   Darrell Etherington, "Amazon Launches Local Register, a Square Competitor with Lower Transaction Rates," TechCrunch, August 13, 2014, https://techcrunch.com/2014/08/13/amazon-local-register/.

7   Shawn Collins, "History of Affiliate Marketing," ClickZ, November 10, 2000, https://www.clickz.com/history-of-affiliate-marketing/.

8   Geno Prussakov, "Amazon Retires aStore Affiliate Tool: Reasons and Lessons to Learn," AM Navigator, October 18, 2017, https://www.amnavigator.com/blog/2017/10/18/amazon-retires-astore-reasons-lessons/.

9   "Amazon Physical Store Locations," Amazon, https://www.amazon.com/find-your-store/b/?node=17608448011.

10 Julia Faria, "Amazon's Global Brand Value from 2006 to 2022," Statista, January 6, 2023, https://www.statista.com/statistics/326086/amazon-brand-value/.

11 Wikipedia, s.v. "Amazon Fresh," last modified January 18, 2023, https://en.wikipedia.org/wiki/Amazon_Fresh.

12 Aran Ali, "AWS: Powering the Internet and Amazon's Profits," Visual Capitalist, July 10, 2022, https://www.visualcapitalist.com/aws-powering-the-internet-and-amazons-profits/.

13 Felix Richter, "Amazon, Microsoft and Google Dominate Cloud Market," Statista, December 23, 2022, https://www.statista.com/chart/18819/worldwide-market-share-of-leading-cloud-infrastructure-service-providers/.

Chapter Fifteen

1   James Currier, "The Network Effects Bible (Updated 2022)," NFX, July 2019, https://www.nfx.com/post/network-effects-bible.

2   James Currier, "The Network Effects Manual: 16 Different Network Effects—2022," NFX, June 2021, https://www.nfx.com/post/network-effects-manual.

3   Robin Good, "Content Curation Approaches: Types and Formats," Medium, February 12, 2018, https://medium.com/content-curation-official-guide/content-curation-approaches-types-and-formats-ae2b33fe6a18.

4   Sarah, "NASA Spinoffs—Everyday Products from NASA," Kennedy Space Center, October 17, 2018, https://www.kennedyspacecenter.com/blog/nasa-spinoffs.

5   Andrew Chen, "The Red Flags and Magic Numbers That Investors Look For in Your Startup's Metrics—80 Slide Deck Included!" @andrewchen, https://andrewchen.com/investor-metrics-deck/.

6   Andrew Chen, *The Cold Start Problem* (New York: HarperBusiness, 2021).

STEP 6

1   Wikipedia, s.v. "General Electric," last modified January 26, 2023, https://en.wikipedia.org/wiki/General_Electric.

2   Services focus has changed GE from a company that in 1980 derived 85 percent of its revenues from the sale of products to one that today is based 70 percent on the sale of services.

3   Wikipedia, s.v. "Jack Welch," last modified January 11, 2023, https://en.wikipedia.org/wiki/Jack_Welch.

4   John McClenahen, "Viewpoint—GE's Welch Leaves Legacy of Aggressive Innovation," *IndustryWeek*, December 21, 2004, https://www.industryweek.com/leadership/companies-executives/article/22008547/viewpoint-ges-welch-leaves-legacy-of-aggressive-innovation.

Chapter Sixteen

1   Branka, "Zoom Statistics—2023," Truelist, last updated January 7, 2023, https://truelist.co/blog/zoom-statistics/.

2   Wikipedia, s.v. "Videotelephony," last modified January 21, 2023, https://en.wikipedia.org/wiki/Videotelephony.

3   Roger Dooley, "How Zoom Conquered Video Conferencing," Forbes, September 30, 2020, https://www.forbes.com/sites/rogerdooley/2020/09/30/how-zoom-conquered-video-conferencing/?sh=4f5c44bc5a97.

4   Wikipedia, s.v. "Innovation," last modified January 31, 2023, https://en.wikipedia.org/wiki/Innovation.

5   Clayton Christensen, *The Innovator's Dilemma: When New Technologies Cause Great Firms to Fail* (Boston: Harvard Business Review Press, 1997).

6   Wikipedia, s.v. "Innovation," last modified January 31, 2023, https://en.wikipedia.org/wiki/Innovation.

7   Ned Smith, "Incubators Heat Up Chances of Small Business Survival," Business News Daily, January 23, 2023, https://www.businessnewsdaily.com/272-incubators-increase-small-business-success.html.

8   Joey Sneddon, "Must Read: 25 Awesome Things Powered by Linux," omg! ubuntu!, January 5, 2021, https://www.omgubuntu.co.uk/2016/08/25-awesome-unexpected-things-powered-linux.

9   Encyclopaedia Britannica, s.v. "Firefox: Internet Browser," last modified August 23, 2022, https://www.britannica.com/technology/Firefox-Web-browser.

10   Richard Farson and Ralph Keyes, "The Failure-Tolerant Leader," *Harvard Business Review*, August 2002, https://hbr.org/2002/08/the-failure-tolerant-leader.

11   Farson and Keyes, "The Failure-Tolerant Leader," https://hbr.org/2002/08/the-failure-tolerant-leader.

12 Shana Lebowitz, "In 1963, Jack Welch Accidentally Blew Up a Factory at GE—and It Taught Him a Lesson About Leadership That's Stuck with Him to This Day," *Business Insider*, March 29, 2018, https://www.yahoo.com/news/1963-jack-welch-accidentally-blew-160316578.html.

13 Steven Levy, "Google's Larry Page on Why Moon Shots Matter," Wired, January 1, 2013, https://www.wired.com/2013/01/ff-qa-larry-page/.

14 Wikipedia, s.v. "Side Project Time" last modified January 30, 3023, https://en.wikipedia.org/wiki/Side_project_time.

15 Ritza Suazo, "10 Corporate Incubator Examples You Should Know About," Bundl, https://www.bundl.com/articles/examples-10-corporate-incubator-examples-you-should-know-about.

16 Wikipedia, s.v. "Steve Pruitt," last modified January 30, 2023, https://en.wikipedia.org/wiki/Steven_Pruitt.

17 David Gardner, "The LEGO Ideas Story: How Brands Can Take a Page out of LEGO's Co-creation and Innovation Playbook," Chaordix, https://chaordix.com/resources/lego-ideas-story-co-creation-and-innovation-playbook.

18 Andrew Leary and Sandro Kaulartz, *IPSOS Views: Introducing the New Era of Lead User Innovation* (New York: IPSOS, January 2019), https://www.ipsos.com/sites/default/files/ct/publication/documents/2019-01/lead-user-innovation-web.pdf.

19 Leary and Kaulartz, *IPSOS Views*, https://www.ipsos.com/sites/default/files/ct/publication/documents/2019-01/lead-user-innovation-web.pdf.

20 "Edison's Lightbulb," Franklin Institute, https://www.fi.edu/history-resources/edisons-lightbulb.

21 Wikipedia, s.v. "Innovation: Sustaining vs Disruptive Innovation," last modified February 2, 2023, https://en.wikipedia.org/wiki/Innovation#Sustaining_vs_disruptive_innovation.

Chapter Seventeen

1 Wikipedia, s.v. "Economy of the British Virgin Islands," last modified November 19, 2022, https://en.wikipedia.org/wiki/Economy_of_the_British_Virgin_Islands.

2 Joanna Partridge and Kari Paul, "$80bn Wiped from Value of Facebook and Instagram Owner Meta," *The Guardian*, October 27, 2022, https://www.theguardian.com/technology/2022/oct/26/meta-earnings-report-facebook-stocks.

3 Lucas Downey, "Google's Incredible YouTube Purchase 15 Years Later," Investopedia, September 2, 2021, https://www.investopedia.com/google-s-incredible-youtube-purchase-15-years-later-5200225.

4 Paulo Santos, "Update: Twitch Is Much Smaller Than Expected," Seeking Alpha, October 29, 2014, https://seekingalpha.com/article/2605505-update-twitch-is-much-smaller-than-expected.

5 Daniel Ruby, "Twitch Users—How Many People Use Twitch (2023)," Demand Sage, January 7, 2023, https://www.demandsage.com/twitch-users/.

6   Graham Kenny, "Don't Make This Common M&A Mistake," *Harvard Business Review*, March 16, 2020, https://hbr.org/2020/03/dont-make-this-common-ma-mistake.

7   Jeff Haxer, Ben Siegal, Kai Grass, and Sarah Yanes, "Healthcare M&A: Record-High Valuations Are Forcing Acquirers to Get Creative," Bain & Company, February 8, 2022, https://www.bain.com/insights/healthcare-m-and-a-report-2022/.

8   Oscar Gonzalez, "Facebook Drops Oculus name as Part of Meta Rebrand," CNET, October 28, 2021, https://www.cnet.com/tech/facebook-drops-oculus-name-as-part-of-meta-rebrand/.

9   Wikipedia, s.v. "List of Mergers and Acquisitions by Alphabet: Key Acquisitions," last modified January 6, 2023, https://en.wikipedia.org/wiki/List_of_mergers_and_acquisitions_by_Alphabet#Key_acquisitions.

10   Jeffrey Dastin and Greg Roumeliotis, "Amazon Buys Startup Ring in $1 Billion Deal to Run Your Home Security," Reuters, February 27, 2018, https://www.reuters.com/article/us-ring-m-a-amazon-com-idUSKCN1GB2VG.

11   Deedee Myers, "Geographic Expansion Via Merger," National Association of Federally-Insured Credit Unions, August 31, 2021, https://www.nafcu.org/nafcuservicesnafcu-services-blog/geographic-expansion-merger.

12   Barb Renner, Curt Fedder, and Shweta Joshi, *Mergers and Acquisitions for Growth* (Deloitte Insights, 2018), https://www.eprentise.com/wp-content/uploads/Deloitte-MA-for-growth.pdf.

13   Wikipedia, s.v. "List of Mergers and Acquisitions by Meta Platforms," last modified November 17, 2022, https://en.wikipedia.org/wiki/List_of_mergers_and_acquisitions_by_Meta_Platforms.

14   Bizz Buzz, "Why Facebook Buys Startups," YouTube video, 2:59, October 18, 2021, https://www.youtube.com/watch?v=OlBDyItD0Ak.

15   Jeffrey S. Young, *Steve Jobs: The Journey Is the Reward* (London: Scott, Foresman and 5Company, 1988).

16   Monica Langley, *Tearing Down the Walls: How Sandy Weill Fought His Way to the Top of the Financial World...and Then Nearly Lost It All* (Florence, MA: Free Press, 2003).

17   Wikipedia, s.v. "Sanford I. Weill," last modified December 14, 2022, https://en.wikipedia.org/wiki/Sanford_I._Weill.

18   Timothy B. Lee, "Zuckerberg Wrote 'Instagram Can Hurt Us' Days Before Acquisition," ARS Technica, July 29, 2022, https://arstechnica.com/tech-policy/2020/07/zuck-email-instagram-deal-could-neutralize-a-potential-competitor/.

19   "This Is Zoox," Zoox, https://zoox.com/about/.

20   "Amazon Agrees to Buy Self-Driving Technology Startup Zoox," Reuters, June 25, 2020, https://www.reuters.com/article/us-zoox-m-a-amazon-com-idUSKBN23X0PI.

21   "3 Companies Own 95% of Car Rental Brands," Guardian Rent-a-Car, August 30, 2015, http://guardianrentacar.com/3-companies-own-95-of-car-rental-brands/.

22   Annie Palmer, "Amazon Acquires Warehouse Machinery and Robotics Maker Cloostermans," CNBC, September 9, 2022, https://www.cnbc.com/2022/09/09/amazon-acquires-warehouse-machinery-and-robotics-maker-cloostermans.html.

23   Katie Tarasov, "Amazon Bought Whole Foods Five Years Ago for $13.7 Billion. Here's What's Changed at the High-End Grocer," CNBC, August 25, 2022, https://www.cnbc.com/2022/08/25/how-whole-foods-has-changed-in-the-five-years-since-amazon-took-over.html.

24   "What Is the Growth Share Matrix?," Boston Consulting Group, https://www.bcg.com/about/overview/our-history/growth-share-matrix.

25   Wikipedia, s.v. "Growth-Share Matrix," last modified April 22, 2022, https://en.wikipedia.org/wiki/Growth%E2%80%93share_matrix.

26   Steve Preda: *Buyable: Your Guide to Building a Self-Managing, Fast-Growing, and High-Profit Business* (Amershire Publishing, Glen Allen, Virginia, 2021)

Chapter Eighteen

1   Wikipedia, s.v. "History of IBM," last modified January 22, 2022, https://en.wikipedia.org/wiki/History_of_IBM.

2   Wikipedia, s.v. "Corning Inc.," last modified January 7, 2023, https://en.wikipedia.org/wiki/Corning_Inc.

3   "The History of Corning Innovation," Corning, https://www.corning.com/au/en/innovation/culture-of-innovation/the-history-of-corning-innovation.html.

4   Zlata Rodionova, "Why Play-Doh Might Be Hasbro's Biggest Success," *The Independent*, February 15, 2016, https://www.independent.co.uk/news/business/news/why-playdoh-might-be-hasbro-s-biggest-success-a6875436.html.

5   Wikipedia, s.v. "Chaebol," last modified January 25, 2023, https://en.wikipedia.org/wiki/Chaebol.

6   Wikipedia, s.v. "LG Corporation," last modified January 17, 2023, https://en.wikipedia.org/wiki/LG_Corporation.

7   "Revenue for LG Electronics (LGLG.F)," CompaniesMarketCap.com, accessed February 1, 2023, https://companiesmarketcap.com/lg-electronics/revenue/.

8   Dave Lee, "Nokia: The Rise and Fall of a Mobile Giant," BBC News, September 3, 2013, https://www.bbc.com/news/technology-23947212.

9   Wikipedia, s.v. "Nokia: Stock," last modified January 30, 2023, https://en.wikipedia.org/wiki/Nokia#Stock.

10   Leslie Cook, "Best Online Banks of 2022–2023," *Money*, November 15, 2022, https://money.com/best-online-bank/.

11   Dashia Milden, "Ally Bank Just Raised High-Yield Savings Rates to 3.30%. What Else to Know About Saving with Ally," NextAdvisor, December 16, 2022, https://time.com/nextadvisor/banking/ally-bank-review/.

12   Wikipedia, s.v. "American Express," last modified January 31, 2023, https://en.wikipedia.org/wiki/American_Express.

13 Wikipedia, s.v. "Starbucks," last modified January 30, 2023, https://en.wikipedia.org/wiki/Starbucks.

14 "Number of International and U.S.-Based Starbucks Stores from 2005 to 2022," Statista, accessed February 1, 2023, https://www.statista.com/statistics/218366/number-of-international-and-us-starbucks-stores/.

15 Anna Kaufman, "When Did Disney Buy Marvel and For How Much? The Historic Deal Explained," USA Today, July 28, 2022, https://www.usatoday.com/story/entertainment/2022/07/28/when-did-disney-buy-marvel/10147483002/.

16 Wikipedia, s.v. "History of Nintendo," last modified February 1, 2023, https://en.wikipedia.org/wiki/History_of_Nintendo.

17 Wikipedia, s.v. "Adobe Inc.," last modified February 1, 2023, https://en.wikipedia.org/wiki/Adobe_Inc.

18 "Adobe Captivate Subscriptions Become the New Normal," Adobe, last updated February 28, 2022, https://helpx.adobe.com/captivate/adobe-captivate-perpetual-license-discontinue.html.

19 "Adobe Market Cap over Time," Google, accessed February 8, 2023, https://ycharts.com/companies/ADBE/market_cap.

20 Wikipedia, s.v. "Slack (software)," last modified January 26, 2023, https://en.wikipedia.org/wiki/Slack_(software).

Index

Strategy OS
Trademarked Terms

Action Designer™
Advanced Profit per X™
Brainstorming Ground Rules™
Brand Promise Articulator™
Business Constraint(s)™
Core Business™
Core Business Lens™
Core Market™
Crux Challenge™
Crux Intuitor™
Economy Quadrant™
Entrepreneur Tools™
Execution Planner™
Expansion Action Board™
Expansion Dimension™
Flywheel Themes™
Focus Quadrant™
Innovation Culture™
Luxury Quadrant™
Mindshare Terms™
Positioning Matrix™
Positioning Statement™
Response Stimulator™
Scaling Loop Optimizer™
Scaling Loop Selector™
Short Phrase Strategy™
Smart M&A™
Strategic Flywheel™

Strategic Implication(s)™
Strategic Position™
Strategy Operating System™
Strategy OS™
Strategy OS App™
SPBG Guide™
Strategy OS Journey™
Strategy OS Toolkit™
Strategy Stack™
Tentacle Spreader™
The 5 Technology Levers™
The 6 Business Levers™
Six Competitive Forces™
Six Competitive Forces Map™
Six Dimensions of Expansion™
UA's™
Unique Activities™
Unique Activity Formulator™
Unique Activity Generator™
Unique Activity Optimizer™
Variety Quadrant™

www.ingramcontent.com/pod-product-compliance
Lightning Source LLC
Chambersburg PA
CBHW050854150626
46549CB00013B/1635